Instructor's Manual

VIRTUAL CHEMLAB
GENERAL CHEMISTRY LABORATORIES v2.1
INORGANIC QUALITATIVE ANALYSIS
FUNDAMENTAL EXPERIMENTS IN QUANTUM CHEMISTRY

BRIAN F. WOODFIELD
MATTHEW C. ASPLUND
HEIDI R. CATLIN
BRIGHAM YOUNG UNIVERSITY

Provo, UT 84602

Prentice
Hall

Upper Saddle River, NJ 07458

Project Manager: Kristen Kaiser
Editor-in-Chief: John Challice
Executive Managing Editor: Kathleen Schiaparelli
Assistant Managing Editor: Dinah Thong
Production Editor: Dana Dunn
Supplement Cover Management/Design: Paul Gourhan
Manufacturing Buyer: Ilene Kahn

© 2004 by Pearson Education, Inc.
Pearson Education, Inc.
Upper Saddle River, NJ 07458

Printed in the United States of America

10 9 8 7 6 5 4

ISBN 0-13-101075-1

Pearson Education Ltd., *London*
Pearson Education Australia Pty. Ltd., *Sydney*
Pearson Education Singapore, Pte. Ltd.
Pearson Education North Asia Ltd., *Hong Kong*
Pearson Education Canada, Inc., *Toronto*
Pearson Educación de Mexico, S.A. de C.V.
Pearson Education—Japan, *Tokyo*
Pearson Education Malaysia, Pte. Ltd.
Pearson Education, *Upper Saddle River, New Jersey*

Table of Contents

Quantum Assignments

Inorganic User's Guide 253

Quantum User's Guide 265

Electronic Lab Book 287

Instructor Utilities Guide 291

Installation and Overview

Overview

Welcome to *Virtual ChemLab,* a collection of realistic simulations of organic synthesis and organic qualitative analysis and five general chemistry laboratories, including inorganic qualitative analysis, quantum mechanics, gases, titrations, and calorimetry. In these laboratories, students are placed in a virtual environment where they are free to make the choices and decisions about situations they would confront in an actual instructional laboratory setting and, in turn, experience the resulting consequences. To date, the inorganic, quantum, and organic laboratories are completed while the others are in various stages of completion. The organic and general chemistry laboratories are currently sold separately. These installation instructions are for the general chemistry laboratory simulations. If both versions are purchased by an institution, instructions for combining the two sets of software so they operate from a unified executable can be obtained by emailing *chemlab@byu.edu.*

The general features of the inorganic simulation include 26 cations that can be added to test tubes in any combination, 11 reagents that can be added to the test tubes in any sequence and any number of times, necessary laboratory manipulations, a lab book for recording results and observations, and a stockroom for creating test tubes with known mixtures, generating practice unknowns, or retrieving instructor assigned unknowns. The simulation uses over 2500 actual pictures to show the results of reactions and over 220 videos to illustrate the different flame tests. With 26 cations that can be combined in any order or combination and 11 reagents that can be added in any order, there are in excess of 10^{16} possible outcomes in the simulation.

The purpose of the quantum laboratory is to allow students to explore and better understand the foundational experiments that led to the development of quantum mechanics. Because of the very sophisticated nature of most of these experiments, the quantum laboratory is the most "virtual" of the *Virtual ChemLab* laboratory simulations. In general, the laboratory consists of an optics table where a source, sample, modifier, and detector combination can be placed to perform different experiments. These devices are located in the stockroom and can be taken out of the stockroom and placed in various locations on the optics table. The emphasis here is to teach the students to probe a sample (e.g., a gas, metal foil, two-slit screen, etc.) with a source (e.g., a laser, electron gun, alpha-particle source, etc.) and detect the outcome with a specific detector (a phosphor screen, spectrometer, etc.). Heat, electric fields, or magnetic fields can also be applied to modify an aspect of the experiment. A partial list of some of the experiments that can be performed in this laboratory includes Thomson's measurement of the charge-to-mass ratio of the electron, Rutherford's backscattering experiment, Planck's blackbody radiation, Millikan's oil drop experiment, the photoelectric effect, emission spectra of gases, two-slit diffraction, plus many others.

Instructor utilities are also provided which allows an instructor to establish classes, make assignments, and view the results, grades, and lab books of the students. Access to this part of the virtual laboratory is allowed only to those individuals with administrative rights.

The purpose of this workbook is to provide students with hundreds of assignments that can be used to explore and learn about the various aspects of general chemistry. Details on the use of the general chemistry simulations are given in separate user guides found at the end of this workbook. The chemistry and physics that can be explored and investigated with *Virtual ChemLab* is nearly unlimited. Enjoy!

System Requirements

Minimum system requirements are as follows:

PC
Pentium 300 MHz (Pentium II or better recommended)
64 Mb RAM (128+ Mb recommended)
CD-ROM drive (for installation)
230 Mb of free disk space
Display capable of **and** set to millions of colors (24-bit color)
Minimum resolution 800 x 600 (1024 x 768 or higher recommended)
Windows 95/98 or Windows NT 4.0 or Windows 2000 Professional/ME or Windows XP
QuickTime 5.0 (installer included on CD)

Mac
PowerPC (G3 or better recommended)
64 Mb RAM (128 Mb recommended)
CD-ROM drive (for installation)
230 Mb of free disk space
Display capable of **and** set to millions of colors (24-bit color)
Recommended minimum resolution 832 x 624 (higher resolution recommended)
OS 8.0 or higher (OSX recommended)
QuickTime 5.0

Server (For network installations)
A file server running an operating system capable of mapped or named drives accessible to all clients in the local area network is required for a network installation. The clients must be running an operating system compatible with the *Virtual ChemLab* software (see above), but it is possible to have mixed platform access to the centralized database. In PC environments, a Novell file server is recommended, but other file servers running operating systems meeting the above requirements are acceptable.

Note: The preceding requirements are the recommended minimum hardware and system software requirements for reasonable execution speeds and reliability. However, it should be noted that the software has been successfully installed and used on computers with significantly lower capabilities than the recommendations given, with corresponding reductions in execution speed and media access time.

Installing *Virtual ChemLab*

Virtual ChemLab comes as a Student version and a Client/Server (Network) version. The Student version is almost identical to the Client/Server version except for two main differences. (1) In a Student version the hallway is bypassed entirely, and the simulation starts in the general chemistry laboratory. (2) No instructor assignments can be given or received.

The student workbook is intended for the Student version; however, the workbook assignments can also be used in the Network version. If students use the Network version instead of the Student version, the program will start in the hallway that leads into the different virtual rooms in *Virtual ChemLab*. To enter the general chemistry laboratory, students must click the "General Chemistry Laboratory" door and then enter a password provided by the instructor. The user guides in this workbook follow from this point.

If the Client/Server version is used for electronic release and submissions of assignments (instead of the workbook), any additional information that may be needed can be found by using the help options within the program or by using the user guides found on the CD or installed with the program. In addition, the *Instructor Utilities* guide is provided at the end of this instructor manual, and the system requirements that follow are for the Client/Server version.

To install the software, locate and run the program "Setup ChemLab" on the CD-ROM drive, then follow the prompts. The following installation options are available:

- **Local Installation.** This option installs all files to the local hard drive and requires approximately 230 Mb of free hard drive space. The CD is not needed to run the program. This option is included for individual use on individual computers. For example, instructors and teaching assistants may wish to have a local installation so that they can familiarize themselves with the program, etc. without affecting the network installation.

- **Network Installation with Client.** This option installs the necessary files to a network server including an installer that can be run from the server to configure clients. In this option, the client software is also installed on the computer from which the network installation originated. The client installation is a full installation on a client computer attached to the network, except the installation configures the software to use a centralized database that was installed on the server to control access to the virtual laboratory. Client installations allow multiple users to access the virtual laboratory and/or Instructor Utilities using IDs (or passwords).

- **Network Installation without Client.** This installation is equivalent to the above network installation except the client is not automatically installed on the local computer. The Client Installer *is* installed on the network server to allow for client installations at a later time on other computers connected to the server.

All users who will be running *Virtual ChemLab* from a client must have read/write/erase privileges to the *Virtual ChemLab* directory (including subdirectories) on the network drive. This does not imply that users must be given access to these files and directories but only that they have read/write/erase privileges to enable the software to run correctly.

Installing *Virtual ChemLab* to the Client

To install *Virtual ChemLab* to a client computer, locate your network installation and run "Install Client" from the client computer. The Client Installer performs a complete installation on the client computer except for the database and backup directories. Instead, the client software is configured to access the centralized database installed and maintained on the server.

Important Installation Notes and Issues

1. The graphics used in the simulations require the monitor to be set to 24-bit true color (millions of colors). Lower color resolutions can be used, but the graphics will not be as sharp.

2. QuickTime 5.0 or later is required for the software to run properly. A QuickTime 5.0 installer for the PC platform has been included on the CD if needed.

3. It should be noted that *Virtual ChemLab* runs more slowly on the Macintosh platform than on a PC, particularly when performing graphics updates and playing QuickTime movies. The reason for this decrease in speed has not been found, but there is significant improvement in performance when using the OSX operating system.

4. In the Server/Client mode, the centralized database containing passwords, assignments, scores, and lab books must be maintained on a server drive accessible by all the clients. In order for the software to work properly, the users on these client machines must have Read/Write/Erase privileges to the folders containing this database. For security reasons, we recommend that these users be prevented from accessing these folders on the server by blocking access to My Computer, Explorer, or the server drive icon on the Macintosh desktop when the server drive is mounted. To hide the server drive icon on a Macintosh (OS9 or OSX), use the following steps: (1) Launch **Resedit** (this is a free utility from Apple), (2) Go to the "Get Info on Files/Folders", and (3) Choose the file or folder and set its attributes to be invisible.

5. For a client installation, the installation routine detects the path to the network installation for use by *Virtual ChemLab*. Consequently, the installation routine should be run from the drive mapping that will be used by the client computer. However, an option is given during the installation to manually specify the path to the network database used by *Virtual ChemLab* if the Client Installer is launched from a different location. (See the Appendices in Instructor Utilities for more details on ChemLab INI files).

6. When the simulation software has been installed on a Windows 2000 Professional operating system, there is better performance and better system stability when the Windows 2000 Support Pack 2 has been installed.

7. When using *Virtual ChemLab* under the Windows 2000 Professional operating system, users must be, at a minimum, a Power User in order for the program to have sufficient rights to run properly. Otherwise, the program will run as a Restricted User, but the fonts will be incorrect along with other minor annoyances. In a server environment where a Restricted User is necessary, we suggest that a separate ChemLab Account be setup to grant the user Power User Status, but only give the user access to the ChemLab software.

8. For unknown reasons, on some machines the QuickTime videos will not play properly if the system QuickTime settings are in their default state. This can be corrected by changing the Video Settings in QuickTime to Normal Mode.

Inorganic Assignments

Virtual ChemLab: Inorganic is a realistic and complete simulation of inorganic qualitative analysis. Chemistry is a laboratory science and as such, it requires that the students participate in meaningful laboratory experiences. One of the fundamental purposes of these instructional laboratories is to teach the cognitive processes or analytical skills that form the foundation of chemistry and other laboratory sciences. In actuality, however, many students go through these laboratories with little thought about what they are suppose to learn, but narrowly follow the written directions for the experiment in order to get their expected results (affectionately called "cookbooking"). The primary purpose of *Virtual ChemLab: Inorganic* is to teach the thinking processes that form the foundation of an inorganic qualitative analysis laboratory. In *Virtual ChemLab: Inorganic*, students are free to make the choices and decisions that they would confront in an actual laboratory environment and, in turn, experience the resulting consequences. By experimenting in the virtual laboratory, students create their own procedures for identifying unknowns. In this way, students develop critical thinking and problem solving skills and eliminate the "cookbooking" tendencies that are prevalent in an actual laboratory setting.

This simulation uses over 2500 actual pictures to show the results of reactions and over 220 videos to show the different flame tests. The general features of the simulation also include the following:
- 26 cations that can be added to test tubes in any combination,
- 11 reagents that can be added to the test tubes in any sequence and any number of times,
- necessary laboratory manipulations,
- a lab book for recording results and observations, and
- a stockroom for creating test tubes with known mixtures, generating practice unknowns, or retrieving instructor assigned unknowns.

To keep the simulation at a manageable size and complexity, a few assumptions and restrictions have been applied:
- The cations are the nitrates and are dissolved in water to form a 0.02 M solution except for NH_4^+ which is a 1 M solution.
- Additional cations cannot be added once the test tube is in the laboratory.
- The reagents have concentrations of 3 M for the HNO_3 and NaOH, 0.1 M for the H_2S, 3% H_2O_2, and 1 M for the NH_3, NaCl, Na_2SO_4, and Na_2CO_3 solutions.
- The pH 4, pH 7, and pH 10 solutions are inert buffers and are added in sufficient quantity to set the pH of the solution to the indicated value.
- Reagents are added in excess.
- After decanting, precipitates are rinsed with an appropriate solution so the precipitate does not dissolve.

With 26 cations that can be combined in any order or combination and 11 reagents that can be added in any order, there are in excess of 10^{16} possible outcomes in the simulation.

The *Instructor Utilities* or stockroom component of *Virtual ChemLab* allows instructors to define and release inorganic qualitative analysis unknowns to a class of students. The *Instructor Utilities Guide* explains how to create these assignments. In order to allow flexibility, instructors can create assignments according to the level of the class and the chemistry that is being studied. Unknown assignments can contain any number and selection of cations for the unknown, and the cation set (the cations that are possible in the unknown) can also vary. Thus, students may begin with less difficult unknowns and then progressively obtain more challenging assignments.

Inorganic Assignments

The largest cation set contains all the cations except for iron (II). When silver (I) and iron (II) are mixed, an oxidation-reduction reaction occurs in which silver (I) is reduced to the silver metal, and iron (II) is oxidized to iron (III). This leaves the original iron (II) indistinguishable from iron (III), which may have already been part of the unknown. Thus, the Full Cation Set does not include iron (II). In addition, it is advised that instructors do not make assignments in which all three cations (Ag^+, Fe^{2+}, and Fe^{3+}) can be present.

The unknowns described in the **Full Cation Set** and the **Additional Assignments** sections of this guide are stored in the Inorganic folder within the Assignments folder. The *Retrieve Assignment* button allows access to these assignments. Instructors can also create and archive their own assignments. See the **Inorganic Assignments** section of the *Instructor Utilities Guide* for details on how to retrieve and archive assignments.

The last section of this manual contains additional reactions of interest. These reactions include oxidation-reduction reactions and cation/cation precipitate reactions. Since many of these reactions involve the interaction between two cations, these reactions are not included within the assignments. However, these reactions are useful in teaching important principles in inorganic chemistry.

Full Cation Set

The Full Cation Set can be separated into four major groups: the Chlorides (Assignment 2), the Acidic Sulfides (Assignment 3), the Basic Hydroxides and Sulfides (Assignment 6), and the last group that forms few precipitates (Assignment 10). Note that Assignments 4 and 5 are subsets of Assignment 3 (the Acidic Sulfides); Assignments 7, 8, and 9 are subsets of Assignment 6 (the Hydroxides and Basic Sulfides); and Assignment 11 is a subset of Assignment 10 (the last group). Thus, Assignments 2 through 11 comprise all the subgroups needed to carry out the Full Cation Set separation and identification. Although The Full Cation Set separation and identification is named Assignment 1, this is the most difficult assignment and should be the last assignment given to the students.

Assignment 1 – Full Cation Set

Difficulty level: 10

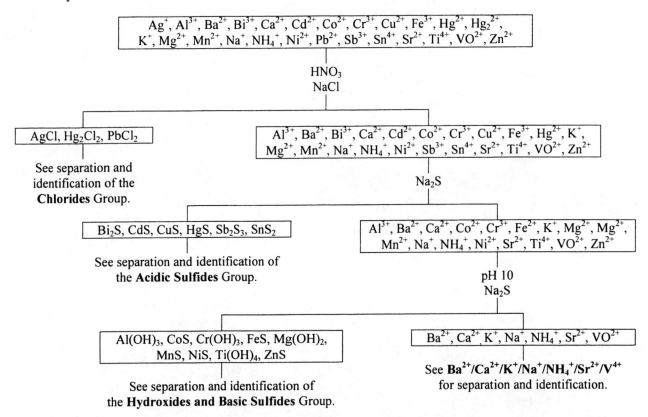

The Full Cation Set can be separated into four major groups: the **Chlorides**, the **Acidic Sulfides**, the **Hydroxides and Basic Sulfides**, and a fourth group that forms few precipitates. From these four groups, each cation can then be separated and or identified. See each group for separation, identification, reactions, and chemistry discussion.

Assignment 2 – Ag$^+$/Hg$_2^{2+}$/Pb^{2+} (The Chlorides)

Difficulty level: 3

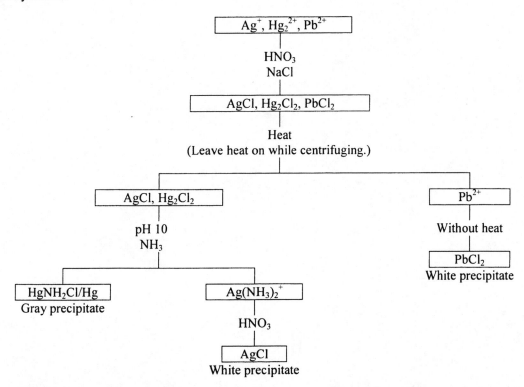

Chloride precipitates out Ag$^+$, Hg$_2^{2+}$, and Pb^{2+}, the first group in the full scheme. Lead chloride is somewhat soluble and is more soluble in hot water. Silver forms a complex with ammonia strong enough to dissolve the silver chloride precipitate. Mercury(I) chloride reacts with ammonia to form mercury and mercury(II) amidochloride. This type of reaction in which an element is both reduced and oxidized is called a disproportionation reaction.

Reactions:

Ag$^+$(aq) + Cl$^-$(aq) → AgCl(s) (white)
AgCl(s) (white) + 2NH$_3$(aq) → Ag(NH$_3$)$_2^+$(aq) + Cl$^-$(aq)

Hg$_2^{2+}$(aq) + 2Cl$^-$(aq) → Hg$_2$Cl$_2$(s) (white)
Hg$_2$Cl$_2$(s) (white) + 2NH$_3$(aq) → HgNH$_2$Cl(s) (white) + Hg(s) (white) + NH$_4^+$(aq) +Cl$^-$(aq)

Pb^{2+}(aq) + 2Cl$^-$(aq) → PbCl$_2$(s) (white)
PbCl$_2$(s) (white) + Heat → Pb^{2+}(aq) + 2Cl$^-$(aq)

Assignment 3 – Bi^{3+}/Cd^{2+}/Cu^{2+}/Hg^{2+}/$Sb3^+$/Sn^{4+} (The Acidic Sulfides)

Difficulty level: 7

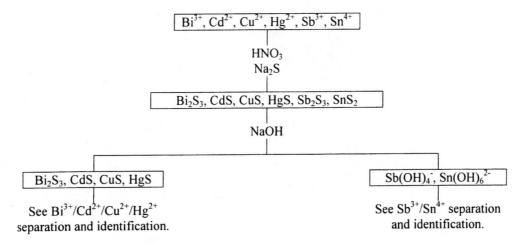

The high insolubility of these sulfide precipitates lets these cations precipitate even in acidic conditions. Upon addition of sodium hydroxide, both tin (IV) and antimony (III) sulfides dissolve to form hydroxide complexes.

Reactions:

$2Bi^{3+}(aq) + 3S^{2-}(aq) \rightarrow Bi_2S_3(s)$ (dark brown)

$Cd^{2+}(aq) + S^{2-}(aq) \rightarrow CdS(s)$ (orange)

$Cu^{2+}(aq)$ (light blue) $+ S^{2-}(aq) \rightarrow CuS(s)$ (dark brown)

$Hg^{2+}(aq) + S^{2-}(aq) \rightarrow HgS(s)$ (black)

$2Sb^{3+}(aq) + 3S^{2-}(aq) + H^+(aq) \rightarrow Sb_2S_3(s)$ (orange) $+ H^+(aq)$
$Sb_2S_3(s)$ (orange) $+ 4OH^-(aq) \rightarrow 2Sb(OH)_4^-(aq) + 3S^{2-}(aq)$

$Sn^{4+}(aq) + 2S^{2-}(aq) + H^+(aq) \rightarrow SnS_2(s)$ (yellow) $+ H^+(aq)$
$SnS_2(s)$ (yellow) $+ 6OH^-(aq) \rightarrow Sb(OH)_6^{2-}(aq) + 2S^{2-}(aq)$

Assignment 4 – $Bi^{3+}/Cd^{2+}/Cu^{2+}/Hg^{2+}$

Difficulty level: 6

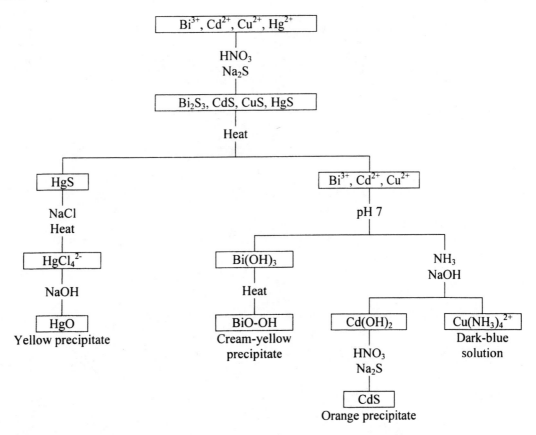

Mercury (II) sulfide is the most insoluble sulfide. It only dissolves in **aqua regia** (a combination of nitric acid and hydrochloric acid) with heat. Bismuth, cadmium, and copper cations dissolve more readily.

Reactions:

$2Bi^{3+}(aq) + 3S^{2-}(aq) \rightarrow Bi_2S_3(s)$ (dark brown)
$Bi_2S_3(s)$ (dark brown) $+ H^+(aq) + Heat \rightarrow 2Bi^{3+}(aq) + 3S(s) + 2NO(g) + 4H_2O$
$Bi^{3+}(aq) + 3OH^-(aq) \rightarrow Bi(OH)_3(s)$ (white)
$Bi(OH)_3(s)$ (white) $+ Heat \rightarrow BiO-OH(s)$ (cream yellow) $+ H_2O$

$Cd^{2+}(aq) + S^{2-}(aq) \rightarrow CdS(s)$ (orange)
$CdS(s)$ (orange) $+ 2H^+(aq) + Heat \rightarrow Cd^{2+}(aq) + H_2S(g)$
$Cd^{2+}(aq) + 2OH^-(aq) \rightarrow Cd(OH)_2(s)$ (white)

$Cu^{2+}(aq)$ (light blue) $+ S^{2-}(aq) \rightarrow CuS(s)$ (dark brown)
$3CuS(s)$ (dark brown) $+ 8H^+(aq) + 2NO_3^-(aq) + Heat \rightarrow 3Cu^{2+}(aq) + 3S(s) + 2NO(g) + 4 H_2O$
$Cu^{2+}(aq)$ (light blue) $+ 2OH^-(aq) \rightarrow Cu(OH)_2(s)$ (blue)
$Cu(OH)_2(s)$ (blue) $+ 4NH_3(aq) \rightarrow Cu(NH_3)_4^{2+}(aq)$ (dark blue) $+ 2OH^-(aq)$

$Hg^{2+}(aq) + S^{2-}(aq) \rightarrow HgS(s)$ (black)
$3HgS(s)$ (black) $+ 8H^+(aq) + 2NO_3^-(aq) + 12Cl^-(aq) + Heat \rightarrow 3HgCl_4^{2-}(aq) + 3S(s) + 2NO(g) + 4H_2O$
$HgCl_4^{2-}(aq) + 2OH^-(aq) \rightarrow HgO(s)$ (yellow) $+ H_2O + 4Cl^-(aq)$

Assignment 5 – Sb^{3+}/Sn^{4+}

Difficulty level: 4

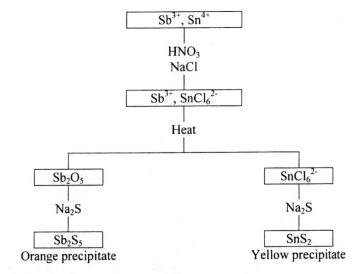

Antimony and tin behave very similarly, which is expected due to their juxtaposition in the periodic table. Both antimony(III) and tin(IV) are soluble in acidic solution with chloride ion; however, upon addition of heat, antimony is oxidized and forms an insoluble oxide precipitate.

Reactions:

$2Sb^{3+}(aq) + 5H_2O + Heat \rightarrow Sb_2O_5(s) \text{ (white)} + 6H^+(aq) + 2H_2(g)$
$Sb_2O_5(s) \text{ (white)} + 5S^{2-}(aq) + H^+(aq) \rightarrow Sb_2S_5(s) \text{ (orange)} + H^+(aq)$

$Sn^{4+}(aq) + H^+(aq) + 6Cl^-(aq) \rightarrow SnCl_6^{2-}(aq) + H^+(aq)$
$SnCl_6^{2-}(aq) + 2S^{2-}(aq) + H^+(aq) \rightarrow SnS_2(s) \text{ (yellow)} + 6Cl^-(aq) + H^+(aq)$

Assignment 6 – $Al^{3+}/Co^{2+}/Cr^{3+}/Fe^{2+}/Fe^{3+}/Mg^{2+}/Mn^{2+}/Ni^{2+}/Ti^{4+}/Zn^{2+}$ (The Hydroxides and Basic Sulfides)

Difficulty level: 8

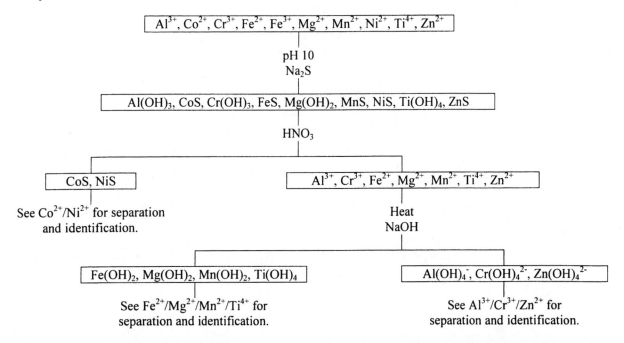

The sulfides in this group (the basic sulfides) are more soluble than the sulfides precipitated out in acid. Cobalt sulfide and nickel sulfide are more insoluble than the other basic sulfides. Even though cobalt sulfide and nickel sulfide cannot be formed in acidic conditions, these sulfides do not dissolve in acid due to their high insolubility. The aluminum(III), chromium(III), and zinc(II) hydroxides are all amphoteric meaning that they dissolve in both acid and base.

Reactions:

$Al^{3+}(aq) + 3OH^-(aq)$ (pH 10) $\rightarrow Al(OH)_3(s)$ (white)
$Al(OH)_3(s)$ (white) $+ OH^-(aq) \rightarrow Al(OH)_4^-(aq)$

$Co^{2+}(aq)$ (pink) $+ S^{2-}(aq) \rightarrow CoS(s)$ (black)

$Cr^{3+}(aq)$ (purple) $+ 3OH^-(aq)$ (pH 10) $\rightarrow Cr(OH)_3(s)$ (gray)
$Cr(OH)_3(s)$ (gray) $+ OH^-(aq) \rightarrow Cr(OH)_4^-(aq)$ (green)

$Fe^{2+}(aq) + S^{2-}(aq) \rightarrow FeS(s)$ (black)
$2Fe^{3+}(aq)$ (yellow) $+ 3S^{2-}(aq) \rightarrow 2FeS(s)$ (black) $+ S(s)$
$FeS(s)$ (black) $+ 2H^+(aq) \rightarrow Fe^{2+}(aq) + H_2S(g)$
$Fe^{2+}(aq) + 2OH^-(aq) \rightarrow Fe(OH)_2(s)$ (pea green)

$Mg^{2+}(aq) + 2OH^-(aq) \rightarrow Mg(OH)_2(s)$ (white gel)

$Mn^{2+}(aq) + S^{2-}(aq) \rightarrow MnS(s)$ (cream yellow)
$MnS(s)$ (cream yellow) $+ 2H^+(aq) \rightarrow Mn^{2+}(aq) + H_2S(g)$
$Mn^{2+}(aq) + 2OH^-(aq) \rightarrow Mn(OH)_2(s)$ (brown/orange)

$Ni^{2+}(aq)$ (green) $+ S^{2-}(aq) \rightarrow NiS(s)$ (black)

$Ti^{4+}(aq) + 4OH^-(aq) \rightarrow Ti(OH)_4(s)$ (white)

$Zn^{2+}(aq) + S^{2-}(aq) \rightarrow ZnS(s)$ (white)
$ZnS(s)$ (white) $+ 2H^+(aq) \rightarrow Zn^{2+}(aq) + H_2S(g)$
$Zn^{2+}(aq) + 4OH^-(aq) \rightarrow Zn(OH)_4^{2-}(aq)$

19

Assignment 7 – Co²⁺/Ni²⁺

Difficulty level: 4

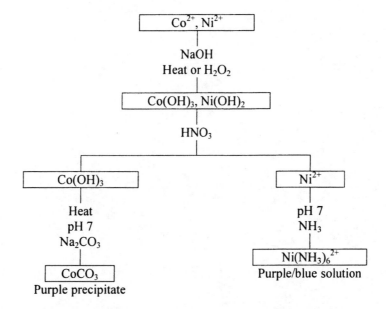

Cobalt and nickel are next to each other in the periodic table, and as expected, they behave very similarly. However, in a basic solution with either heat or hydrogen peroxide, cobalt (II) is oxidized and forms a very insoluble hydroxide. Nickel cannot be oxidized, but it forms nickel(II) hydroxide that dissolves readily in acid.

Reactions:

Co^{2+}(aq) (pink) + $2OH^-$(aq) → $Co(OH)_2$(s) (pink/tan)
$4Co(OH)_2$(s) (pink/tan) + $2H_2O$ + O_2(g) + OH^-(aq) + Heat → $4Co(OH)_3$(s) (dark brown) + OH^-(aq)
$2Co(OH)_2$(s) (pink/tan) + H_2O_2(aq) + OH^-(aq) → $2Co(OH)_3$(s) (dark brown) + OH^-(aq)

Ni^{2+}(aq) (green) + $2OH^-$(aq) → $Ni(OH)_2$(s) (light green)
Ni^{2+}(aq) (green) + $6NH_3$(aq) → $Ni(NH_3)_6^{2+}$(aq) (purple/blue)

Assignment 8 – $Fe^{2+}/Mg^{2+}/Mn^{2+}/Ti^{4+}$

Difficulty level: 6

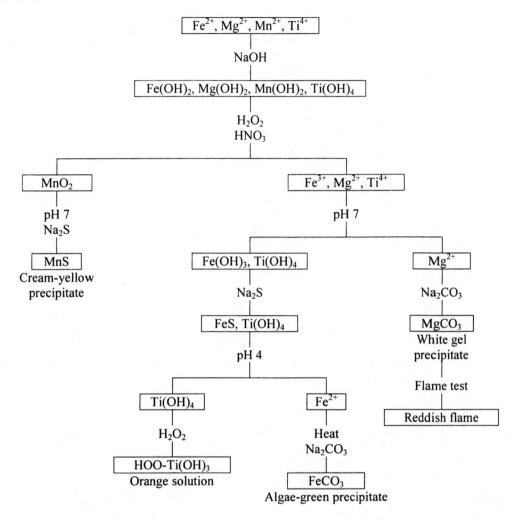

Manganese is oxidized by hydrogen peroxide in basic solution. Iron, magnesium, and titanium are separated according to their solubility in water. Both iron (III) and titanium form insoluble hydroxides at pH 4, but iron (II) does not. Thus, sulfide ion is used to reduce iron (III) to iron (II).

Reactions:

$Fe^{2+}(aq) + 2OH^-(aq) \rightarrow Fe(OH)_2(s)$ (pea green)
$2Fe(OH)_2(s)$ (pea green) $+ H_2O_2(aq) + OH^-(aq)$
       $\rightarrow 2Fe(OH)_3(s)$ (red/orange) $+ OH^-(aq)$
$2Fe^{3+}(aq) + 3S^{2-}(aq) \rightarrow 2FeS(s)$ (black) $+ S(s)$
$Fe^{2+}(aq) + CO_3^{2-}(aq) \rightarrow FeCO_3(s)$ (algae green)

$Mg^{2+}(aq) + 2OH^-(aq) \rightarrow Mg(OH)_2(s)$ (white gel)
$Mg^{2+}(aq) + CO_3^{2-}(aq) \rightarrow MgCO_3(s)$ (white gel)

$Mn^{2+}(aq) + 2OH^-(aq) \rightarrow Mn(OH)_2(s)$ (brown/orange)
$Mn(OH)_2(s)$ (brown/orange) $+ H_2O_2(aq) + OH^-(aq)$
       $\rightarrow MnO_2(s)$ (dark brown) $+ 2H_2O + OH^-(aq)$

$MnO_2(s)$ (dark brown) $+ 4H^+(aq) + 2S^{2-}(aq)$
       $\rightarrow MnS(s)$ (cream yellow) $+ S(s) + 2H_2O$

$Ti^{4+}(aq) + 4OH^-(aq) \rightarrow Ti(OH)_4(s)$ (white)
$Ti(OH)_4(s)$ (white) $+ H_2O_2$ (pH 4)
       $\rightarrow HOO\text{-}Ti(OH)_3(s)$ (orange) $+ H_2O$

Assignment 9 – $Al^{3+}/Cr^{3+}/Zn^{2+}$

Difficulty level: 4

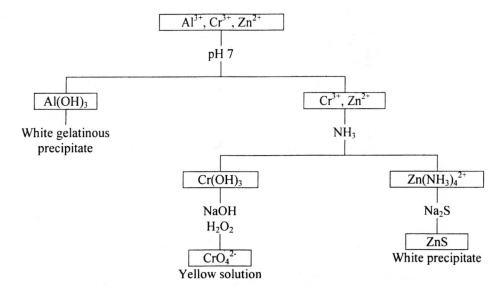

The aluminum(III), chromium(III), and zinc(II) all form amphoteric hydroxides, meaning that they dissolve in both acid and base. Aluminum forms a very insoluble hydroxide that does not dissolve in solution at pH 7. Oxidation of chromium to chromate is a simple way to confirm the presence of chromium. Zinc forms an ammonia complex, which allows separation from the other amphoteric hydroxides.

Reactions:

$Al^{3+}(aq) + 3OH^-(aq) \rightarrow Al(OH)_3(s)$ (white)

$Cr^{3+}(aq)$ (purple) $+ 3NH_3(aq) + 3H_2O \rightarrow Cr(OH)_3(s)$ (gray) $+ 3NH_4^+(aq)$
$Cr(OH)_3(s)$ (gray) $+ OH^-(aq) \rightarrow Cr(OH)_4^-(aq)$ (green)
$2Cr(OH)_4^-(aq)$ (green) $+ 3H_2O_2(aq) + 2OH^-(aq) \rightarrow 2CrO_4^{2-}(aq)$ (yellow) $+ 8H_2O$

$Zn^{2+}(aq) + 4NH_3(aq) \rightarrow Zn(NH_3)_4^{2+}(aq)$

Assignment 10 – Ba^{2+}/Ca^{2+}/K^+/Na^+/NH_4^+/Sr^{2+}/V^{4+}

Difficulty level: 5

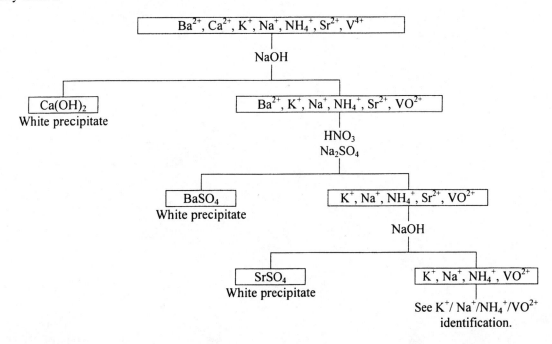

Calcium ion precipitates out in very basic solution. Barium and strontium have very similar chemistry. Both cations precipitate out with sulfate, but strontium sulfate is more soluble. In acidic solution, there is not as much free sulfate due to the formation of bisulfate: $H^+ + SO_4^{2-} \rightarrow HSO_4$. Thus, in acidic solution, strontium will not precipitate out with sulfate, but barium sulfate will precipitate due to its greater insolubility.

Reactions:

$Ba^{2+}(aq) + SO_4^{2-}(aq) \rightarrow BaSO_4(s)$ (white)

$Ca^{2+}(aq) + 2OH^-(aq) \rightarrow Ca(OH)_2(s)$ (white)

$Sr^{2+}(aq) + SO_4^{2-}(aq) \rightarrow SrSO_4(s)$ (white)

Assignment 11 – K⁺/Na⁺/NH₄⁺/V⁴⁺

Difficulty level: 2

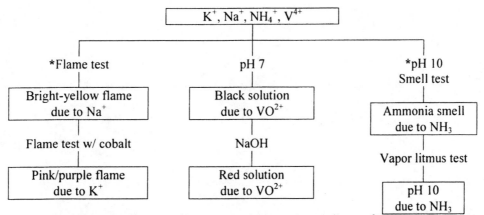

*Use original solution when testing for Na⁺ or NH₄⁺. If Ti⁴⁺ or Bi³⁺ are in the solution, make solution pH 7 and centrifuge. Use supernatant only for flame tests.

The original solution should be used for testing sodium and ammonia since these cations can be added in the laboratory room. However, since Ti^{4+} and Bi^{3+} both have bright flame tests like Na^+, these cations must be removed from the solution to not confuse them for Na^+. Although none of the cations in this group can be precipitated, they can be identified by flame tests, pH tests, and solution color.

Additional Assignments

These assignments are included with *Virtual ChemLab: Inorganic* for convenience. The organization of the assignments by difficulty level allows for easy access to an appropriate assignment for the level of the class. Increasingly difficult assignments challenge students and help them to develop critical thinking skills. Note that the header for each assignment includes the difficulty level for easy reference.

Assignment 12 – Fe^{2+}/Fe^{3+}

Difficulty level: 1

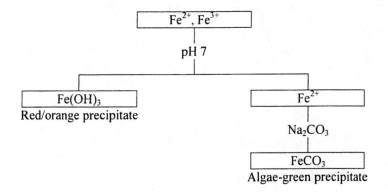

The +2 and +3 oxidation states of iron significantly change the solution chemistry of iron. Iron (III) forms a red/orange hydroxide precipitate in water. Iron (II) forms a green hydroxide, but only in basic solution. In addition, iron (III) does not form a carbonate precipitate, but iron (II) does form a carbonate precipitate.

Reactions:

$Fe^{2+}(aq) + CO_3^{2-}(aq) \rightarrow FeCO_3(s)$ (algae green)

Fe^{3+}(yellow) $+ 3H_2O \rightarrow Fe(OH)_3(s)$ (red/orange) $+ 3H^+(aq)$

Assignment 13 – Hg_2^{2+}/Hg^{2+}

Difficulty level: 1

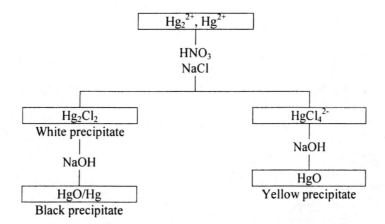

Mercury (I) forms a white chloride precipitate in acidic condition, while mercury (II) forms a soluble complex with chloride. Upon addition of sodium hydroxide, mercury (II) forms mercuric oxide, a yellow precipitate.

Reactions:

$Hg_2^{2+}(aq) + 2Cl^-(aq) \rightarrow Hg_2Cl_2(s)$ (white)

$Hg^{2+}(aq) + 4Cl^-(aq) \rightarrow HgCl_4^-(aq)$
$HgCl_4^{2-}(aq) + 2OH^-(aq) \rightarrow HgO(s)$ (yellow) $+ H_2O + 4Cl^-(aq)$

Assignment 14 – K$^+$/Na$^+$

Difficulty level: 1

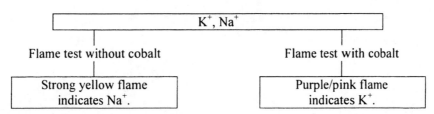

Sodium and potassium can only be detected by their flame tests. Sodium gives a strong yellow flame. Potassium gives a purple/pink flame. The bright sodium flame can mask out the potassium flame, but cobalt glass can be used, which absorbs most of the bright color from the sodium.

Assignment 15 − K⁺/Na⁺/V⁴⁺

Difficulty level: 1

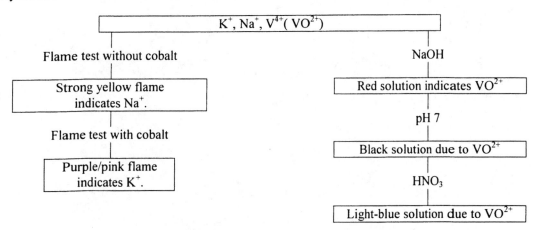

Although these cations do not form precipitates, they can be identified by flame tests and by solution color. Sodium gives a strong yellow flame, and potassium gives a purple/pink flame behind cobalt glass. Vanadium (IV) exists as VO2+ in solution, and this complex changes color according to pH.

Assignment 16 – Ag⁺/Cu²⁺/NH₄⁺

Difficulty level: 2

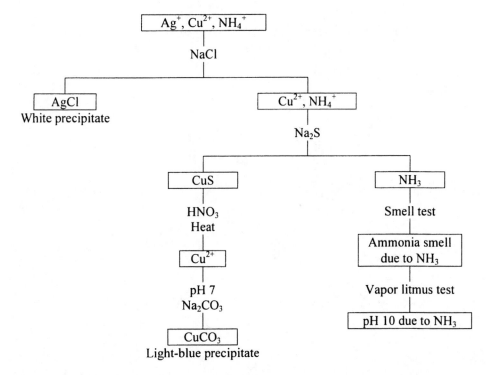

Silver (I) is one of the few cations that forms a chloride precipitate, allowing for an easy separation from many other cations. Copper (II) can be detected in various ways; it will precipitate out with several of the reagents while ammonia stays in solution.

Reactions:

$Ag^+(aq) + Cl^-(aq) \rightarrow AgCl(s)$ (white)

$Cu^{2+}(aq)$ (light blue) $+ S^{2-}(aq) \rightarrow CuS(s)$ (dark brown)
$3CuS(s)$ (dark brown) $+ 8H^+(aq) + 2NO_3^-(aq) + Heat \rightarrow 3Cu^{2+}(aq) + 3S(s) + 2NO(g) + 4 H_2O$
$Cu^{2+}(aq)$ (light blue) $+ CO_3^{2-}(aq) \rightarrow CuCO_3(s)$ (light blue)

Assignment 17 – Al³⁺/Mg²⁺/Na⁺

Difficulty level: 2

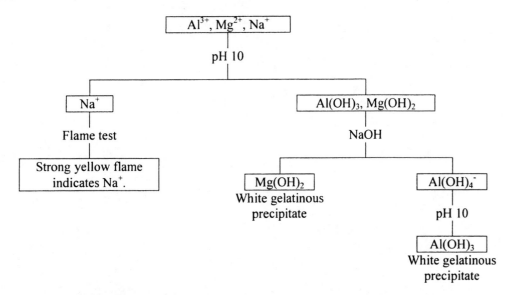

Aluminum (III) and magnesium (II) both form hydroxide precipitates, but aluminum (III) hydroxide dissolves in excess base. The characteristic bright-yellow flame indicates sodium is present.

Reactions:

Al^{3+}(aq) + 3OH⁻(aq) (pH 10) $\rightarrow$ Al(OH)₃(s) (white gel)
Al^{3+}(aq) + 4OH⁻(aq) $\rightarrow$ Al(OH)₄⁻(aq)

Mg^{2+}(aq) + 2OH⁻(aq) $\rightarrow$ Mg(OH)₂(s) (white gel)

Assignment 18 – Ba²⁺/Co²⁺/Hg₂²⁺

Difficulty level: 2

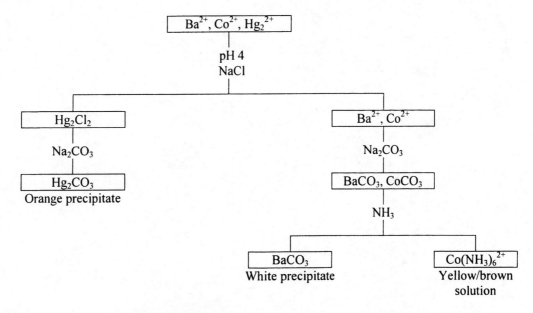

Mercury (I) is one of the few cations that forms a chloride precipitate. Barium (II) and cobalt (II) form carbonate precipitates. Cobalt (II) forms a complex with ammonia that dissolves the carbonate precipitate.

Reactions:

$Ba^{2+}(aq) + CO_3^{2-}(aq) \rightarrow BaCO_3(s)$

$Co^{2+}(aq) + CO_3^{2-}(aq) \rightarrow CoCO_3(s)$ (purple)
$CoCO_3(s)$ (purple) $+ 6NH_3(aq) \rightarrow Co(NH_3)_6^{2+}(aq)$ (yellow/brown) $+ CO_3^{2-}(aq)$

$Hg_2^{2+}(aq) + 2Cl^-(aq) \rightarrow Hg_2Cl_2(s)$ (white)
$Hg_2Cl_2(s)$ (white) $+ CO_3^{2-}(aq) \rightarrow Hg_2CO_3(s)$ (orange)

Assignment 19 – $Ca^{2+}/Cu^{2+}/Sn^{4+}$

Difficulty level: 2

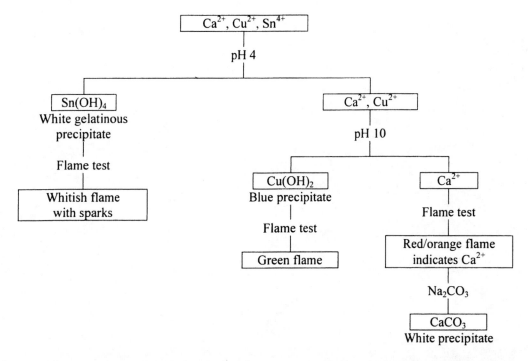

Calcium, copper, and tin are spread out over the periodic table, and their chemistry is appreciably different. Tin (IV) is very acidic and forms a hydroxide precipitate even in acidic solution. Copper (II) forms a hydroxide precipitate at pH 10, but calcium (II) will not form a hydroxide precipitate except under very basic conditions. Calcium (II) will also form a carbonate precipitate. Flame tests of each cation can further identify the cations, since each has a unique flame.

Reactions:

$Ca^{2+}(aq) + CO_3^{2-}(aq) \rightarrow CaCO_3(s)$ (white)

$Cu^{2+}(aq) + 2OH^-(aq) \rightarrow Cu(OH)_2(s)$ (white)

$Sn^{4+}(aq) + 4H_2O \rightarrow Sn(OH)_4(s)$ (white) $+ 4H^+(aq)$

Assignment 20 – $Cr^{3+}/Ti^{4+}/V^{4+}$

Difficulty level: 2

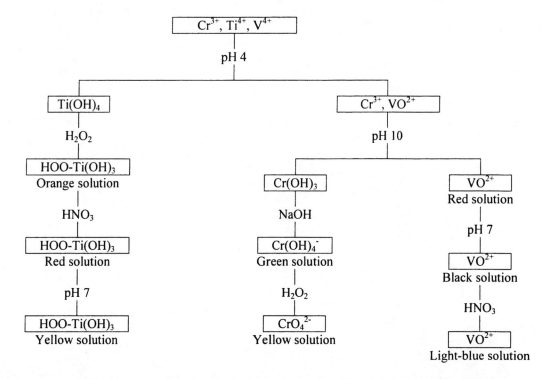

Chromium, titanium, and vanadium lay next to each other in the periodic table. The chemistry of these cations is quite different, but they all have bright-colored solutions. Titanium (IV) is more acidic than chromium (III) and vanadium (IV), and its hydroxide forms even in acidic conditions. Chromium (III) also forms a hydroxide precipitate, but only at pH 10. Upon addition of hydrogen peroxide, titanium (IV) forms a complex that changes color according to pH. Vanadium (IV) exists as VO^{2+} in solution, and this complex also changes color according to pH. Chromium also has several colors of solution. The chromium (III) cation gives a purple solution. Upon addition of excess base, a green chromium hydroxide complex is formed. Hydrogen peroxide oxidizes chromium (III) forming chromate, which gives a yellow solution.

Reactions:

$Cr^{3+}(aq)$ (purple) $+ 3OH^-(aq) \rightarrow Cr(OH)_3(s)$ (gray)
$Cr(OH)_3(s)$ (gray) $+ OH^-(aq) \rightarrow Cr(OH)_4^-(aq)$ (green)
$2Cr(OH)_4^-(aq)$ (green) $+ 3H_2O_2(aq) + 2OH^-(aq) \rightarrow 2CrO_4^{2-}(aq)$ (yellow) $+ 8H_2O$

$Ti^{4+}(aq) + 4OH^-(aq) \rightarrow Ti(OH)_4(s)$ (white)
$Ti(OH)_4(s)$ (white) $+ H_2O_2$ (pH 4) $\rightarrow HOO\text{-}Ti(OH)_3(s)$ (orange) $+ H_2O$

$V^{4+}(aq) + H_2O \rightarrow VO^{2+}(aq)$ (green) $+ 2H^+(aq)$

Assignment 21 – $Cu^{2+}/K^+/Ti^{4+}$

Difficulty level: 2

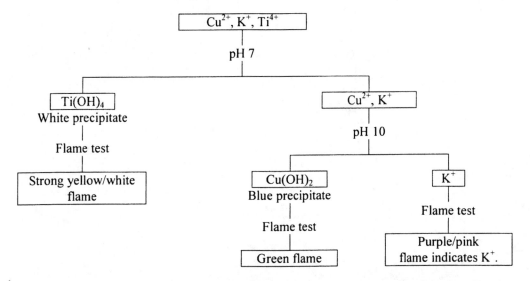

Titanium (IV) forms a hydroxide precipitate in water. Copper (II) forms a hydroxide precipitate in basic solution. The distinctive flame tests of copper, potassium, and titanium cations indicate the presence of these cations. Copper gives a green flame. Titanium gives a strong yellow/white flame. Potassium gives a purple/pink flame.

Reactions:

$Cu^{2+}(aq)$ (light blue) $+ 2OH^-(aq) \rightarrow Cu(OH)_2(s)$ (blue)

$Ti^{4+}(aq) + 4H_2O \rightarrow Ti(OH)_4(s)$ (white) $+ 4H^+(aq)$

Assignment 22 – $Fe^{2+}/NH_4^+/Sr^{2+}$

Difficulty level: 2

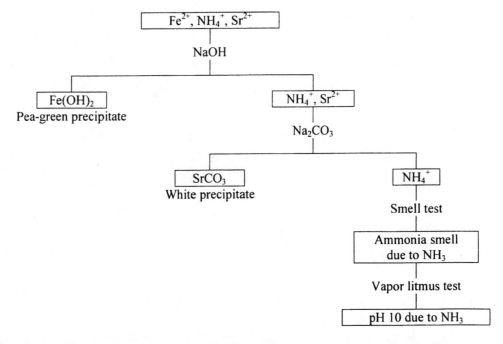

The chemistry of these cations is very different making their separation simple. Iron (II) forms a pea-green hydroxide precipitate in basic solution. Strontium (II) forms a white carbonate precipitate upon addition of carbonate. Ammonia does not precipitate out, but it can be identified by its characteristic smell or its basic vapor.

Reactions:

$Fe^{2+}(aq) + 2OH^-(aq) \rightarrow Fe(OH)_2(s)$ (pea green)

$Sr^{2+}(aq) + CO_3^{2-}(aq) \rightarrow SrCO_3(s)$ (white)

Assignment 23 – Ag$^+$/Ni^{2+}/Sr^{2+}

Difficulty level: 3

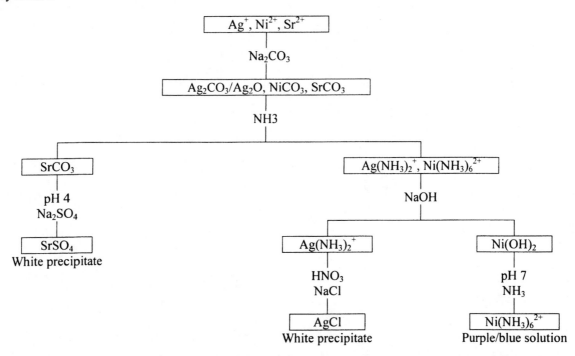

All three cations form insoluble carbonates. However, nickel (II) and silver (I) dissolve in ammonia and strontium (II) does not. The chemistry of these cations is appreciably different, so these cations may be separated and identified in various ways.

Reactions:

$2Ag^+(aq) + 2OH^-(aq) \rightarrow Ag_2O(s)$ (brown) $+ H_2O$

$Ag_2O(s)$ (brown) $+ 4NH_3(aq) + H_2O \rightarrow 2Ag(NH_3)_2^+(aq) + 2OH^-(aq)$

$2Ag^+(aq) + CO_3^{2-}(aq)$ (pH 10) $\rightarrow Ag_2CO_3(s)$ (cream yellow)

$Ag_2CO_3(s)$ (cream yellow) $+ 4NH_3(aq) \rightarrow 2Ag(NH_3)_2^+(aq) + CO_3^{2-}(aq)$

$Ag(NH_3)_2^+(aq) + 2H^+(aq) \rightarrow Ag^+(aq) + 2NH_4^+(aq)$

$Ag^+(aq) + Cl^-(aq) \rightarrow AgCl(s)$ (white)

$Ni^{2+}(aq)$ (green) $+ CO_3^{2-}(aq) \rightarrow NiCO_3(s)$ (light green)

$NiCO_3(s)$ (light green) $+ NH_3(aq) \rightarrow Ni(NH_3)_6^{2+}(aq)$ (purple/blue)

$Ni(NH_3)_6^{2+}(aq)$ (purple/blue) $+ OH^-(aq) \rightarrow Ni(OH)_2(s)$ (light green)

$Sr^{2+}(aq) + CO_3^{2-}(aq) \rightarrow SrCO_3(s)$ (white)

$SrCO_3(s)$ (white) $+ 2H^+(aq) \rightarrow Sr^{2+}(aq) + H_2O + CO_2(g)$

$Sr^{2+}(aq) + SO_4^{2-}(aq) \rightarrow SrSO_4(s)$ (white)

Assignment 24 – Al³⁺/Cr³⁺/Zn²⁺

Difficulty level: 3

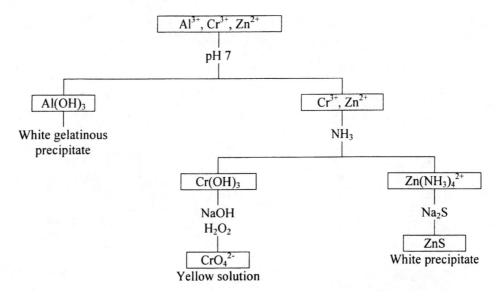

All three cations form hydroxide precipitates and dissolve in excess base. Zinc (II) dissolves in ammonia, but aluminum (III) and chromium (III) do not. The sulfide anion precipitates out the zinc cation, forming zinc sulfide. Chromium is separated from aluminum by oxidizing it to the chromate anion, which is soluble and yellow.

Reactions:

$Al^{3+}(aq) + 3OH^{-}(aq)$ (pH 10) $\rightarrow Al(OH)_3(s)$ (white gel)

$Cr^{3+}(aq) + 3OH^{-}(aq)$ (pH 10) $\rightarrow Cr(OH)_3(s)$ (gray)
$Cr^{3+}(aq) + 4OH^{-}(aq) \rightarrow Cr(OH)_4^{-}(aq)$ (green)
$2Cr(OH)_4^{-}(aq)$ (green) $+ 3H_2O_2(aq) + 2OH^{-}(aq) \rightarrow 2CrO_4^{2-}(aq)$ (yellow) $+ 8H_2O$

$Zn^{2+}(aq) + 4NH_3(aq) \rightarrow Zn(NH_3)_4^{2+}(aq)$
$Zn(NH_3)_4^{2+}(aq) + S^{2-}(aq) \rightarrow ZnS(s)$ (white) $+ 4NH_3(aq)$

Assignment 25 – Ba^{2+}/Sr^{2+}

Difficulty level: 3

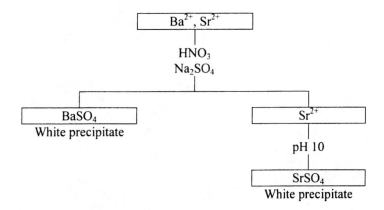

Barium and strontium have similar chemistry. They both form carbonate and sulfate precipitates. The relative solubilities of barium (II) sulfate and strontium (II) sulfate allow for their separation. Barium (II) sulfate forms even in acidic solution, when there is not as much free sulfate. In acidic solution, some of the sulfate anions form bisulfate anions according to the reaction $H^+ + SO_4^{2-} \rightarrow HSO_4^-$. Strontium (II) sulfate, which is more soluble than barium sulfate, does not precipitate out in acidic solution.

Reactions:

$Ba^{2+}(aq) + SO_4^{2-}(aq) \rightarrow BaSO_4(s)$ (white)

$Sr^{2+}(aq) + SO_4^{2-}(aq) \rightarrow SrSO_4(s)$ (white)

Assignment 26 – Bi³⁺/Hg²⁺/Pb²⁺

Difficulty level: 3

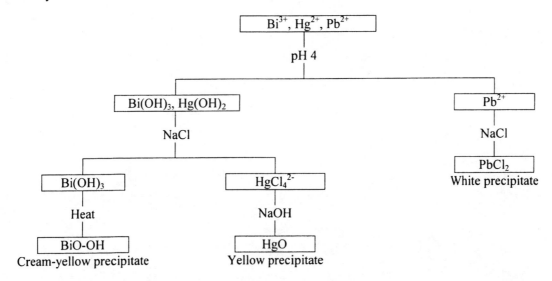

All three cations form hydroxide precipitates, but the bismuth (III) and mercury (II) hydroxides are very insoluble as they form even under acidic conditions. The lead (II) chloride precipitate identifies lead (II), as lead (II) is one of the few cations that forms a chloride precipitate. Mercury (II) forms a complex with chloride, allowing for its separation from white bismuth (III) hydroxide. In basic conditions, yellow mercuric oxide identifies the presence of mercury (II).

Reactions:

$Bi^{3+}(aq) + 3H_2O \rightarrow Bi(OH)_3(s)$ (white) $+ 3H^+(aq)$
$Bi(OH)_3(s)$ (white) $+ Heat \rightarrow BiO\text{-}OH(s)$ (cream yellow) $+ H_2O$

$Hg^{2+}(aq) + H_2O \rightarrow Hg(OH)_2(s)$ (cream yellow)
$Hg(OH)_2(s)$ (cream yellow) $+ 4Cl^-(aq) \rightarrow HgCl_4^{2-}(aq) + 2OH^-(aq)$
$HgCl_4^{2-}(aq) + 2OH^-(aq) \rightarrow HgO(s)$ (yellow) $+ H_2O + 4Cl^-(aq)$

$Pb^{2+}(aq) + 2Cl^-(aq) \rightarrow PbCl_2(s)$ (white)

Assignment 27 – $Ca^{2+}/K^{+}/Mg^{2+}/Na^{+}$

Difficulty level: 3

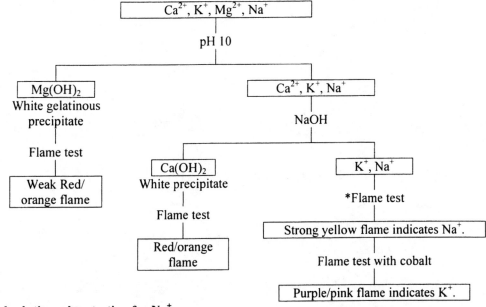

*Use original solution when testing for Na^{+}.

Calcium (II) and magnesium (II) both form hydroxide precipitates. Magnesium (II) hydroxide is less soluble and thus forms at a lower pH than calcium (II). Potassium and sodium cations can be identified by their distinctive flame tests. However, the original solution must be used for the sodium flame test, since sodium hydroxide was added as a reagent.

Reactions:

$Ca^{2+}(aq) + 2OH^{-}(aq) \rightarrow Ca(OH)_2(s)$ (white)

$Mg^{2+}(aq) + 2OH^{-}(aq) \rightarrow Mg(OH)_2(s)$ (white gel)

Assignment 28 – $Ca^{2+}/K^+/Ti^{4+}/V^{4+}$

Difficulty level: 3

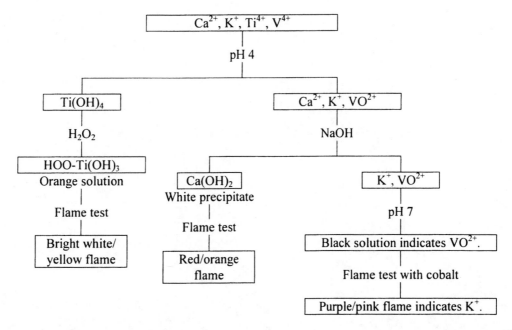

Potassium, calcium, titanium, and vanadium are all within the same row in the periodic table. Titanium (IV) and calcium (II) both form hydroxide precipitates, but calcium (II) will only form a hydroxide precipitate in very basic conditions. Vanadium (IV) always exists as VO^{2+} in solution, and this complex changes according to pH, making vanadium (IV) identifiable. A purple/pink flame behind cobalt glass identifies the presence of potassium.

Reactions:

$Ca^{2+}(aq) + 2OH^-(aq) \rightarrow Ca(OH)_2(s)$ (white)

$Ti^{4+}(aq) + 4H_2O \rightarrow Ti(OH)_4(s)$ (white) $+ 4H^+(aq)$
$Ti(OH)_4(s)$ (white) $+ H_2O_2$ (pH 4) $\rightarrow HOO\text{-}Ti(OH)_3(s)$ (orange) $+ H_2O$

$V^{4+}(aq) + 2OH^-(aq) \rightarrow VO^{2+}(aq)$ (green) $+ H_2O$

Assignment 29 – Cd^{2+}/Co^{2+}/Cu^{2+}

Difficulty level: 3

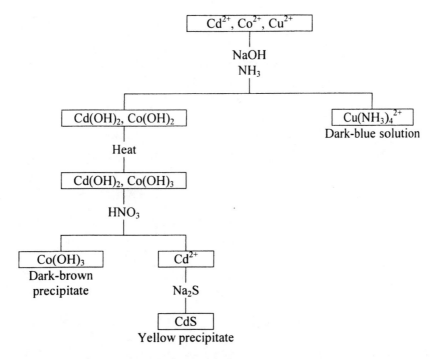

These cations form soluble complexes with ammonia at pH 10. However, cadmium (II) and cobalt (II) form hydroxide precipitates at high pH, while copper (II) remains dissolved in solution. Heat oxidizes cobalt (II) hydroxide to cobalt (III) hydroxide, which is very insoluble. Cobalt (III) hydroxide does not dissolve in acid, unless heated. Cadmium (II) hydroxide dissolves readily in acid and is identified by its yellow sulfide precipitate.

Reactions:

$Cd^{2+}(aq) + 2OH^-(aq) \rightarrow Cd(OH)_2(s)$ (white)
$Cd^{2+}(aq) + S^{2-}(aq) \rightarrow CdS(s)$ (yellow)

$Co^{2+}(aq)$ (pink) $+ 2OH^-(aq) \rightarrow Co(OH)_2(s)$ (pink/tan)
$Co(OH)_2(s)$ (pink/tan) $+ 6NH_3(aq)$ (pH 10) $\rightarrow Co(NH_3)_6^{2+}(aq) + 2OH^-(aq)$
$Co(NH_3)_6^{2+}(aq) + 2OH^-(aq) \rightarrow Co(OH)_2(s)$ (pink/tan) $+ 6NH_3(aq)$
$4Co(OH)_2(s)$ (pink/tan) $+ 2H_2O + O_2(g) + OH^-(aq) + Heat \rightarrow 4Co(OH)_3(s)$ (dark brown) $+ OH^-(aq)$

$Cu^{2+}(aq)$ (light blue) $+ 2OH^-(aq) \rightarrow Cu(OH)_2(s)$ (blue)
$Cu(OH)_2(s)$ (blue) $+ 4NH_3(aq) \rightarrow Cu(NH_3)_4^{2+}(aq)$ (dark blue) $+ 2OH^-(aq)$

Assignment 30 – Cd^{2+}/Hg^{2+}/Zn^{2+}

Difficulty level: 3

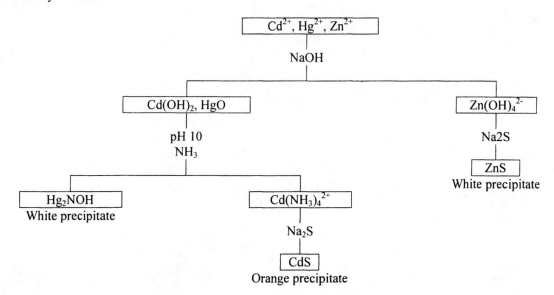

Cadmium, mercury, and zinc lie within the same period of the periodic table, but the chemistry of their cations is very different. Cadmium (II), mercury (II), and zinc (II) hydroxides all precipitate out at pH 10, but zinc (II) hydroxide dissolves in excess base. Formation of a white zinc (II) sulfide precipitate identifies the presence of zinc. Cadmium (II) complexes with ammonia dissolving the cadmium (II) hydroxide precipitate at pH 10. The cadmium (II) sulfide precipitate is stronger than the cadmium (II) ammonia complex, so formation of an orange precipitate upon addition of sulfide identifies the presence of cadmium. Mercuric oxide (HgO) does not dissolve in ammonia, but it forms a white precipitate.

Reactions:

Cd^{2+}(aq) + 2OH$^-$(aq) → $Cd(OH)_2$(s) (white)
$Cd(OH)_2$(s) (white) + 4NH$_3$(aq) → $Cd(NH_3)_4^{2+}$(aq) + 2OH$^-$(aq)
$Cd(NH_3)_4^{2+}$(aq) + S^{2-}(aq) → CdS(s) (orange) + 4NH$_3$(aq)

Hg^{2+}(aq) + 2OH$^-$(aq) → HgO(s) (yellow) + H$_2$O
2HgO(s) (yellow) + NH$_3$(aq) (pH 10)→ Hg$_2$NOH(s) (white) + H$_2$O

Zn^{2+}(aq) + 4OH$^-$(aq) → $Zn(OH)_4^{2-}$(aq)
$Zn(OH)_4^{2-}$(aq) + S^{2-}(aq) → ZnS(s) (white) + 4OH$^-$(aq)

Assignment 31 – $Co^{2+}/Cr^{3+}/Cu^{2+}$

Difficulty level: 3

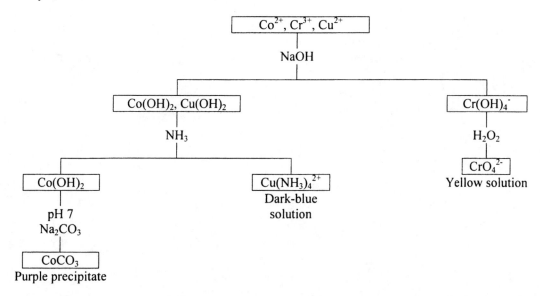

Cobalt (II), chromium (III), and copper all form hydroxide precipitates at pH 10, but chromium (III) dissolves in excess base. The chromium (III) hydroxide complex is green but further detection of chromium is made by oxidizing chromium (III) to the yellow chromate anion. Cobalt (II) and copper (II) both form complexes with ammonia, but only the copper (II) ammonia complex forms in excess base. The dark-blue copper ammonia complex identifies the presence of copper. The cobalt (II) hydroxide precipitate is tan, but by lowering the pH and adding carbonate, a purple precipitate is formed.

Reactions:

Co^{2+}(aq) (pink) + $2OH^-$(aq) → $Co(OH)_2$(s) (pink/tan)
Co^{2+}(aq) (pink) + CO_3^{2-}(aq) → $CoCO_3$(s) (purple)

Cu^{2+}(aq) (light blue) + $2OH^-$(aq) → $Cu(OH)_2$(s) (blue)
$Cu(OH)_2$(s) (blue) + $4NH_3$(aq) → $Cu(NH_3)_4^{2+}$(aq) (dark blue) + $2OH^-$(aq)

Cr^{3+}(aq) (purple) + $4OH^-$(aq) → $Cr(OH)_4^-$(aq) (green)
$2Cr(OH)_4^-$(aq) (green) + $3H_2O_2$(aq) + $2OH^-$(aq) → $2CrO_4^{2-}$(aq) (yellow) + $8H_2O$

Assignment 32 – $Cr^{3+}/Fe^{3+}/Ni^{2+}$

Difficulty level: 3

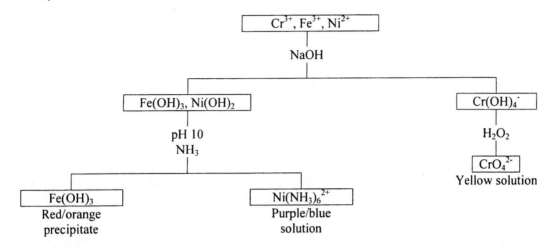

Chromium (III), iron (III), and nickel (II) form hydroxides in basic solutions, but chromium (III) dissolves in excess base. Hydrogen peroxide oxidizes chromium (III) to chromium (VI), which forms the yellow chromate anion. Iron (II) and nickel (II) hydroxides are separated upon the addition of ammonia at pH 10, since nickel (II) hydroxide dissolves as it forms a purple/blue complex with ammonia. A remaining red/orange precipitate is iron (III) hydroxide.

Reactions:

$Cr^{3+}(aq)$ (purple) + $4OH^{-}(aq) \rightarrow Cr(OH)_4^{-}(aq)$ (green)
$2Cr(OH)_4^{-}(aq)$ (green) + $3H_2O_2(aq)$ + $2OH^{-}(aq) \rightarrow 2CrO_4^{2-}(aq)$ (yellow) + $8H_2O$

$Fe^{3+}(aq)$ (yellow) + $3OH^{-}(aq) \rightarrow Fe(OH)_3(s)$ (red/orange)

$Ni^{2+}(aq)$ (green) + $2OH^{-}(aq) \rightarrow Ni(OH)_2(s)$ (light green)
$Ni^{2+}(aq)$ (green) + $6NH_3(aq) \rightarrow Ni(NH_3)_6^{2+}(aq)$ (purple/blue)

Assignment 33 – $Cr^{3+}/Mg^{2+}/Mn^{2+}$

Difficulty level: 3

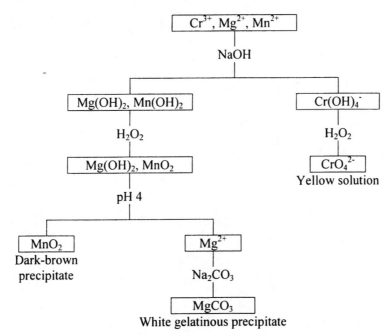

At pH 10, all three cations for hydroxide precipitate, but chromium (III) hydroxide dissolves in excess base while magnesium (II) hydroxide and manganese (II) hydroxide do not. The chromium (III) hydroxide complex is green, and further detection of chromium is made by oxidizing chromium (III) to the yellow chromate anion. Magnesium and manganese can be separated by oxidizing manganese (II) to manganese (IV), which forms a very insoluble oxide. Manganese (IV) oxide does not dissolve in acid, but magnesium (II) hydroxide dissolves readily in acid. Upon the addition of carbonate, white magnesium (II) carbonate identifies the presence of magnesium.

Reactions:

$Cr^{3+}(aq)$ (purple) $+ 4OH^-(aq) \rightarrow Cr(OH)_4^-(aq)$ (green)
$2Cr(OH)_4^-(aq)$ (green) $+ 3H_2O_2(aq) + 2OH^-(aq) \rightarrow 2CrO_4^{2-}(aq)$ (yellow) $+ 8H_2O$

$Mg^{2+}(aq) + 2OH^-(aq) \rightarrow Mg(OH)_2(s)$ (white gel)
$Mg^{2+}(aq) + CO_3^{2-}(aq) \rightarrow MgCO_3(s)$ (white gel)

$Mn^{2+}(aq) + 2OH^-(aq) + 2H_2O \rightarrow Mn(OH)_2(s)$ (brown/orange) $+ 2NH_4^+(aq)$
$Mn(OH)_2(s)$ (brown/orange) $+ H_2O_2(aq) + OH^-(aq) \rightarrow MnO_2(s)$ (dark brown) $+ 2H_2O + OH^-(aq)$

Assignment 34 – $Cu^{2+}/Fe^{3+}/Ni^{2+}$

Difficulty level: 3

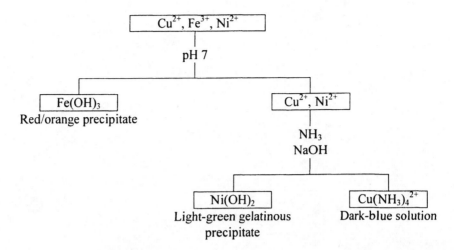

Iron (III) forms a red/orange hydroxide precipitate in water, but copper (II) and nickel (II) only form hydroxide precipitates in basic solution. Copper (II) and nickel (II) both form complexes with ammonia, but nickel (II) favors the hydroxide precipitate in excess base, while copper (II) remains in solution in the ammonia complex. Nickel (II) hydroxide is a light-green gelatinous precipitate, and the copper ammonia complex gives a dark-blue solution.

Reactions:

Cu^{2+}(aq) (light blue) + $4NH_3$(aq) → $Cu(NH_3)_4{}^{2+}$(aq) (dark blue)

Fe^{3+}(yellow) + $3H_2O$ → $Fe(OH)_3$(s) (red/orange) + $3H^+$(aq)

Ni^{2+}(aq) (green) + $2OH^-$(aq) → $Ni(OH)_2$(s) (light-green gel)

Assignment 35 – Al^{3+}/Bi^{3+}/Cr^{3+}/Sb^{3+}

Difficulty level: 4

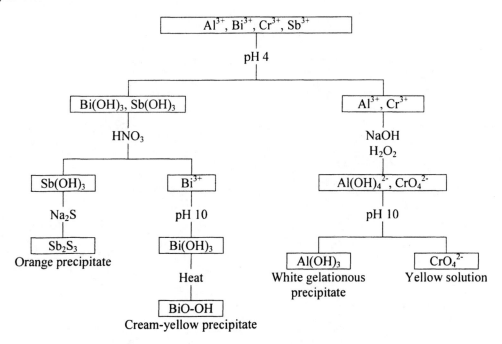

All four cations form hydroxide precipitates. Antimony (III) will form hydroxide precipitates readily, even at low pH. The other three cations are not as acidic, but they will form hydroxide precipitates in basic solutions. Chromium (III) can be separated and identified by oxidizing it to the bright-yellow chromate anion.

Reactions:

$Al^{3+}(aq) + 3OH^-(aq)$ (pH 10) $\rightarrow Al(OH)_3(s)$ (white gel)
$Al^{3+}(aq) + 4OH^-(aq) \rightarrow Al(OH)_4^-(aq)$

$Bi^{3+}(aq) + 3H_2O \rightarrow Bi(OH)_3(s)$ (white) $+ 3H^+(aq)$
$Bi(OH)_3 + heat \rightarrow BiO\text{-}OH(s)$ (cream yellow) $+ H_2O$

$Cr^{3+}(aq) + 4OH^-(aq) \rightarrow Cr(OH)_4^-(aq)$ (green)
$2Cr(OH)_4^-(aq)$ (green) $+ 3H_2O_2(aq) + 2OH^-(aq) \rightarrow 2CrO_4^{2-}(aq)$ (yellow) $+ 8H_2O$

$Sb^{3+}(aq) + 3H_2O \rightarrow Sb(OH)_3(s)$ (white) $+ 3H^+(aq)$
$2Sb(OH)_3(s)$ (white) $+ 6H^+(aq) + 3S^{2-}(aq) \rightarrow Sb_2S_3(s)$ (orange) $+ 6H_2O$

Assignment 36 – Al^{3+}/Cr^{3+}/Mg^{2+}/Ti^{4+}

Difficulty level: 4

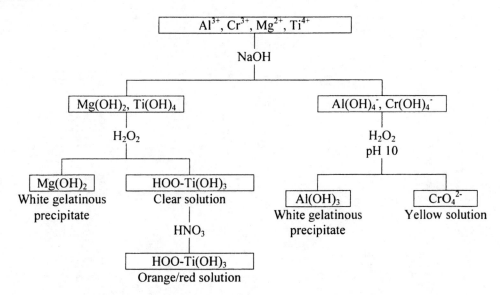

Aluminum (III) and chromium (III) cations are both amphoteric. (Their hydroxide precipitates will dissolve in both acid and base.) Titanium (IV) can be separated from many hydroxides since it forms a soluble complex with hydrogen peroxide. The pH-dependent color of the complex identifies the presence of the titanium cation. Chromium (III) can be oxidized to the soluble chromate anion, which can be separated from the aluminum hydroxide precipitate at pH 10.

Reactions:

Al^{3+}(aq) + 3OH$^-$(aq) (pH 10) → Al(OH)$_3$(s) (white gel)
Al^{3+}(aq) + 4OH$^-$(aq) → Al(OH)$_4^-$(aq)

Cr^{3+}(aq) + 4OH$^-$(aq) → Cr(OH)$_4^-$(aq) (green)
2Cr(OH)$_4^-$(aq) (green) + 3H$_2$O$_2$(aq) + 2OH$^-$(aq) → 2CrO$_4^{2-}$(aq) (yellow) + 8H$_2$O

Mg^{2+}(aq) + 2OH$^-$(aq) → Mg(OH)$_2$(s) (white gel)

Ti^{4+}(aq) + 4OH$^-$(aq) → Ti(OH)$_4$(s) (white)
Ti(OH)$_4$(s) (white) + H$_2$O$_2$(aq) → HOO-Ti(OH)$_3$(aq) + H$_2$O

Assignment 37 – $Al^{3+}/Cr^{3+}/Fe^{3+}/NH_4^+$

Difficulty level: 4

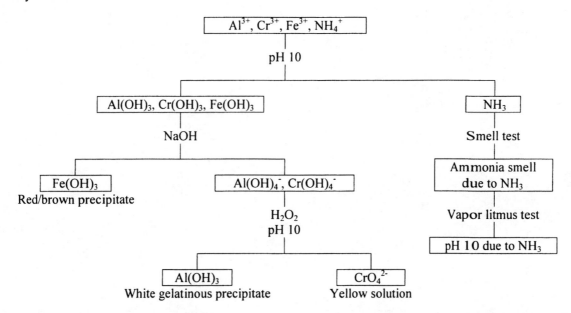

Aluminum (III), chromium (III), and iron (III) cations all form hydroxide precipitates, but aluminum (III) and chromium (III) both dissolve in excess base. Base and hydrogen peroxide oxidize chromium (III) to chromium (VI), which forms the soluble chromate anion. Ammonia does not precipitate out, but it is identified by its smell or basic vapor.

Reactions:

$Al^{3+}(aq) + 3OH^-(aq) \rightarrow Al(OH)_3(s)$ (white)
$Al(OH)_3(s)$ (white) $+ OH^-(aq) \rightarrow Al(OH)_4^-(aq)$

$Fe^{3+}(aq) + 3OH^-(aq) \rightarrow Fe(OH)_3(s)$ (red/brown)

$Cr^{3+}(aq) + 3OH^-(aq)$ (pH 10) $\rightarrow Cr(OH)_3(s)$ (gray)
$Cr(OH)_3(s)$ (gray) $+ OH^-(aq) \rightarrow Cr(OH)_4^-(aq)$ (green)
$2Cr(OH)_4^-(aq)$ (green) $+ 3H_2O_2(aq) + 2OH^-(aq) \rightarrow 2CrO_4^{2-}(aq)$ (yellow) $+ 8H_2O$

$NH_4^+(aq) + OH^-(aq) \rightarrow NH_3(aq) + H_2O$

Assignment 38 – $Al^{3+}/Cr^{3+}/Pb^{2+}/Zn^{2+}$

Difficulty level: 4

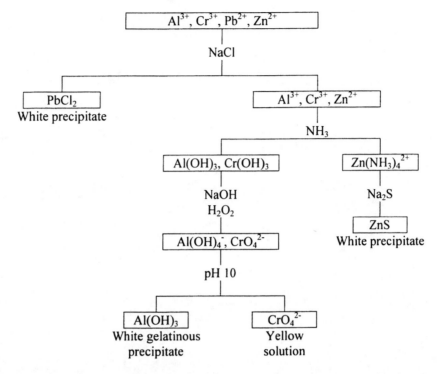

All four cations form hydroxide precipitates and dissolve in excess base. Lead (II) is one of the few cations that forms a chloride precipitate. Zinc (II) dissolves in ammonia, but aluminum (III) and chromium (III) do not. Sulfide precipitates out zinc (II), forming zinc sulfide. Chromium (III) is separated from aluminum (III) by oxidizing it to the chromate anion, which is soluble and yellow.

Reactions:

$Al^{3+}(aq) + 3OH^-(aq)$ (pH 10) $\rightarrow Al(OH)_3(s)$ (white gel)
$Al^{3+}(aq) + 4OH^-(aq) \rightarrow Al(OH)_4^-(aq)$

$Cr^{3+}(aq) + 3OH^-(aq)$ (pH 10) $\rightarrow Cr(OH)_3(s)$ (gray)
$Cr^{3+}(aq) + 4OH^-(aq) \rightarrow Cr(OH)_4^-(aq)$ (green)
$2Cr(OH)_4^-(aq)$ (green) $+ 3H_2O_2(aq) + 2OH^-(aq) \rightarrow 2CrO_4^{2-}(aq)$ (yellow) $+ 8H_2O$

$Pb^{2+}(aq) + 2Cl^-(aq) \rightarrow PbCl_2(s)$ (white)

$Zn^{2+}(aq) + 4NH_3(aq) \rightarrow Zn(NH_3)_4^{2+}(aq)$
$Zn(NH_3)_4^{2+}(aq) + S^{2-}(aq) \rightarrow ZnS(s)$ (white) $+ 4NH_3(aq)$

Assignment 39 – Ba²⁺/Bi³⁺/Hg²⁺/Pb²⁺

Difficulty level: 4

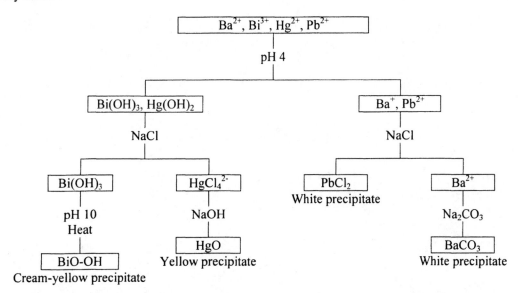

Bismuth (III) and mercury (II) both form hydroxide precipitates readily, even in acidic solution. Mercury (II) forms a complex with chloride in acidic solution. Lead (II) is one of the few cations that forms a chloride precipitate. The barium (II) carbonate precipitate indicates the presence of barium.

Reactions:

$Ba^{2+}(aq) + CO_3^{2-}(aq) \rightarrow BaCO_3(s)$ (white)

$Bi^{3+}(aq) + 3H_2O \rightarrow Bi(OH)_3(s)$ (white) $+ 3H^+(aq)$
$Bi(OH)_3 + Heat \rightarrow BiO\text{-}OH(s)$ (cream yellow) $+ H_2O$

$Hg^{2+}(aq) + H_2O \rightarrow Hg(OH)_2(s)$ (white) $+ 2H^+(aq)$
$Hg(OH)_2(s)$ (white) $+ 4Cl^-(aq) \rightarrow HgCl_4^{2-}(aq) + 2OH^-(aq)$
$HgCl_4^{2-}(aq) + 2OH^-(aq) \rightarrow HgO(s)$ (yellow) $+ H_2O + 4Cl^-(aq)$

$Pb^{2+}(aq) + 2Cl^-(aq) \rightarrow PbCl_2(s)$ (white)

Assignment 40 – $Ba^{2+}/K^+/Na^+/Sr^{2+}/V^{4+}$

Difficulty level: 4

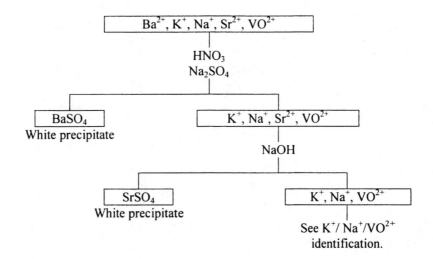

Barium and strontium have very similar chemistry. Both cations precipitate out with sulfate, but strontium (II) sulfate is more soluble. In acidic solution, there is not as much free sulfate due to the formation of bisulfate: $H^+ + SO_4^{2-} \rightarrow HSO_4$. Thus, in acidic solution, strontium (II) will not precipitate out with sulfate, but barium (II) sulfate will precipitate due to its greater insolubility. Potassium, sodium, and vanadium cations do not ever precipitate out with the available reagents, but they can be identified.

Reactions:

$Ba^{2+}(aq) + SO_4^{2-}(aq) \rightarrow BaSO_4(s)$ (white)

$Sr^{2+}(aq) + SO_4^{2-}(aq) \rightarrow SrSO_4(s)$ (white)

Assignment 41 – Bi^{3+}/Fe^{3+}/Hg^{2+}

Difficulty level: 4

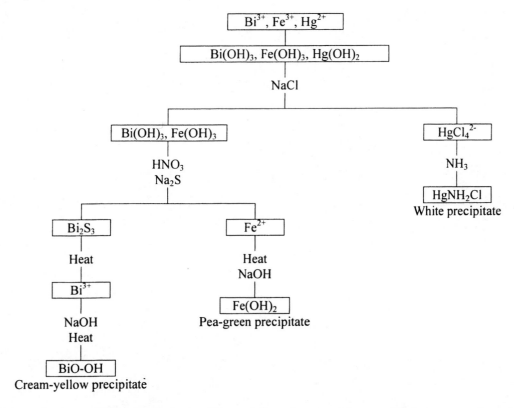

All three cations are acidic and form hydroxide precipitates in water. Mercury (II) forms a complex with chloride, allowing for its separation. Bismuth (III) forms a sulfide precipitate in acidic sulfide solution, but iron only precipitates out with sulfide in basic solution. However, sulfide reduces iron (III) to iron (II). Iron (II) is detected by its pea-green hydroxide.

Reactions:

$Bi^{3+}(aq) + 3H_2O \rightarrow Bi(OH)_3(s)$ (white) $+ 3H^+(aq)$
$2Bi^{3+}(aq) + 3S^{2-}(aq) \rightarrow Bi_2S_3(s)$ (dark brown)
$Bi_2S_3(s)$ (dark brown) $+ H^+(aq) + Heat \rightarrow 2Bi^{3+}(aq) + 3S(s) + 2NO(g) + 4H_2O$
$Bi(OH)_3(s)$ (white) $+ Heat \rightarrow BiO\text{-}OH(s)$ (cream yellow) $+ H_2O$

$Fe^{3+}(aq) + 3H_2O \rightarrow Fe(OH)_3(s)$ (red/brown) $+ 3H^+(aq)$
$2Fe^{3+}(aq)$ (yellow) $+ H_2S(aq) \rightarrow 2Fe^{2+}(aq) + 2H^+(aq) + S(s)$
$Fe^{2+}(aq) + 2OH^-(aq) \rightarrow Fe(OH)_2(s)$ (pea green)

$Hg^{2+}(aq) + H_2O \rightarrow Hg(OH)_2(s)$ (cream yellow)
$Hg(OH)_2(s)$ (cream yellow) $+ 4Cl^-(aq) \rightarrow HgCl_4^{2-}(aq) + 2OH^-(aq)$
$HgCl_4^{2-}(aq) + NH_3(aq) \rightarrow HgNH_2Cl(s)$ (white) $+ H^+(aq) + 3Cl^-(aq)$

Assignment 42 – $Cd^{2+}/Mn^{2+}/Pb^{2+}$

Difficulty level: 4

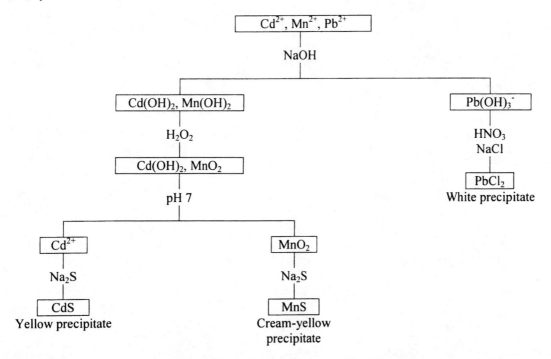

Cadmium (II), manganese (II), and lead (II) all form hydroxide precipitates at pH 10, but lead (II) is amphoteric and therefore dissolves in excess base. The white lead (II) chloride precipitate identifies the presence of lead. Cadmium (II) hydroxide dissolves in ammonia at pH 10 since cadmium (II) forms a complex with ammonia. A brown/orange precipitate after addition of ammonia is manganese (II) hydroxide. Addition of sulfide to the cadmium (II) ammonia complex will cause orange cadmium (II) sulfide to precipitate.

Reactions:

$Cd^{2+}(aq) + 2OH^-(aq) \rightarrow Cd(OH)_2(s)$ (white)
$Cd^{2+}(aq) + S^{2-}(aq) \rightarrow CdS(s)$ (orange)

$Mn^{2+}(aq) + 2OH^-(aq) \rightarrow Mn(OH)_2(s)$ (brown/orange)
$Mn(OH)_2(s) + H_2O_2(aq) + OH^-(aq) \rightarrow MnO_2(s)$ (dark brown) $+ 2H_2O + OH^-(aq)$
$MnO_2(s)$ (dark brown) $+ 4H^+(aq) + 2S^{2-}(aq) \rightarrow MnS(s)$ (cream yellow) $+ S(s) + 2H_2O$

$Pb^{2+}(aq) + 3OH^-(aq) \rightarrow Pb(OH)_3^-(aq)$
$Pb^{2+}(aq) + 2Cl^-(aq) \rightarrow PbCl_2(s)$ (white)

Assignment 43 – $Cd^{2+}/Sb^{3+}/Sn^{4+}$

Difficulty level: 4

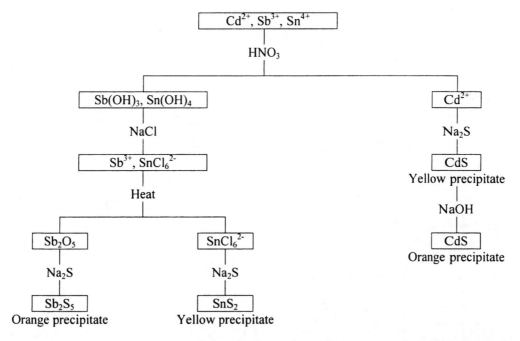

Cadmium, antimony, and tin are found in the same row in the periodic table. Antimony (III) and tin (IV) are more acidic than cadmium (II), and their hydroxide precipitates do not readily dissolve in acidic solution. Cadmium (II) precipitates out in acidic conditions with sulfide, forming a yellow precipitate. Antimony (III) and tin (IV) hydroxides dissolve in strong acidic solution in the presence of chloride. Heat oxidizes antimony (III) to antimony (V), which forms an insoluble oxide precipitate. The insoluble antimony (V) oxide can then be separated from the tin (IV) chloride complex. Both cations can be identified by their bright sulfide precipitates in acidic solution.

Reactions:

Cd^{2+}(aq) + H^+(aq) + S^{2-}(aq) → CdS(s) (yellow) + H^+(aq)
CdS(s) (yellow) + OH^-(aq) → CdS(s) (orange) + OH^-(aq)

Sb^{3+}(aq) + $3H_2O$ → $Sb(OH)_3$(s) (white) + $3H^+$(aq)
$Sb(OH)_3$(s) (white) + $3H^+$(aq) + Cl^-(aq) → Sb^{3+}(aq) + $3H_2O$ + Cl^-(aq)
$2Sb^{3+}$(aq) + $5H_2O$ + Heat → Sb_2O_5(s) (white) + $6H^+$(aq) + $2H_2$(g)
Sb_2O_5(s) (white) + $5S^{2-}$(aq) + H^+(aq) → Sb_2S_5(s) (orange) + H^+(aq)

Sn^{4+}(aq) + H_2O → $Sn(OH)_4$(s) (white gel) + $4H^+$(aq)
$Sn(OH)_4$(s) + $4H^+$(aq) + $6Cl^-$(aq) → $SnCl_6^{2-}$(aq) + $4H_2O$
$SnCl_6^{2-}$(aq) + $2S^{2-}$(aq) + H^+(aq) → SnS_2(s) (yellow) + $6Cl^-$(aq) + H^+(aq)

Assignment 44 – Co²⁺/Cu²⁺/Ni²⁺

Difficulty level: 4

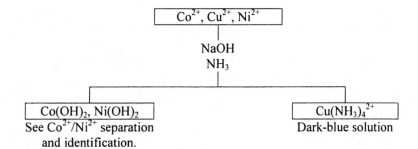

The blue copper (II) ammonia complex stays in solution in very basic solution, but cobalt (II) and nickel (II) hydroxides precipitate out. Cobalt and nickel have similar chemistry, but they can be separated by oxidizing cobalt (II) to cobalt (III), which forms an insoluble hydroxide.

Reactions:

$Co^{2+}(aq)$ (pink) + $6NH_3(aq) \rightarrow Co(NH_3)_6^{2+}(aq)$ (yellow/brown)

$Cu^{2+}(aq)$ (light blue) + $4NH_3(aq) \rightarrow Cu(NH_3)_4^{2+}(aq)$ (dark blue)

$Ni^{2+}(aq)$ (green) + $6NH_3(aq) \rightarrow Ni(NH_3)_6^{2+}(aq)$ (purple/blue)

Assignment 45 – Co^{2+}/Fe^{2+}/Hg_2^{2+}/Pb^{2+}

Difficulty level: 4

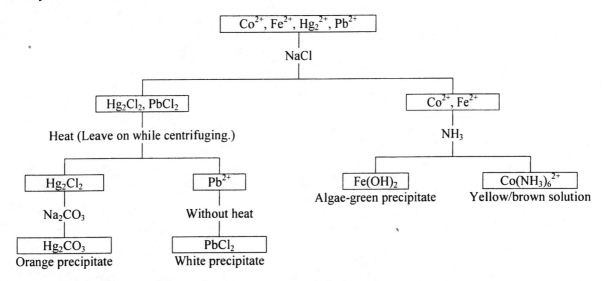

Mercury (I) and lead (II) both form chloride precipitates. As lead (II) chloride is much more soluble than mercury (I) chloride, it will dissolve upon addition of heat while mercury (I) chloride remains insoluble. When heat is taken away, lead (II) chloride will form again. Mercury (I) will form an orange carbonate precipitate upon the addition of carbonate. Cobalt (I) and iron (II) both form hydroxides in basic solution, but cobalt (II) forms a complex with ammonia if the solution is not too basic. An algae-green precipitate indicates iron (II) hyrdoxide, and a yellow/brown solution indicates cobalt is present.

Reactions:

$Co^{2+}(aq)$ (pink) + $6NH_3(aq) \rightarrow Co(NH_3)_6^{2+}(aq)$ (yellow/brown)

$Fe^{2+}(aq) + 2NH_3(aq) + 2H_2O \rightarrow Fe(OH)_2(s)$ (algae green) + $2NH_4^+(aq)$

$Hg_2^{2+}(aq) + 2Cl^-(aq) \rightarrow Hg_2Cl_2(s)$ (white)
$Hg_2Cl_2(s)$ (white) + $CO_3^{2-}(aq) \rightarrow Hg_2CO_3(s)$ (orange) + $2Cl^-(aq)$

$Pb^{2+}(aq) + 2Cl^-(aq) \rightarrow PbCl_2(s)$ (white)
$PbCl_2(s)$ (white) + Heat $\rightarrow Pb^{2+}(aq) + 2Cl^-(aq)$

Assignment 46 – $Fe^{2+}/Mn^{2+}/Zn^{2+}$

Difficulty level: 4

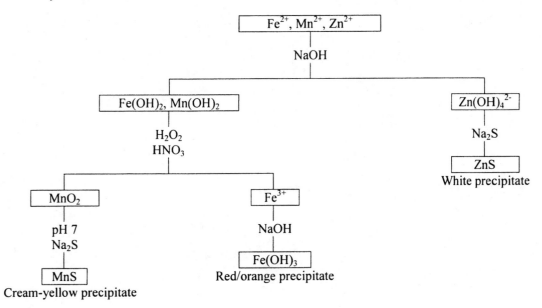

Zinc (II) hydroxide dissolves in excess base, but it will precipitate out with sulfide. In basic solution, hydrogen peroxide oxides iron (II) hydroxide and manganese (II) hydroxide to iron (III) hydroxide and manganese (IV) oxide respectively. Iron (III) hydroxide is more soluble than manganese (IV) oxide; it will dissolve in acid, while manganese (IV) oxide will not. Sulfide reduces manganese (IV) back to manganese (II), and manganese (II) sulfide is formed. Iron (III) forms a red/orange hydroxide.

Reactions:

$Fe^{2+}(aq) + 2OH^-(aq) \rightarrow Fe(OH)_2(s)$ (pea green)
$2Fe(OH)_2(s)$ (pea green) $+ H_2O_2(aq) + OH^-(aq) \rightarrow 2Fe(OH)_3(s)$ (red/orange) $+ OH^-(aq)$

$Mn^{2+}(aq) + 2OH^-(aq) \rightarrow Mn(OH)_2(s)$ (brown/orange)
$Mn(OH)_2(s)$ (brown/orange) $+ H_2O_2(aq) + OH^-(aq) \rightarrow MnO_2(s)$ (dark brown) $+ 2H_2O + OH^-(aq)$
$MnO_2(s)$ (dark brown) $+ 4H^+(aq) + 2S^{2-}(aq) \rightarrow MnS(s)$ (cream yellow) $+ S(s) + 2H_2O$

$Zn^{2+}(aq) + 4OH^-(aq) \rightarrow Zn(OH)_4^{2-}(aq)$
$Zn(OH)_4^{2-}(aq) + S^{2-}(aq) \rightarrow ZnS(s)$ (white) $+ 4OH^-(aq)$

Assignment 47 – Mn²⁺/NH₄⁺/Pb²⁺/Zn²⁺

Difficulty level: 4

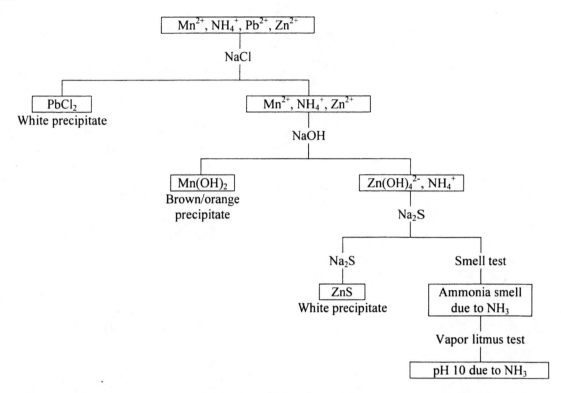

Lead (II) forms a white chloride precipitate. Manganese (II) forms a brown/orange hydroxide in excess base. Zinc (II) also forms a hydroxide in basic solution, but it forms a hydroxide complex in excess base. Zinc (II) forms white zinc (II) sulfide upon addition of sulfide even in excess base. Ammonia does not precipitate out, but it can be identified by its characteristic smell or its basic vapor.

Reactions:

$Pb^{2+}(aq) + 2Cl^-(aq) \rightarrow PbCl_2(s)$ (white)

$Mn^{2+}(aq) + 2OH^-(aq) \rightarrow Mn(OH)_2(s)$ (brown/orange)

$Zn^{2+}(aq) + 4OH^-(aq) \rightarrow Zn(OH)_4^{2-}(aq)$
$Zn(OH)_4^{2-}(aq) + S^{2-}(aq) \rightarrow ZnS(s)$ (white) $+ 4OH^-(aq)$

Assignment 48 – Co²⁺/Fe²⁺/Mn²⁺

Difficulty level: 4

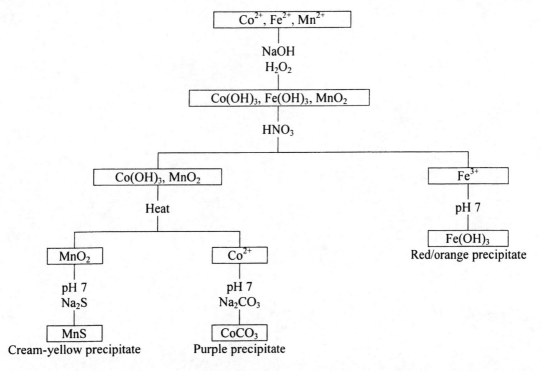

In basic solution, hydrogen peroxide oxidizes cobalt (II), iron (II), and manganese (II). The oxidized forms can be separated according to their relative solubilities. Iron (III) hydroxide readily dissolves in acid. Cobalt (III) hydroxide only dissolves in acid with heat. Even with heat and acid, manganese (IV) oxide will not dissolve, but manganese (IV) can be reduced back to manganese (II) by sulfide in basic conditions.

Reactions:

$2Co(OH)_2(s)$ (pink/tan) $+ H_2O_2(aq) + OH^-(aq) \rightarrow 2Co(OH)_3(s)$ (dark brown) $+ OH^-(aq)$
$4Co(OH)_3(s)$ (dark brown) $+ 8H^+(aq) + Heat \rightarrow 4Co^{2+}(aq)$ (pink) $+ 10H_2O + O_2(g)$
$Co^{2+}(aq)$ (pink) $+ CO_3^{2-}(aq) \rightarrow CoCO_3(s)$ (purple)

$2Fe^{2+}(aq) + H_2O_2(aq) + 4OH^-(aq) \rightarrow 2Fe(OH)_3(s)$ (red/orange)

$Mn^{2+}(aq) + H_2O_2(aq) + 2OH^-(aq) \rightarrow MnO_2(s)$ (dark brown) $+ 2H_2O$
$MnO_2(s)$ (dark brown) $+ 4H^+(aq) + 2S^{2-}(aq) \rightarrow MnS(s)$ (cream yellow) $+ S(s) + 2H_2O$

Assignment 49 – $Ag^+/Cd^{2+}/Sb^{3+}/Sn^{4+}$

Difficulty level: 5

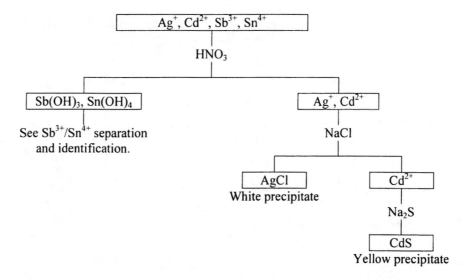

Antimony (III) and tin (IV) cations can be separated from most other cations because of their insoluble hydroxides (even at low pH). Silver (I) is one of the three cations that forms a precipitate with chloride. Although cadmium (II) forms a bright-yellow sulfide in acidic conditions, it forms an orange precipitate with sulfide in basic conditions.

Reactions:

$Ag^+(aq) + Cl^-(aq) \rightarrow AgCl(s)$ (white)

$Cd^{2+}(aq) + S^{2-}(aq) \rightarrow CdS(s)$ (orange)

$Sb^{3+}(aq) + 3H_2O \rightarrow Sb(OH)_3(s)$ (white) $+ 3H^+(aq)$

$Sn^{4+}(aq) + 4H_2O \rightarrow Sn(OH)_4(s)$ (white) $+ 4H^+(aq)$

Assignment 50 – $Ba^{2+}/Ca^{2+}/Mg^{2+}/Sr^{2+}$

Difficulty level: 5

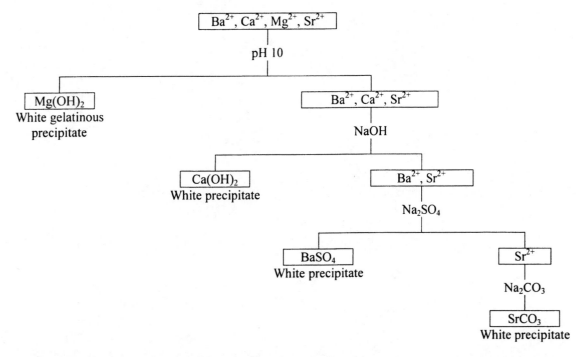

Barium, calcium, magnesium, and strontium are all Group II elements in the periodic table. Going down the periodic table, the hydroxides become more and more soluble. Barium and strontium have very similar chemistry. Both cations precipitate out with sulfate, but strontium (II) does not precipitate in very basic sulfate solution.

Reactions:

$Ba^{2+}(aq) + SO_4^{2-}(aq) \rightarrow BaSO_4(s)$ (white)

$Ca^{2+}(aq) + 2OH^-(aq) \rightarrow Ca(OH)_2(s)$ (white)

$Mg^{2+}(aq) + 2OH^-(aq) \rightarrow Mg(OH)_2(s)$ (white gel)

$Sr^{2+}(aq) + CO_3^{2-}(aq) \rightarrow SrCO_3(s)$ (white)

Assignment 51 – Ba²⁺/Hg²⁺/Pb²⁺/Sr²⁺

Difficulty level: 5

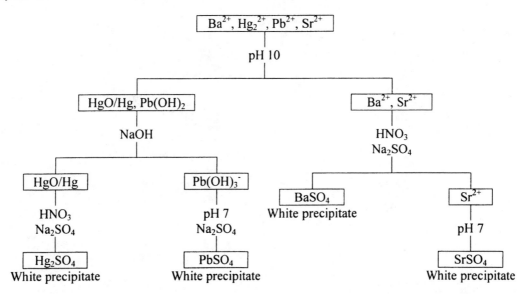

Both lead (II) and mercury (I) are insoluble at pH 10. Mercury (I) disproportionates in basic solution to form mercury (Hg) and mercuric oxide (HgO). Lead (II) forms a hydroxide precipitate at pH 10, but it dissolves in excess base. Barium and strontium have similar chemistry, but strontium (II) sulfate is more soluble than barium (II) sulfate. Thus, strontium sulfate will not precipitate out under acidic conditions, while the more insoluble barium sulfate will precipitate.

Reactions:

$Ba^{2+}(aq) + SO_4^{2-}(aq) \rightarrow BaSO_4(s)$ (white)

$Hg_2^{2+}(aq) + 2OH^-(aq) \rightarrow HgO/Hg(s)$ (black) $+ H_2O$
$HgO/Hg(s)$ (black) $+ 2H^+(aq) + SO_4^{2-}(aq) \rightarrow Hg_2SO_4(s)$ (white) $+ H_2O$

$Sr^{2+}(aq) + SO_4^{2-}(aq) \rightarrow SrSO_4(s)$ (white)

$Pb^{2+}(aq) + 2OH^-(aq)$ (pH 10) $\rightarrow Pb(OH)_2(s)$ (white)
$Pb(OH)_2(s) + OH^-(aq) \rightarrow Pb(OH)_3^-(s)$ (white)
$Pb^{2+}(aq) + SO_4^{2-}(aq) \rightarrow PbSO_4(s)$ (white)

Assignment 52 – Ba^{2+}/K$^+$/Na$^+$/NH$_4^+$/Sr^{2+}/V^{4+}

Difficulty level: 5

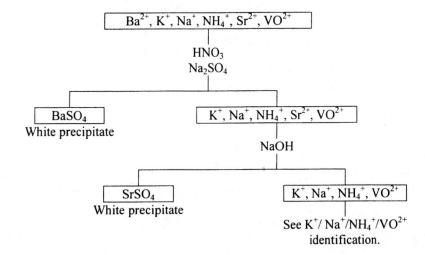

Barium and strontium have very similar chemistry. Both cations precipitate out with sulfate, but strontium (II) sulfate is more soluble. In acidic solution, there is not as much free sulfate due to the formation of bisulfate: $H^+ + SO_4^{2-} \rightarrow HSO_4^-$. Thus, in acidic solution, strontium (II) will not precipitate out with sulfate, but barium (II) sulfate will precipitate due to its greater insolubility. Potassium, sodium, ammonium, and vanadium cations do not ever precipitate out with the available reagents, but they can be identified.

Reactions:

$Ba^{2+}(aq) + SO_4^{2-}(aq) \rightarrow BaSO_4(s) \text{ (white)}$

$Sr^{2+}(aq) + SO_4^{2-}(aq) \rightarrow SrSO_4(s) \text{ (white)}$

Assignment 53 – $Ba^{2+}/K^+/Na^+/Sr^{2+}/V^{4+}$

Difficulty level: 5

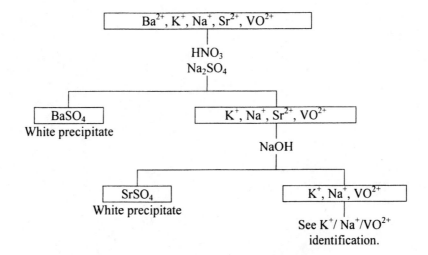

Barium and strontium have very similar chemistry. Both cations precipitate out with sulfate, but strontium (II) sulfate is more soluble. In acidic solution, there is not as much free sulfate due to the formation of bisulfate: $H^+ + SO_4^{2-} \rightarrow HSO_4$. Thus, in acidic solution, strontium (II) will not precipitate out with sulfate, but barium (II) sulfate will precipitate due to its greater insolubility. Potassium, sodium, and vanadium cations do not ever precipitate out with the available reagents, but they can be identified.

Reactions:

$Ba^{2+}(aq) + SO_4^{2-}(aq) \rightarrow BaSO_4(s)$ (white)

$Sr^{2+}(aq) + SO_4^{2-}(aq) \rightarrow SrSO_4(s)$ (white)

Assignment 54 – Bi^{3+}/Pb^{2+}/Sb^{3+}/Sn^{4+}

Difficulty level: 5

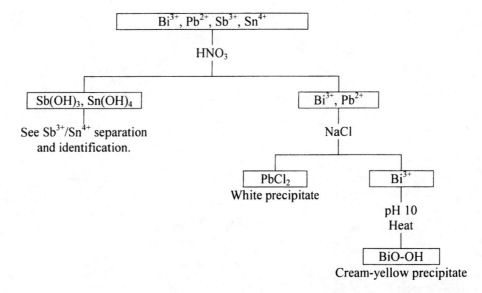

These cations are all close together in the periodic table and have similar chemistry. All four cations form hydroxide precipitates, but antimony (III) and tin (IV) are the most acidic as they form hydroxide precipitates even at very low pH. Addition of chloride will precipitate out lead (II) in acid. The formation of bismuth (III) hydroxide in basic solution identifies the presence of the bismuth cation.

Reactions:

$Bi^{3+}(aq) + 3OH^-(aq) \rightarrow Bi(OH)_3(s)$ (white)
$Bi(OH)_3(s)$ (white) + Heat $\rightarrow$ BiO-OH(s) (cream yellow) + H_2O

$Pb^{2+}(aq) + 2Cl^-(aq) \rightarrow PbCl_2(s)$ (white)

117

Assignment 55 – $Co^{2+}/Cu^{2+}/Fe^{3+}/Ni^{2+}$

Difficulty level: 5

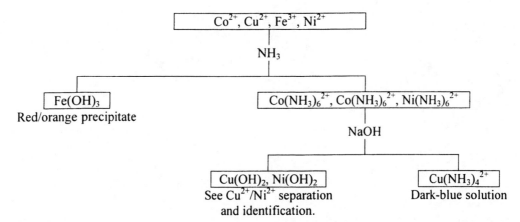

Cobalt (II), copper (II), iron (III), and nickel (II) all form hydroxide precipitates at pH 10, but cobalt (II), copper (II), and nickel (II) hydroxides dissolve in ammonia since these cations form complexes with ammonia. A red/orange precipitate after the addition on ammonia indicates the presence of iron (III). The blue copper (II) ammonia complex stays in solution in very basic solution, but cobalt (II) and nickel (II) hydroxides precipitate out. Cobalt and nickel have similar chemistry, but they can be separated by oxidizing cobalt (II) to cobalt (III), which forms an insoluble hydroxide.

Reactions:

$Co^{2+}(aq)$ (pink) + $6NH_3(aq) \rightarrow Co(NH_3)_6^{2+}(aq)$ (yellow/brown)

$Cu^{2+}(aq)$ (light blue) + $4NH_3(aq) \rightarrow Cu(NH_3)_4^{2+}(aq)$ (dark blue)

$Fe^{3+}(aq)$ (yellow) + $3NH_3(aq) + 3H_2O \rightarrow Fe(OH)_3(s)$ (red/orange) + $3NH_4^+(aq)$

$Ni^{2+}(aq)$ (green) + $6NH_3(aq) \rightarrow Ni(NH_3)_6^{2+}(aq)$ (purple/blue)

Assignment 56 – Cu^{2+}/Fe^{2+}/Hg_2^{2+}/Ni^{2+}

Difficulty level: 5

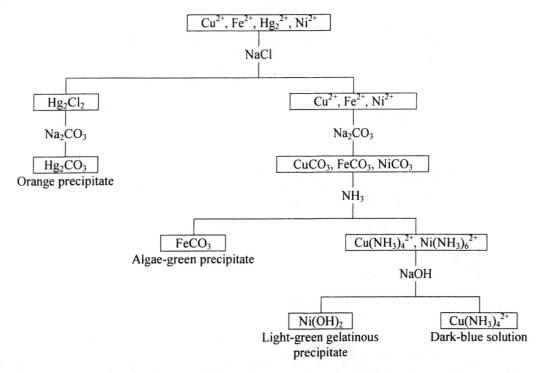

Mercury (I) precipitates out with chloride. The formation of mercurous carbonate, an orange precipitate, confirms the presence of mercury (I), when carbonate is added to the white mercurous chloride precipitate. Copper (II), iron (II), and nickel (II) also form carbonates. The copper (II) and nickel (II) carbonates dissolve in ammonia, since these cations form ammonia complexes. An algae-green precipitate formed after the addition of ammonia is iron (II) carbonate. In excess base, nickel (II) hydroxide precipitates out, but copper (II) remains in solution in the ammonia complex. Nickel (II) hydroxide is a light-green gelatinous precipitate, and the copper ammonia complex gives a dark-blue solution.

Reactions:

$Cu^{2+}(aq) + CO_3^{2-}(aq) \rightarrow CuCO_3(s)$ (pale blue)
$CuCO_3(s)$ (pale blue) $+ 4NH_3(aq) \rightarrow Cu(NH_3)_4^{2+}(aq)$ (dark blue) $+ CO_3^{2-}(aq)$

$Fe^{2+}(aq) + CO_3^{2-}(aq) \rightarrow FeCO_3(s)$ (algae green)

$Hg_2^{2+}(aq) + 2Cl^-(aq) \rightarrow Hg_2Cl_2(s)$ (white)
$Hg_2Cl_2(s)$ (white) $+ CO_3^{2-}(aq) \rightarrow Hg_2CO_3(s)$ (white) $+ 2Cl^-(aq)$

$Ni^{2+}(aq)$ (green) $+ CO_3^{2-}(aq) \rightarrow NiCO_3(s)$ (light-green gel)
$NiCO_3(s)$ (light-green gel) $\rightarrow Ni(NH_3)_6^{2+}(aq)$ (purple/blue)
$Ni(NH_3)_6^{2+}(aq)$ (purple/blue) $+ 2OH^-(aq) \rightarrow Ni(OH)_2(s)$ (light-green gel) $+ 6NH_3(aq)$

Assignment 57 – $Co^{2+}/Fe^{2+}/Mn^{2+}/Ni^{2+}/Zn^{2+}$

Difficulty level: 6

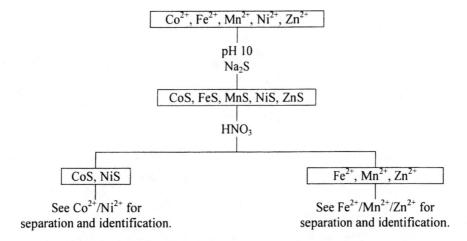

The sulfides of iron (II), manganese (II), and zinc (II) are more soluble than cobalt (II) and nickel (II) sulfides. Although, cobalt (II) and nickel (II) do not form sulfide precipitates in acidic solution, these sulfide precipitates do not readily dissolve once formed.

Reactions:

$Co^{2+}(aq)$ (pink) $+ S^{2-}(aq) \rightarrow CoS(s)$ (black)

$Fe^{2+}(aq) + S^{2-}(aq) \rightarrow FeS(s)$ (black)
$FeS(s)$ (black) $+ 2H^{+}(aq) \rightarrow Fe^{2+}(aq) + H_2S(g)$

$Mn^{2+}(aq) + S^{2-}(aq) \rightarrow MnS(s)$ (cream-yellow)
$MnS(s)$ (cream-yellow) $+ 2H^{+}(aq) \rightarrow Mn^{2+}(aq) + H_2S(g)$

$Ni^{2+}(aq)$ (green) $+ S^{2-}(aq) \rightarrow NiS(s)$ (black)

$Zn^{2+}(aq) + S^{2-}(aq) \rightarrow ZnS(s)$ (white)
$ZnS(s)$ (white) $+ 2H^{+}(aq) \rightarrow Zn^{2+}(aq) + H_2S(g)$

Assignment 58 – Ag$^+$/Co^{2+}/Cr^{3+}/Cu^{2+}/Hg$_2$$^{2+}$/Pb^{2+}

Difficulty level: 6

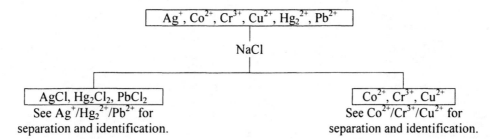

Silver (I), mercury (I) and lead (II) are the few cations that form chloride precipitates, and this allows for an easy separation of these cations from other cations.

Reactions:

$Ag^+(aq) + Cl^-(aq) \rightarrow AgCl(s)$ (white)

$Hg_2^{2+}(aq) + 2Cl^-(aq) \rightarrow Hg_2Cl_2(s)$ (white)

$Pb^{2+}(aq) + 2Cl^-(aq) \rightarrow PbCl_2(s)$ (white)

Assignment 59 – Al^{3+}/Ba^{2+}/Co^{2+}/Cr^{3+}/Hg_2^{2+}/Pb^{2+}/Zn^{2+}

Difficulty level: 6

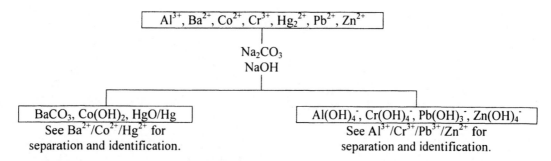

Aluminum (III), chromium (III), lead (II), and zinc (II) are amphoteric, meaning that their hydroxide precipitates dissolve in both acid and base. Barium (II), cobalt (II), and mercury (I) form carbonate precipitates. However, at high pH, barium (II) cobalt favors the hydroxide precipitate and mercury (I) disproportionates to form mercury and mercuric oxide.

Reactions:

$Al^{3+}(aq) + 3CO_3^{2-}(aq) + 3H_2O \rightarrow Al(OH)_3(s)$ (white gel) $+ HCO_3^-(aq)$
$Al(OH)_3(s)$ (white gel) $+ OH^-(aq) \rightarrow Al(OH)_4^-(aq)$

$Ba^{2+}(aq) + CO_3^{2-}(aq) \rightarrow BaCO_3(s)$ (white)

$Co^{2+}(aq) + CO_3^{2-}(aq) \rightarrow CoCO_3(s)$ (purple)
$CoCO_3(s)$ (purple) $+ 2OH^-(aq) \rightarrow Co(OH)_2(s)$ (tan) $+ CO_3^{2-}(aq)$

$Cr^{3+}(aq)$ (purple) $+ 3CO_3^{2-}(aq) + 3H_2O \rightarrow Cr(OH)_3(s)$ (gray) $+ HCO_3^-(aq)$
$Cr(OH)_3(s)$ (gray) $+ OH^-(aq) \rightarrow Cr(OH)_4^-(aq)$ (green)

$Hg_2^{2+}(aq) + CO_3^{2-}(aq) \rightarrow Hg_2CO_3(s)$ (orange)
$2Hg_2CO_3(s)$ (orange) $+ 2OH^-(aq) \rightarrow HgO/Hg(s)$ (black) $+ 2CO_3^{2-}(aq) + H_2O$

$Pb^{2+}(aq) + CO_3^{2-}(aq) \rightarrow PbCO_3(s)$ (white)
$PbCO_3(s)$ (white) $+ 3OH^-(aq) \rightarrow Pb(OH)_3^-(aq) + CO_3^{2-}(aq)$

$Zn^{2+}(aq) + CO_3^{2-}(aq) \rightarrow ZnCO_3(s)$ (white)
$ZnCO_3(s)$ (white) $+ 4OH^-(aq) \rightarrow Zn(OH)_4^{2-}(aq) + CO_3^{2-}(aq)$

Assignment 60 – $Al^{3+}/Co^{2+}/Cr^{3+}/Fe^{3+}/Ni^{2+}/Zn^{2+}$

Difficulty level: 6

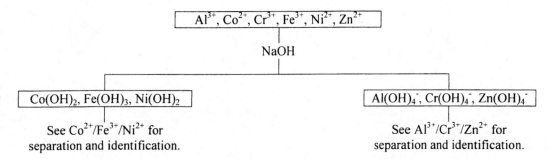

Aluminum (III), chromium (III), and zinc (II) are amphoteric, meaning that their hydroxide precipitates dissolve in both acid and base. The hydroxides of cobalt (II), iron (III), and nickel (II) will dissolve in acid, but not in base.

Reactions:

$Al^{3+}(aq) + 4OH^{-}(aq) \rightarrow Al(OH)_4^{-}(aq)$

$Co^{2+}(pink) + 2OH^{-}(aq) \rightarrow Co(OH)_2(s)$ (tan)

$Cr^{3+}(aq)$ (purple) $+ 4OH^{-}(aq) \rightarrow Cr(OH)_4^{-}(aq)$ (green)

$Fe^{3+}(aq)$ (yellow) $+ 3OH^{-}(aq) \rightarrow Fe(OH)_3(s)$ (red/orange)

$Ni^{2+}(aq)$ (green) $+ 2OH^{-}(aq) \rightarrow Ni(OH)_2(s)$ (light green)

$Zn^{2+}(aq) + 4OH^{-}(aq) \rightarrow Zn(OH)_4^{-}(aq)$

Assignment 61 − Cd^{2+}/Co^{2+}/Cu^{2+}/Ni^{2+}/Zn^{2+}

Difficulty level: 6

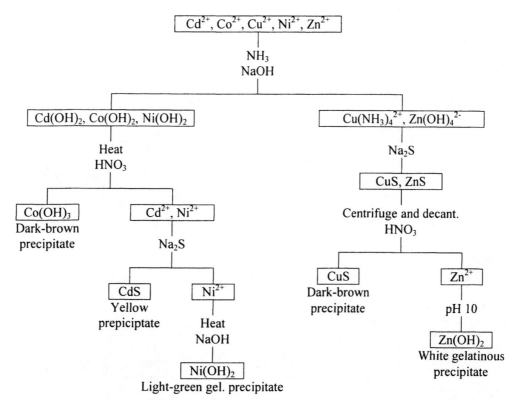

All five cations form ammonia complexes but only copper (II) and zinc (II) stay in solution at high pH. Copper and zinc can be separated based on their relative sulfide precipitate solubilties. As copper (II) sulfide is much less soluble than zinc (II) sulfide, it does not dissolve in acid while zinc (II) sulfide does dissolve in acid. A white precipitate at pH 10 identifies the presence of zinc. Heat oxidizes cobalt (II) hydroxide to cobalt (III) hydroxide, which is very insoluble. Cobalt (III) hydroxide can be separated from cadmium (II) hydroxide and nickel (II) hydroxide since these hydroxides dissolve in acid, but cobalt (III) hydroxide does not. Cadmium and nickel can be separated by adding sulfide, since cadmium (II) sulfide precipitates in acidic solution, but nickel (II) sulfide only precipitates out in basic solution.

Reactions:

$Cd^{2+}(aq) + 4NH_3(aq) \rightarrow Cd(NH_3)_4^{2+}(aq)$
$Cd(NH_3)_4^{2+}(aq) + 2OH^-(aq)$
$\qquad\qquad \rightarrow Cd(OH)_2(s)$ (white) $+ 4NH_3(aq)$
$Cd^{2+}(aq) + S^{2-}(aq) \rightarrow CdS(s)$ (orange)

$Co^{2+}(aq)$ (pink) $+ 4NH_3(aq)$
$\qquad\qquad \rightarrow Co(NH_3)_4^{2+}(aq)$ (yellow/brown)
$Co(NH_3)_4^{2+}(aq)$ (yellow/brown) $+ 2OH^-(aq)$
$\qquad\qquad \rightarrow Co(OH)_2(s)$ (pink/tan) $+ 4NH_3(aq)$
$4Co(OH)_2(s)$ (pink/tan) $+ 2H_2O + O_2(g) + OH^-(aq) +$
$\qquad$ Heat $\rightarrow 4Co(OH)_3(s)$ (dark brown) $+ OH^-(aq)$

$Cu^{2+}(aq)$ (light blue) $+ 4NH_3(aq)$
$\qquad\qquad \rightarrow Cu(NH_3)_4^{2+}(aq)$ (dark blue)

$Cu(NH_3)_4^{2+}(aq)$ (dark blue) $+ S^{2-}(aq)$
$\qquad\qquad \rightarrow CuS(s)$ (dark brown) $+ 4NH_3(aq)$

$Ni^{2+}(aq)$ (green) $+ 6NH_3(aq)$
$\qquad\qquad \rightarrow Ni(NH_3)_6^{2+}(aq)$ (purple/blue)
$Ni(NH_3)_6^{2+}(aq)$ (purple/blue) $+ 2OH^-(aq)$
$\qquad\qquad \rightarrow Ni(OH)_2(s)$ (light green) $+ 6NH_3(aq)$
$Ni^{2+}(aq)$ (green) $+ 2OH^-(aq) \rightarrow Ni(OH)_2(s)$ (light green)

$Zn^{2+}(aq) + 4NH_3(aq) \rightarrow Zn(NH_3)_4^{2+}(aq)$
$Zn(NH_3)_4^{2+}(aq) + 4OH^-(aq)$
$\qquad\qquad \rightarrow Zn(OH)_4^{2-}(aq) + 4NH_3(aq)$
$Zn(OH)_4^{2-}(aq) + S^{2-}(aq) \rightarrow ZnS(s)$ (white) $+ 4OH^-(aq)$
$ZnS(s)$ (white) $+ 2H^+(aq) + $ Heat $\rightarrow Zn^{2+}(aq) + H_2S(g)$
$Zn^{2+}(aq) + 2OH^-(aq)$ (pH 10) $\rightarrow Zn(OH)_2(s)$ (white gel)

131

Assignment 62 – $Cd^{2+}/Mn^{2+}/Pb^{2+}/Sb^{3+}/Sn^{4+}$

Difficulty level: 6

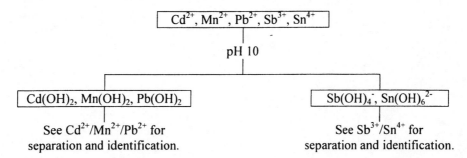

All six cations form hydroxide precipitates, but the hydroxides of antimony (III) and tin (IV) dissolve readily in basic solution. Lead (II) also forms a hydroxide complex in basic solution, but at a higher pH.

Reactions:

$Cd^{2+}(aq) + 2OH^-(aq) \rightarrow Cd(OH)_2(s)$ (white)

$Mn^{2+}(aq) + 2OH^-(aq) \rightarrow Mn(OH)_2(s)$ (brown/orange)

$Pb^{2+}(aq) + 2OH^-(aq)$ (pH 10) $\rightarrow Pb(OH)_2(s)$ (white)

$Sb^{3+}(aq) + 4OH^-(aq) \rightarrow Sb(OH)_4^-(aq)$

$Sn^{4+}(aq) + 6OH^-(aq) \rightarrow Sn(OH)_6^{2-}(aq)$

Assignment 63 – $Cd^{2+}/Co^{2+}/Cr^{3+}/Cu^{2+}/Fe^{3+}/Pb^{2+}/Zn^{2+}$

Difficulty level: 7

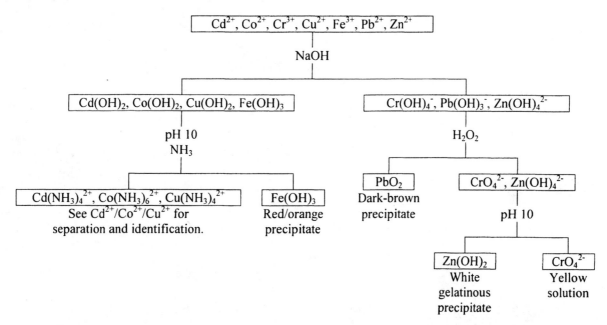

All of these cations form hydroxide precipitates at pH 10. However, chromium (III), lead (II), and zinc (II) are amphoteric and therefore dissolve in excess base. Hydrogen peroxide in basic solution oxidizes lead (II) to the insoluble lead (IV). Hydrogen peroxide in basic solution also oxidizes chromium (III) to chromium (VI), which exists as the soluble chromate anion. Cadmium (II), cobalt (II) and copper (II) can be separated from red iron (III) hydroxide since these cations all form soluble complexes with ammonia at pH 10.

Reactions:

$Cd^{2+}(aq) + 2OH^-(aq) \rightarrow Cd(OH)_2(s)$ (white)
$Cd(OH)_2(s)$ (white) $+ 4NH_3(aq)$ (pH 10) $\rightarrow Cd(NH_3)_4^{2+}(aq) + 2OH^-(aq)$

$Co^{2+}(aq)$ (pink) $+ 2OH^-(aq) \rightarrow Co(OH)_2(s)$ (pink/tan)
$Co(OH)_2(s)$ (pink/tan) $+ 6NH_3(aq)$ (pH 10) $\rightarrow Co(NH_3)_6^{2+}(aq) + 2OH^-(aq)$
$Co(NH_3)_6^{2+}(aq) + 2OH^-(aq) \rightarrow Co(OH)_2(s)$ (pink/tan) $+ 6NH_3(aq)$
$4Co(OH)_2(s)$ (pink/tan) $+ 2H_2O + O_2(g) + OH^-(aq) + Heat \rightarrow 4Co(OH)_3(s)$ (dark brown) $+ OH^-(aq)$

$Cr^{3+}(aq)$ (purple) $+ 3OH^-(aq)$ (pH 10) $\rightarrow Cr(OH)_3(s)$ (gray)
$Cr(OH)_3(s)$ (gray) $+ OH^-(aq) \rightarrow Cr(OH)_4^-(aq)$ (green)
$2Cr(OH)_4^-(aq)$ (green) $+ 3H_2O_2(aq) + 2OH^-(aq) \rightarrow 2CrO_4^{2-}(aq)$ (yellow) $+ 8H_2O$

$Cu^{2+}(aq)$ (light blue) $+ 2OH^-(aq) \rightarrow Cu(OH)_2(s)$ (blue)
$Cu(OH)_2(s)$ (blue) $+ 4NH_3(aq) \rightarrow Cu(NH_3)_4^{2+}(aq)$ (dark blue) $+ 2OH^-(aq)$

$Fe^{3+}(aq)$ (yellow) $+ 3OH^-(aq) \rightarrow Fe(OH)_3(s)$ (red/brown)

$Pb^{2+}(aq) + 3OH^-(aq) \rightarrow Pb(OH)_3^-(aq)$
$Pb(OH)_3^-(aq) + H_2O_2(aq) \rightarrow PbO_2(s)$ (dark brown) $+ 2H_2O + OH^-(aq)$

$Zn^{2+}(aq) + 4OH^-(aq) \rightarrow Zn(OH)_4^{2-}(aq)$
$Zn(OH)_4^{2-}(aq)$ (pH 10) $\rightarrow Zn(OH)_2(s)$ (white) $+ 2OH^-(aq)$

Assignment 64 – $Co^{2+}/Cr^{3+}/Cu^{2+}/Fe^{3+}/Ni^{2+}/V^{4+}$

Difficulty level: 7

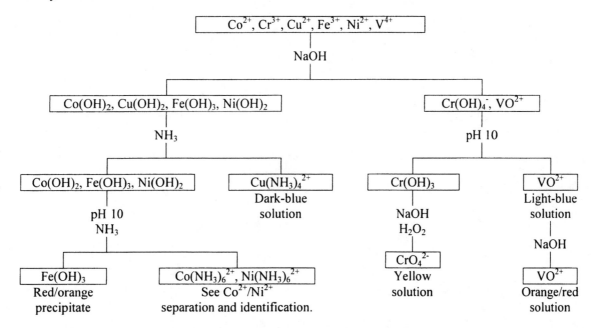

In excess base, cobalt(II), copper (II), iron (III), and nickel (II) form hydroxide precipitates, and chromium (III) and vanadium (IV) form soluble complexes. Vanadium (IV) exists as VO^{2+} in solution, and this complex changes color according to pH, making vanadium identifiable. Chromium (III) forms a gray hydroxide precipitate at pH, but it can also be identified by oxidizing it to the yellow chromate anion. Cobalt (II), copper (II), and nickel (II) can be separated from copper by adding ammonia, which forms a blue complex with copper even in very basic conditions. Cobalt (II) and nickel (II) also form complexes with ammonia, but only at pH 10. A red/orange precipitate indicates iron (III) is present. Cobalt and nickel have similar chemistry, but they can be separated by oxidizing cobalt (II) to cobalt (III), which forms an insoluble hydroxide.

Reactions:

Co^{2+}(aq) (pink) + $2OH^-$(aq) → $Co(OH)_2$(s) (pink/tan)
$Co(OH)_2$(s) (pink/tan) + $6NH_3$(aq) (pH 10) → $Co(NH_3)_6^{2+}$(aq) (yellow/brown) + $2OH^-$(aq)

Cr^{3+}(aq) (purple) + $4OH^-$(aq) → $Cr(OH)_4^-$(aq) (green)
$Cr(OH)_4^-$(aq) (green) (pH 10) → $Cr(OH)_3$(s) (gray) + OH^-(aq)
$2Cr(OH)_4^-$(aq) (green) + $3H_2O_2$(aq) + $2OH^-$(aq) → $2CrO_4^{2-}$(aq) (yellow) + $8H_2O$

Cu^{2+}(aq) (light blue) + $2OH^-$(aq) → $Cu(OH)_2$(s) (blue)
$Cu(OH)_2$(s) (blue) + $4NH_3$(aq) → $Cu(NH_3)_4^{2+}$(aq) (dark blue) + $2OH^-$(aq)

Fe^{3+}(aq) (yellow) + $3OH^-$(aq) → $Fe(OH)_3$(s) (red/orange)

Ni^{2+}(aq) (green) + $2OH^-$(aq) → $Ni(OH)_2$(s) (light green)
$Ni(OH)_2$(s) (light green) + $6NH_3$(aq) (pH 10) → $Ni(NH_3)_6^{2+}$(aq) (purple/blue) + $2OH^-$(aq)

V^{4+}(aq) (green) + $2OH^-$(aq) → VO^{2+}(aq) (orange/red)
VO^{2+}(aq) (orange/red) (pH 10) → VO^{2+}(aq) (light blue)

Assignment 65 – $Co^{2+}/Fe^{2+}/Mn^{2+}/Ni^{2+}/Zn^{2+}$

Difficulty level: 7

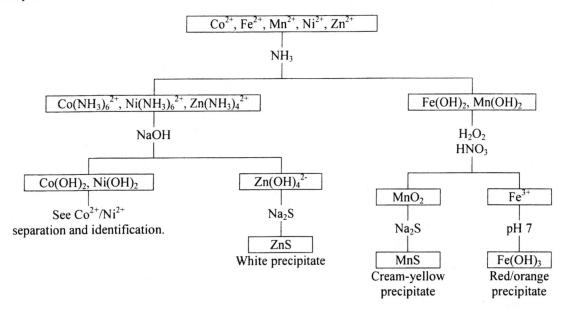

Cobalt (II), nickel (II), and zinc (II) form complexes with ammonia, while iron (II) and manganese (II) form hyrdoxide precipitates upon the addition of ammonia. In excess base, zinc (II) forms a hydroxide complex and cobalt and nickel form hydroxide precipitates. Addition of sulfide to the supernatant tests for zinc, since zinc (II) precipitates out with sulfide even in very basic conditions. Cobalt and nickel have similar chemistry, but they can be separated by oxidizing cobalt (II) to cobalt (III), which forms a very insoluble hydroxide. In basic solution, hydrogen peroxide oxidizes both iron (II) and manganese (II). Manganese (IV) oxide and iron (III) hyrdoxide can be separated according to their relative slubilities. Iron (III) hyrdoxide is more soluble and dissolves in acid, but manganese (IV) oxide does not dissolve in acid.

Reactions:

$Co^{2+}(aq)$ (pink) $+ 6NH_3(aq) \rightarrow Co(NH_3)_6^{2+}(aq)$ (yellow/brown)
$Co(NH_3)_6^{2+}(aq)$ (yellow/brown) $+ 2OH^-(aq) \rightarrow Co(OH)_2(s)$ (pink/tan) $+ 6NH_3(aq)$

$Fe^{2+}(aq) + 2NH_3(aq) + 2H_2O \rightarrow Fe(OH)_2(s)$ (algae green) $+ 2NH_4^+(aq)$
$2Fe(OH)_2(s)$ (pea green) $+ H_2O_2(aq) + OH^-(aq) \rightarrow 2Fe(OH)_3(s)$ (red/orange) $+ OH^-(aq)$

$Mn^{2+}(aq) + 2NH_3(aq) + 2H_2O \rightarrow Mn(OH)_2(s)$ (brown/orange) $+ 2NH_4^+(aq)$
$Mn(OH)_2(s)$ (brown/orange) $+ H_2O_2(aq) + OH^-(aq) \rightarrow MnO_2(s)$ (dark brown) $+ 2H_2O + OH^-(aq)$
$MnO_2(s)$ (dark brown) $+ 4H^+(aq) + 2S^{2-}(aq) \rightarrow MnS(s)$ (cream yellow) $+ S(s) + 2H_2O$

$Ni^{2+}(aq)$ (green) $+ 6NH_3(aq) \rightarrow Ni(NH_3)_6^{2+}(aq)$ (purple/blue)
$Ni(NH_3)_6^{2+}(aq)$ (purple/blue) $+ 2OH^-(aq) \rightarrow Ni(OH)_2(s)$ (light green) $+ 6NH_3(aq)$

$Zn^{2+}(aq) + 4NH_3(aq) \rightarrow Zn(NH_3)_4^{2+}(aq)$
$Zn(NH_3)_4^{2+}(aq) + 4OH^-(aq) \rightarrow Zn(OH)_4^{2-}(aq) + 4NH_3(aq)$
$Zn(OH)_4^{2-}(aq) + S^{2-}(aq) \rightarrow ZnS(s)$ (white) $+ 4OH^-(aq)$

Assignment 66 – $Ba^{2+}/Cu^{2+}/Fe^{2+}/Hg_2^{2+}/Ni^{2+}/Pb^{2+}/Sr^{2+}$

Difficulty level: 7

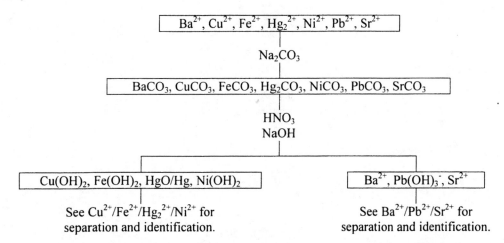

These cations are similar in that they all form carbonate precipitates. Copper (II), iron (II), and nickel (II) form hydroxide precipitates in base. Mercury (I) disproportionates in basic solution to form mercuric oxide (HgO) and mercury (Hg). Lead (II) also forms a hydroxide precipitate, but it dissolves in excess base.

Reactions:

$2H^+(aq) + CO_3^{2-}(aq) \rightarrow H_2O + CO_2(g)$

$Ba^{2+}(aq) + CO_3^{2-}(aq) \rightarrow BaCO_3(s)$ (white)

$Cu^{2+}(aq)$ (light blue) $+ CO_3^{2-}(aq) \rightarrow CuCO_3(s)$ (pale blue)
$Cu^{2+}(aq)$ (light blue) $+ 2OH^-(aq) \rightarrow Cu(OH)_2(s)$ (blue)

$Fe^{2+}(aq) + CO_3^{2-}(aq) \rightarrow FeCO_3(s)$ (algae green)
$Fe^{2+}(aq) + 2OH^-(aq) \rightarrow Fe(OH)_2(s)$ (pea green)

$Hg_2^{2+}(aq) + CO_3^{2-}(aq) \rightarrow Hg_2CO_3(s)$ (algae green)
$2Hg_2^{2+}(aq) + 2OH^-(aq) \rightarrow HgO/Hg(s)$ (black) $+ H_2O$

$Ni^{2+}(aq)$ (green) $+ CO_3^{2-}(aq) \rightarrow NiCO_3(s)$ (light green)
$Ni^{2+}(aq)$ (green) $+ 2OH^-(aq) \rightarrow Ni(OH)_2(s)$ (light green)

$Pb^{2+}(aq) + CO_3^{2-}(aq) \rightarrow PbCO_3(s)$ (white)
$Pb^{2+}(aq) + 3OH^-(aq) \rightarrow Pb(OH)_3^-(aq)$

$Sr^{2+}(aq) + CO_3^{2-}(aq) \rightarrow SrCO_3(s)$ (white)

Assignment 67 – $Co^{2+}/Cu^{2+}/Fe^{2+}/Mg^{2+}/Mn^{2+}/Ni^{2+}/Ti^{4+}$

Difficulty level: 7

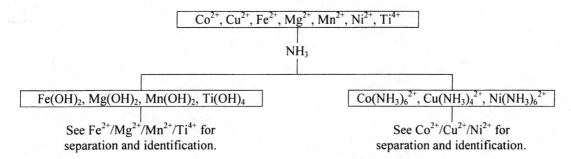

All seven cations form hydroxide precipitates in basic solution, but cobalt (II), copper (II), and nickel (II) form ammonia complexes that dissolve their hydroxide precipitates.

Reactions:

Co^{2+}(aq) (pink) + $6NH_3$ → $Co(NH_3)_6^{2+}$(aq) (yellow/brown)

Cu^{2+}(aq) (light blue) + $4NH_3$ → $Co(NH_3)_4^{2+}$(aq) (dark blue)

Fe^{2+}(aq) + $2NH_3$(aq) + $2H_2O$ → $Fe(OH)_2$(s) (algae green) + $2NH_4^+$(aq)

Mg^{2+}(aq) + $2NH_3$(aq) + $2H_2O$ → $Mg(OH)_2$(s) (white gel) + $2NH_4^+$(aq)

Mn^{2+}(aq) + $2NH_3$(aq) + $2H_2O$ → $Mn(OH)_2$(s) (brown/orange) + $2NH_4^+$(aq)

Ni^{2+}(aq) (green) + $6NH_3$(aq) → $Ni(NH_3)_6^{2+}$(aq) (purple/blue)

Ti^{4+}(aq) + $4NH_3$(aq) + $4H_2O$ → $Ti(OH)_2$(s) (brown/orange) + $4NH_4^+$(aq)

Assignment 68 – $Ba^{2+}/Bi^{3+}/Co^{2+}/Cr^{3+}/Cu^{2+}/Fe^{3+}/Hg^{2+}/K^+/Na^+/Sr^{2+}/V^{4+}$

Difficulty level: 7

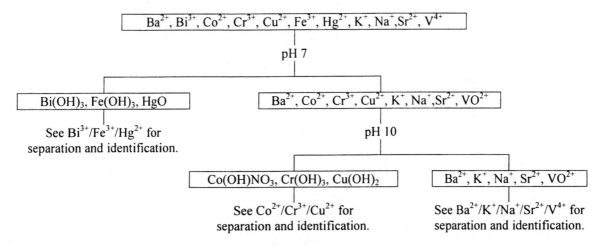

These cations can be split into three main groups according to their solubility at different pHs. Bismuth (III), iron(III), and mercury (II) are acidic and readily form hydroxide precipitates in water. Cobalt (II), chromium (III), and copper (II) only form hydroxide precipitates in basic solution. Barium (II), potassium (I), sodium (I), strontium (II), and vanadium (IV) cations do not form hydroxide precipitates, even in very basic conditions.

Reactions:

$Bi^{3+}(aq) + 3H_2O \rightarrow Bi(OH)_3(s)$ (white) $+ 3H^+(aq)$

$Co^{2+}(aq)$ (pink) $+ NO_3^-(aq) + OH^-(aq)$ (pH 10) $\rightarrow Co(OH)NO_3(s)$ (aqua blue)

$Cr^{3+}(aq)$ (purple) $+ 3OH^-(aq)$ (pH 10) $\rightarrow Cr(OH)_3(s)$ (gray)

$Cu^{2+}(aq)$ (light blue) $+ 2OH^-(aq) \rightarrow Cu(OH)_2(s)$ (blue)

$Fe^{3+}(aq) + 3H_2O \rightarrow Fe(OH)_3(s)$ (red/orange) $+ 3H^+(aq)$

$Hg^{2+}(aq) + H_2O \rightarrow HgO(s)$ (yellow) $+ 2H^+(aq)$

Assignment 69 – $Ba^{2+}/Ca^{2+}/Co^{2+}/Cu^{2+}/Fe^{2+}/Mn^{2+}/Ni^{2+}/V^{4+}$

Difficulty level: 8

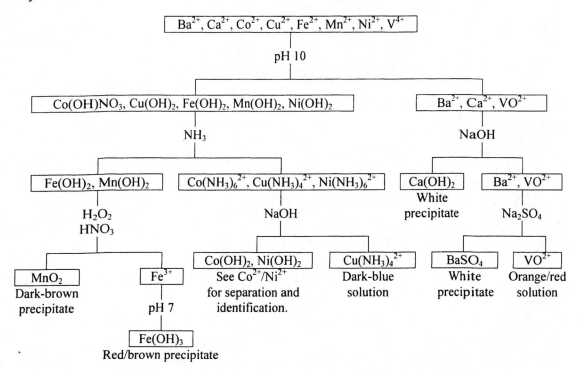

Cobalt, copper, iron, manganese, and nickel are all located next to each other in the periodic table. They all form hydroxide precipitates at pH 10, but only cobalt (II), copper (II), and nickel (II) form complexes with ammonia. In excess base, cobalt (II) and nickel (II) once again form hydroxide precipitates, but copper stays dissolved in the ammonia complex. Cobalt and nickel behave very similarly, and manganese and iron also behave very similarly, as can be predicted by their juxtapositions in the periodic table. However, both sets of cations can be separated because of differences in solubility after oxidation. Barium (II), calcium (II), and vanadium (IV) are three of the few cations that do not form hydroxide precipitates at pH 10. Calcium (II) does form a hydroxide precipitate, but only in very basic solution. Sulfate precipitates out barium (II). The bright-orange/red vanadium solution distinguishes the vanadium cation.

Reactions:

$Ba^{2+}(aq) + SO_4^{2-}(aq) \rightarrow BaSO_4(s)$ (white)

$Ca^{2+}(aq) + 2OH^-(aq) \rightarrow Ca(OH)_2(s)$ (white)

$Co^{2+}(aq) + NO_3^-(aq) + OH^-(aq)$ (pH 10)
$\qquad \rightarrow Co(OH)NO_3(s)$ (aqua blue)
$Co(OH)NO_3(s)$ (aqua blue) $+ 6NH_3(aq)$
$\qquad \rightarrow Co(NH_3)_6^{2+}(aq)$ (yell/brn) $+ NO_3^-(aq) + OH^-(aq)$
$Co(NH_3)_6^{2+}(aq)$ (yellow/brown) $+ 2OH^-(aq)$
$\qquad \rightarrow Co(OH)_2(s)$ (pink/tan) $+ 6NH_3(aq)$

$Cu^{2+}(aq)$ (light blue) $+ 2OH^-(aq) \rightarrow Cu(OH)_2(s)$ (blue)
$Cu(OH)_2(s)$ (blue) $+ 4NH_3(aq)$
$\qquad \rightarrow Cu(NH_3)_4^{2+}(aq)$ (dark blue) $+ 2OH^-(aq)$

$Fe^{2+}(aq) + 2OH^-(aq) \rightarrow Fe(OH)_2(s)$ (pea green)
$2Fe(OH)_2(s)$ (pea green) $+ H_2O_2(aq) + OH^-(aq)$
$\qquad \rightarrow 2Fe(OH)_3(s)$ (red/orange) $+ OH^-(aq)$
$Fe(OH)_3(s)$ (red/brown) $+ 3H^+(aq) \rightarrow Fe^{3+}(aq) + 3H_2O$

$Mn^{2+}(aq) + 2OH^-(aq) \rightarrow Mn(OH)_2(s)$ (brown/orange)
$Mn(OH)_2(s)$ (brown/orange) $+ H_2O_2(aq) + OH^-(aq)$
$\qquad \rightarrow MnO_2(s)$ (dark brown) $+ 2H_2O + OH^-(aq)$

$Ni^{2+}(aq)$ (green) $+ 2OH^-(aq) \rightarrow Ni(OH)_2(s)$ (light green)
$Ni(OH)_2(s)$ (light green) $+ 6NH_3(aq)$ (pH 10)
$\qquad \rightarrow Ni(NH_3)_6^{2+}(aq)$ (purple/blue) $+ 2OH^-(aq)$
$Ni(NH_3)_6^{2+}(aq)$ (purple/blue) $+ 2OH^-(aq)$
$\qquad \rightarrow Ni(OH)_2(s)$ (light green) $+ 6NH_3(aq)$

Assignment 70 – $Cd^{2+}/Co^{2+}/Cr^{3+}/Cu^{2+}/Mg^{2+}/Mn^{2+}/Ni^{2+}/Zn^{2+}$

Difficulty level: 8

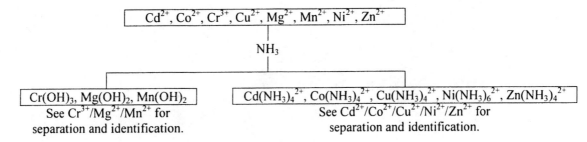

All eight cations form hydroxide precipitates at pH 10, but cadmium (II), cobalt (II), copper (II), nickel (II), and zinc (II) favor the ammonia complex when ammonia is present.

Reactions:

$Cd^{2+}(aq) + 4NH_3(aq) \rightarrow Cd(NH_3)_4^{2+}(aq)$

$Co^{2+}(aq)$ (pink) $+ 4NH_3(aq) \rightarrow Co(NH_3)_4^{2+}(aq)$ (yellow/brown)

$Cr^{3+}(aq)$ (purple) $+ 3NH_3(aq) + 3H_2O \rightarrow Cr(OH)_3(s)$ (gray) $+ 3NH_4^+(aq)$

$Cu^{2+}(aq)$ (light blue) $+ 4NH_3(aq) \rightarrow Cu(NH_3)_4^{2+}(aq)$ (dark blue)

$Mg^{2+}(aq) + 2NH_3(aq) + 2H_2O \rightarrow Mg(OH)_2(s)$ (white gel) $+ 2NH_4^+(aq)$

$Mn^{2+}(aq) + 2NH_3(aq) + 2H_2O \rightarrow Mn(OH)_2(s)$ (brown/orange) $+ 2NH_4^+(aq)$

$Ni^{2+}(aq)$ (green) $+ 6NH_3(aq) \rightarrow Ni(NH_3)_6^{2+}(aq)$ (purple/blue)

$Zn^{2+}(aq) + 4NH_3(aq) \rightarrow Zn(NH_3)_4^{2+}(aq)$

Assignment 71 – $Al^{3+}/Ba^{2+}/Bi^{3+}/Cd^{2+}/Cr^{3+}/Cu^{2+}/Hg^{2+}/K^+/Na^+/NH_4^+/Pb^{2+}/Sb^{3+}/Sn^{4+}/Sr^{2+}/V^{4+}/Zn^{2+}$

Difficulty level: 8

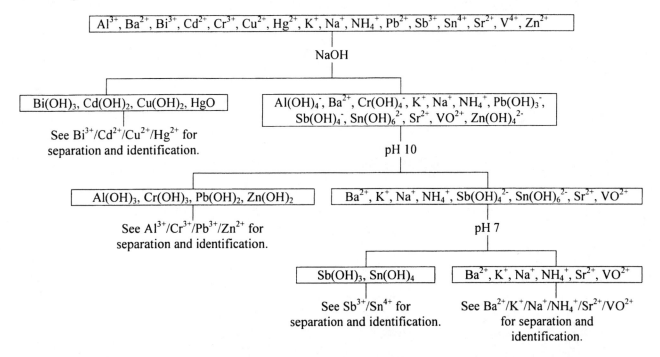

These cations can be split into four main groups according to their solubility at different pHs. Bismuth (III), cadmium (II), copper (II), and mercury (II) precipitate in basic conditions. Aluminum (III), chromium (III), lead (II), and zinc (II) also precipitate in basic solution, but these hydroxides dissolve in excess base since they are amphoteric. Antimony (III) and tin (IV) are also amphoteric, but their hydroxides dissolve more readily in basic solutions. Barium (II), potassium (I), sodium (I), ammonium, strontium (II), and vanadium (IV) cations do not form hydroxide precipitates at any pH.

Reactions:

$Al^{3+}(aq) + 4OH^-(aq) \rightarrow Al(OH)_4^-(aq)$
$Al(OH)_4^-(aq) + H^+(aq)$ (pH 10)
$\qquad\qquad \rightarrow Al(OH)_3(s)$ (white) $+ H_2O$

$Bi^{3+}(aq) + 3OH^-(aq) \rightarrow Bi(OH)_3(s)$ (white)

$Cd^{2+}(aq) + 2OH^-(aq) \rightarrow Cd(OH)_2(s)$ (white)

$Cr^{3+}(aq) + 4OH^-(aq) \rightarrow Cr(OH)_4^-(aq)$ (green)
$Cr(OH)_4^-(aq)$ (green) $+ H^+(aq)$ (pH 10)
$\qquad\qquad \rightarrow Cr(OH)_3(s)$ (gray) $+ H_2O$

$Cu^{2+}(aq)$ (light blue) $+ 2OH^-(aq) \rightarrow Cu(OH)_2(s)$ (blue)

$Hg^{2+}(aq) + 2OH^-(aq) \rightarrow HgO(s)$ (yellow) $+ H_2O$

$Pb^{2+}(aq) + 3OH^-(aq) \rightarrow Pb(OH)_3^-(aq)$
$Pb(OH)_3^-(aq) + H^+(aq)$ (pH 10) $\rightarrow Pb(OH)_2(s)$ (white)

$Sb^{3+}(aq) + 4OH^-(aq) \rightarrow Sb(OH)_4^-(aq)$
$Sb(OH)_4^-(aq) + H^+(aq)$ (pH 7)
$\qquad\qquad \rightarrow Sb(OH)_3(s)$ (white) $+ H_2O$

$Sn^{4+}(aq) + 6OH^-(aq) \rightarrow Sn(OH)_6^{2-}(aq)$
$Sn(OH)_6^{2-}(aq) + 2H^+(aq)$ (pH 7)
$\qquad\qquad \rightarrow Sn(OH)_4(s)$ (white gel) $+ 2H_2O$

$Zn^{2+}(aq) + 4OH^-(aq) \rightarrow Zn(OH)_4^{2-}(aq)$
$Zn(OH)_4^{2-}(aq) + 2H^+(aq)$ (pH 10)
$\qquad\qquad \rightarrow Zn(OH)_2(s)$ (white gel) $+ 2H_2O$

Assignment 72 – Ag^+/Al^{3+}/Co^{2+}/Cr^{3+}/Cu^{2+}/Hg_2^{2+}/Ni^{2+}/Pb^{2+}/Sb^{3+}/ Sn^{4+}/Zn^{2+}

Difficulty level: 8

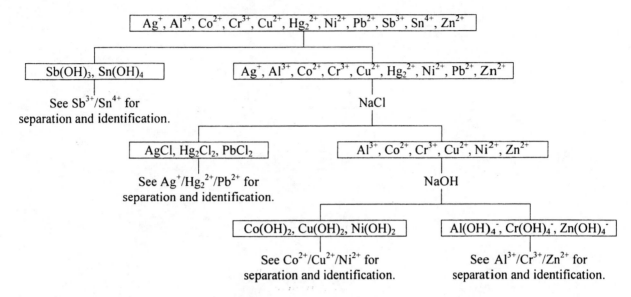

Antimony (III) and tin (IV) are acidic and form hydroxides in water. Adding chloride is a simple way to separate out silver (I), mercury (I), and lead (II). The remaining cations all form hydroxide precipitates in basic solution, but aluminum (III), chromium (III), and zinc (II) are amphoteric and will dissolve in excess base.

Reactions:

$Ag^+(aq) + Cl^-(aq) \rightarrow AgCl(s)$ (white)

$Al^{3+}(aq) + 4OH^-(aq) \rightarrow Al(OH)_4^-(aq)$

$Co^{2+}(aq)$ (pink) $+ NaOH \rightarrow Co(OH)_2(s)$ (tan)

$Cr^{3+}(aq)$ (purple) $+ 4OH^-(aq) \rightarrow Cr(OH)_4^-(aq)$ (green)

$Cu^{2+}(aq)$ (light blue) $+ 2OH^-(aq) \rightarrow Cu(OH)_2(s)$ (blue)

$Hg_2^{2+}(aq) + 2Cl^-(aq) \rightarrow Hg_2Cl_2(s)$ (white)

$Ni^{2+}(aq)$ (green) $+ 2OH^-(aq) \rightarrow Ni(OH)_2(s)$ (light green)

$Pb^{2+}(aq) + 2Cl^-(aq) \rightarrow PbCl_2(s)$ (white)

$Sb^{3+}(aq) + 3H_2O \rightarrow Sb(OH)_3(s)$ (white) $+ 3H^+(aq)$

$Sn^{4+}(aq) + 4H_2O \rightarrow Sn(OH)_4(s)$ (white gel) $+ 4H^+(aq)$

$Zn^{2+}(aq) + 4OH^-(aq) \rightarrow Zn(OH)_4^-(aq)$

Assignment 73 – $Ag^+/Bi^{3+}/Cd^{2+}/Co^{2+}/Cu^{2+}/Fe^{3+}/Hg^{2+}/Hg_2^{2+}/$ $Mn^{2+}/Ni^{2+}/Pb^{2+}/Sb^{3+}/Sn^{4+}/Zn^{2+}$ (The Sulfides)

Difficulty level: 9

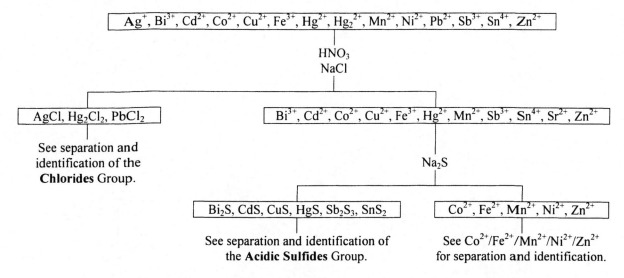

These are all cations that form sulfide precipitates. Adding chloride is a simple way to separate out silver (I), mercury (I), and lead (II) since these are the only cations that form chloride precipitates. The other cations can be divided into two groups according to their sulfide solubilties. In acidic solution, there is not as much free sulfide since it associates with hydrogen to form hydrogen sulfide ($2H^+ + S^{2-} \rightarrow H_2S$). Thus, the more insoluble sulfides precipitate in acidic solution, but the more soluble sulfides only precipitate in basic sulfide.

Reactions:

$Ag^+(aq) + Cl^-(aq) \rightarrow AgCl(s)$ (white)

$2Bi^{3+}(aq) + 3S^{2-}(aq) \rightarrow Bi_2S_3(s)$ (dark brown)

$Cd^{2+}(aq) + S^{2-}(aq) \rightarrow CdS(s)$ (orange)

$Cu^{2+}(aq)$ (light blue) $+ S^{2-}(aq) \rightarrow CuS(s)$ (dark brown)

$Hg^{2+}(aq) + S^{2-}(aq) \rightarrow HgS(s)$ (black)

$Hg_2^{2+}(aq) + 2Cl^-(aq) \rightarrow Hg_2Cl_2(s)$ (white)

$Pb^{2+}(aq) + 2Cl^-(aq) \rightarrow PbCl_2(s)$ (white)

$2Sb^{3+}(aq) + 3S^{2-}(aq) + H^+(aq) \rightarrow Sb_2S_3(s)$ (orange) $+ H^+(aq)$

$Sn^{4+}(aq) + 2S^{2-}(aq) + H^+(aq) \rightarrow SnS_2(s)$ (yellow) $+ H^+(aq)$

Additional Reactions

Although *Vitual ChemLab: Inorganic* is primarily focused on inorganic qualitative analysis, many possible reactions are not used in the qualitative analysis schemes. Among these reactions are oxidation-reduction reactions and reactions involving the formation of precipitates containing two cations. Thus, instructors can use *Vitual ChemLab: Inorganic* in the classroom to demonstrate these reactions while teaching the chemical principles behind them.

Oxidation-Reduction Reactions

Oxidation-reduction reactions are reactions in which one substance is oxidized and the other substance is reduced. One of the previous reactions found in the assignments is an example:

$$2Fe^{3+}(aq) + 3S^{2-}(aq) \rightarrow 2FeS(s) \text{ (black)} + S(s)$$

(Remember that in oxidation-reduction reactions, both charge and mass must be balanced.) In this example, one sulfide ion is oxidized and iron (III) is reduced. In this case, the sulfide ion is the reducing agent and iron (III) is the oxidizing reagent. Hydrogen peroxide is another reagent involved in oxidation-reduction reactions. However, hydrogen peroxide can act as either a reducing agent or an oxidizing reagent:

$$Mn^{2+}(aq) + 2OH^{-}(aq) + H_2O_2(aq) \rightarrow MnO_2(s) \text{ (dark brown)} + 2H_2O$$

$$MnO_2(s) \text{ (dark brown)} + 2H^{+}(aq) + H_2O_2(aq) \rightarrow Mn^{2+}(aq) + 2H_2O + O_2(g)$$

In this case, hydrogen peroxide acts as an oxidizing agent in basic solution; the oxygen is reduced (from the -1 oxidation state to –2) and manganese (II) is oxidized. However, in acidic solution, hydrogen peroxide acts as a reducing reagent; the oxygen is oxidized (from the -1 oxidation state to 0) and manganese (IV) is reduced.

Not only do the available cations undergo oxidation-reduction reactions with the reagents, but the cations themselves can interact to carry out oxidation-reduction reactions. One main example is silver (I) and iron (II):

$$Ag^{+}(aq) + Fe^{2+}(aq) \rightarrow Ag/Ag_2O(s) \text{ (brown)} + Fe^{3+}(aq) \text{ (yellow)}$$

In this reaction, iron (II) is oxidized and silver (I) is reduced to silver metal. Notice that not all of the silver is reduced, but a combination of silver metal and silver (I) oxide is produced. (The reaction is not completely balanced.) The following cation/cation oxidation-reduction reactions occur in basic solution:

$$2Hg_2^{2+}(aq) + Sb(OH)_3(s) \text{ (white)} + 3OH^{-}(aq) \rightarrow 2Hg(s) \text{ (gray)} + Sb(OH)_6^{-}(aq)$$

$$Hg^{2+}(aq) + 2VO^{2+}(blue) + OH^{-}(aq) + 2H_2O \rightarrow Hg(s) \text{ (gray)} + 2V^{5+}(aq) + 5OH^{-}(aq)$$

In these last two reactions, the mercury cations (the mercurous ion in the first reaction and the mercuric ion in the second reaction) are reduced to mercury metal and the other cations are oxidized.

Cation/Cation Precipitates

Cations can also interact with each other to form precipitates. This occurs when a cation precipitates with a polyatomic anion that contains another cation. A polyatomic anion is a negatively charged molecule composed of more than one atom. Sodium hydroxide and hydrogen peroxide oxidize both chromium (III) and vanadium (IV) to chromium (VI) and vanadium (V) respectively. Chromium (VI) forms CrO_4^{2-} (chromate), a polyatomic anion. Vanadium (V) can exist as the polyatomic anion VO_3^-. Both CrO_4^{2-} and VO_3^- form precipitates with several of the other cations.

BaCrO$_4$ – $Ba^{2+} + Cr^{3+} + NaOH + H_2O_2$:

$Ba^{2+}(aq) + Cr^{3+}(aq)$ (purple) $+ 4OH^-(aq) \rightarrow Ba^{2+}(aq) + Cr(OH)_4^-(aq)$ (green)

$2Ba^{2+}(aq) + 2Cr(OH)_4^-(aq)$ (green) $+ 3H_2O_2(aq) + 2OH^-(aq) \rightarrow 2BaCrO_4^{2-}(s)$ (cream/yellow) $+ 8H_2O$

CuCrO$_4$ - $Cu^{2+} + Cr^{3+} + NaOH + H_2O_2$ then pH 7:

$Cu^{2+}(aq)$ (blue) $+ 2Cr^{3+}(aq)$ (purple) $+ 10OH^-(aq) + 3H_2O_2(aq) \rightarrow$
$Cu(OH)_2(s)$ (green) $+ 2CrO_4^{2-}(aq)$ (yellow) $+ 8H_2O$

$Cu(OH)_2(s)$ (green) $+ CrO_4^{2-}(aq)$ (yellow) $+ 2H^+(aq)$ (pH 7) $\rightarrow CuCrO_4(s)$ (red/orange) $+ 2H_2O$

Ba(VO$_3$)$_2$ – $Ba^{2+} + V^{4+} + NaOH + H_2O_2$:

$Ba^{2+}(aq) + 2VO^{2+}(aq)$ (green) $+ H_2O_2$ (aq) $+ 6OH^-(aq) \rightarrow Ba(VO_3)_2(s)$ (white) $+ 4H_2O$

Cu(VO$_3$)$_2$ – $Cu^{2+} + V^{4+} + NaOH + H_2O_2$:

$Cu^{2+}(aq)$ (blue) $+ 2VO^{2+}(aq)$ (green) $+ H_2O_2$ (aq) $+ 6OH^-(aq) \rightarrow Cu(VO_3)_2(s)$ (pea green) $+ 4H_2O$

Quantum Assignments

Virtual ChemLab: Quantum is a set of simulated physical chemistry experiments that demonstrate many of the concepts and ideas that led to the development of atomic theory and quantum mechanics. Because of the very sophisticated nature of most of these experiments, the quantum laboratory is the most "virtual" of the *Virtual ChemLab* laboratory simulations. In general, the laboratory consists of an optics table where a source, sample, modifier, and detector combination can be placed to perform different experiments. These devices are located in the stockroom and can be taken out of the stockroom and placed in various locations on the optics table. The emphasis here is to help students learn to probe a sample (e.g., a gas, metal foil, two-slit screen, etc.) with a source (e.g., a laser, electron gun, alpha-particle source, etc.) and detect the outcome with a specific detector (a phosphor screen, spectrometer, etc.). Heat, electric fields, or magnetic fields can also be applied to modify an aspect of the experiment.

The quantum assignments in this workbook guide students through foundational experiments in quantum chemistry. The virtual laboratory provides a safe environment in which students can learn about and visualize these fundamental experiments at their level. The assignments will help them explore and understand the ideas that led to the development of quantum mechanics, as they link laboratory results with atomic theory.

The level of the chemistry experiments in *Virtual ChemLab: Quantum* can be very basic or very sophisticated, depending on the level of the class and the purpose for performing the experiments. In this workbook, there are usually several assignments for each type of experiment. These assignments are numbered by increasing difficulty, so assignments can be selected according to the level of the students.

The *Instructor Utilities* or stockroom component of *Virtual ChemLab* allows the instructor to define and release text-based instructions (or assignments) for performing a number of simulated experiments that demonstrate many of the concepts and ideas that led to the development of quantum mechanics. Each of the assignments in this workbook can be given to students electronically through *Instructor Utilities*. These assignments are received by the students using the clipboard in the quantum stockroom, and a student's work on these assignments is recorded (by the student) in the lab book. A new section is created in the lab book for each assignment accepted by the student. The *Instructor Utilities Guide* explains in further detail how to access and distribute these assignments.

In many experiments, answers will vary since students can choose certain variables of the experiment. Thus, only example answers are given for these experiments. However, final answers (such as derived constants) derived from the students' experiments should vary only in the last digit.

Thomson – 1

As scientists began to examine atoms, their first discovery was that they could extract negatively charged particles from atoms. They called these particles electrons. In order to understand the nature of these particles, they wanted to know how much they weighed, and how much charge they carried. Thomson showed that if you could measure how much a beam of electrons were bent in an electric and magnetic field, you could figure out the ratio of mass to charge for the particles. You will repeat some of Thomson's experiments in this lab.

1. Set up the optics table for this experiment by selecting *Thomson Experiment* on the clipboard of preset experiments.

   What source is used in this experiment? ___ ***The electron gun*** _____

   What type of charge do electrons have? ___ ***Negative*** _____

   What detector is used in this experiment and what does it do? ___ ***The phosphor screen detects***

   electrons, and it glows momentarily at the positions where the electrons impact the screen. ___

   Where is the signal on the detector? ___ ***In the center of the screen*** _____

2. Push the grid button on the phosphor screen, then turn on the magnetic field to 30 μT.

   What happens to the spot from the electron gun? ___ ***It shifts to the right.*** _____

3. Turn off the magnetic field, and turn on the voltage of the electric field to 10 V.

   What happens to the spot from the electron? ___ ***It shifts to the left.*** _____

   In an electric field, the displacement of the electrons is related to their charge, mass, and velocity. The purpose of the Thomson experiment is to calculate the mass to charge ratio of the electron. The displacement of the electrons can be observed in this experiment, and the velocity can be calculated from the electric and magnetic fields. The forces produced by the electric and magnetic fields are qE and $q \cdot v \times B$, respectively (where q is the charge of the electron, v is its velocity, E is the electric field, and B is the magnetic field). If the electric and magnetic forces are equal, then the velocity of the electron can be calculated from E and B ($v = E/B$).

   What two fundamental properties of the electron does its displacement depend on? ___ ***The mass and***

   charge of the electron determine its displacement. _____

   Which way is the electric field aligned in this experiment? ___ ***Into the computer screen*** _____

   Which way is the magnetic field aligned in this experiment? ___ ***Out of the computer screen*** _____

   Where should the signal on the phosphor screen be if the electric and magnetic forces are balanced?

   In the center of the screen _____

4. Increase the voltage of the electric field until the signal reaches the edge of the phosphor screen.

   What voltage is required to deflect the electrons to the edge of the screen?   __15.5 V__

5. Increase the magnetic field until the beam of electrons reaches the center of the screen.

   What magnetic field creates a magnetic force that balances the electric force?   __52.3 μT__

   When the electric and magnetic forces are equal, what does the ratio of the electric field to magnetic field (E/B) give?   __The velocity of the electron__

   What is the purpose of the Thomson experiment?   __The purpose of this experiment is to find the charge-to-mass ratio of the electron.__

Thomson – 2

As scientists began to examine atoms, their first discovery was that they could extract negatively charged particles from atoms. They called these particles electrons. In order to understand the nature of these particles, they wanted to know how much they weighed and how much charge they carried. Thomson showed that if you could measure how much a beam of electrons were bent in an electric and magnetic field, you could figure out the ratio of mass to charge for the particles. You will repeat some of Thomson's experiments in this lab.

1. Set up the optics table for the Thomson experiment by placing the electron gun on the table, aimed at the phosphor screen, and placing the electric and magnetic fields between them right in front of the phosphor screen.

2. Turn on the phosphor screen, and push the grid button.

3. Set the electron gun energy to 100 eV with an intensity of 1 nA.

4. Increase the voltage of the electric field to 10 V.

   What happens to the spot from the electron gun? __***It shifts to the left.***__

   How is the electric field calculated from the applied voltage? __***$E = V/d_{plates}$***__

   Which direction is the electric field pointing? __***Out of the computer screen***__

   What is the force produced by an electric field? __***$F = qE$***__

   What voltage do you have to apply to move the spot to the first line in the grid? __***2.56 V***__

   What voltage is necessary to move it just off the screen? __***16.0 V***__

5. Increase the electron gun energy to 500 eV.

   How does increasing the electron gun energy change the speed of the electrons? __***The speed of the electrons increases.***__

   How does this increase change the deflection of the electrons? __***They are deflected less.***__

   Why does the deflection change? __***As the speed of the electrons increases, the electrons are not in the electric field as long, so the electric force acts on the electrons for a shorter time.***__

   What voltage do you need to deflect the electrons to the edge of the screen? __***77.5 V***__

   To the first grid line? __***12.7 V***__

Quantum Assignments

6. Decrease the electron gun energy to 10 eV.

   *How does this change the deflection of the electrons?*___***The electrons are deflected more.***___

   _____

7. Choose at least five other electron energies, and find the voltages necessary to deflect the electron beam to the edge of the screen. Then plot a graph of electron energy versus voltage.

e⁻ Energy	Voltage
50 eV	*7.73 V*
100 eV	*15.5 V*
150 eV	*23.3 V*
200 eV	*31.0 V*
250 eV	*38.7 V*
300 eV	*46.5 V*
350 eV	*54.3 V*
400 eV	*62.0 V*
450 eV	*69.8 V*
500 eV	*77.5 V*

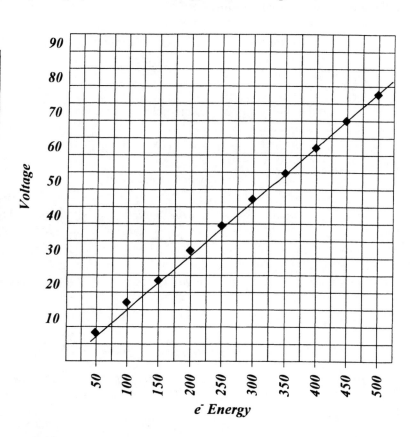

   *What is the trend of the data?*___***The data are linear.***___

8. Using your graph, predict the voltage necessary to deflect a 235 eV electron beam to the edge of the screen, and then test to determine whether your prediction is right. Finally, predict the electron energy necessary to have the beam deflected to the edge of the screen by a voltage of 20 V, and test to determine whether your prediction is right.

   *(235 eV electron beam) Voltage prediction:*___***36 V***___   *Measured voltage:*___***36.4 V***___

   *(20 V) Electron energy prediction:*___***135 eV***___   *Measured electron energy:*___***130 eV***___

9. Turn off the electric field, and repeat the experiment with the magnetic field. Set the electron gun energy back to 100 eV, and turn the magnetic field on to 20 μT.

   *What happens to the spot from the electron gun?*___***It shifts to the right.***___

Which direction is the magnetic field pointing? __*Into the optics table*__

What is the force produced by a magnetic field? __$F = q \cdot v \times B$__

10. As before, choose several electron energies, and find the magnetic fields necessary to deflect the electron beam to the edge of the screen. Then, plot a graph of electron energy versus field.

e⁻ Energy	Magnetic field
50 eV	*37.0 µT*
100 eV	*52.5 µT*
150 eV	*64.0 µT*
200 eV	*74.5 µT*
250 eV	*83.0 µT*
300 eV	*91.0 µT*
350 eV	*98.0 µT*
400 eV	*105 µT*
450 eV	*111 µT*
500 eV	*117 µT*

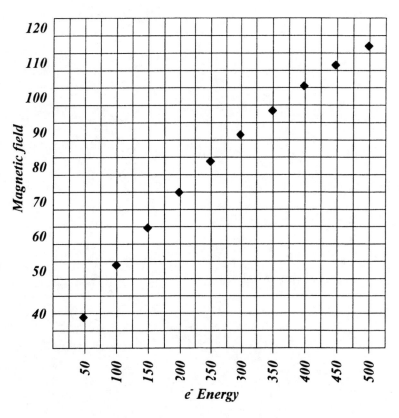

How does the magnetic field change the electron beam differently than the electric field? __*The*__

__*magnetic field does not have a linear relationship to electron energy, but the electric field does.*__

Thomson Experiment

Thomson – 3

As scientists began to examine atoms, their first discovery was that they could extract negatively charged particles from atoms. They called these electrons. In order to understand the nature of these particles, they wanted to know how much they weighed and how much charge they carried. Thomson showed that if you could measure how much a beam of electrons is bent in an electric and magnetic field, you could figure out the ratio of mass to charge for the particles. You will repeat some of Thomson's experiments in this lab. Some of the information you will need for the calculations is found in the *Quantum User Guide* or in the Help Menu (page 13 of *The Simulation*).

1. Set up the optics table for the Thomson experiment by placing the electron gun on the table, aimed at the phosphor screen, and placing the electric and magnetic fields between them right in front of the phosphor screen.

2. Turn on the phosphor screen, and push the grid button.

3. Turn the electron energy to 200 eV. Use the electric field to deflect the beam to the edge of the screen. Now turn on the magnetic field, and increase it until the beam is back in the center of the screen. Calculate the ratio of electric field to magnetic field. Increase the electric field to twice what it currently is, and change the magnetic field to again center the electron beam. Calculate the ratio again. Repeat for three other values of electric field.

Electric field	620 V	1240 V	300 V	900 V	1500 V
Magnetic field	$74.2 \times 10^{-6}\,T$	$148 \times 10^{-6}\,T$	$35.9 \times 10^{-6}\,T$	$107.5 \times 10^{-6}\,T$	$179 \times 10^{-6}\,T$
Ratio	8.36×10^6	8.38×10^6	8.36×10^6	8.37×10^6	8.38×10^6

Conclusions: __*The ratio remains constant.*__

4. Change the electron kinetic energy to 100 eV. Repeat the previous steps.

Electric field	310 V	620 V	440 V	800 V	1000 V
Magnetic field	$52.3 \times 10^{-6}\,T$	$104.5 \times 10^{-6}\,T$	$74.2 \times 10^{-6}\,T$	$135 \times 10^{-6}\,T$	$169 \times 10^{-6}\,T$
Ratio	5.93×10^6	5.93×10^6	5.93×10^6	5.93×10^6	5.92×10^6

Is the ratio still the same? Is this what you predicted? __*The ratio is not the same as before, but it*__

__*still remains constant for a set electron kinetic energy.*__

You can show that the ratio of electric to magnetic fields is related to the ratio of the charge to mass of the electron.

What else would you need to know in order to know the mass of an electron? __*The charge of the*__

__*electron*__

Now calculate the charge-to-mass ratio of the electron. Do the calculation for several different electron energies.

Quantum Assignments

Calculations:

$$\frac{q}{m_e} = \frac{2Ez}{B^2 l^2},$$

where

q = *the charge on the electron in coulombs,*
m_e = *the mass of the electron in kg,*
E = *is the magnitude of the electric field calculated using* $E = V/d$,
V = *voltage applied to the electric plates in volts,*
d = *the spacing between the electric plates in m and is specified as an INI variable in Lab.ini (default setting is 0.050 m),*
B = *the applied magnetic field in T,*
l = *the length of the electric and magnetic fields and is also specified as an INI variable in Lab.ini. (default setting is 0.050 m),*
z = *the deflection of the electron beam as the beam exits the electric and magnetic fields*

$$z = \frac{x}{1 + 2b/l},$$

x = *the deflection of the electron beam as measured at the phosphor screen,*
b = *the distance from the electric and magnetic field to the phosphor screen and is specified as an INI variable in Lab.ini (default setting is 0.762 m).*

Results:

Electron energy	200 eV	100 eV	150 eV	300 eV
q/m	1.72×10^{11}	1.73×10^{11}	1.72×10^{11}	1.73×10^{11}

Rutherford Backscattering – 1

A key experiment in understanding the nature of atomic structure was completed by Ernest Rutherford in 1911. He set up an experiment that directed a beam of alpha particles (helium nuclei) through a gold foil and then onto a detector screen. According to the "plum pudding" atomic model, electrons float around in a cloud of positive charge. Based on this model, Rutherford expected that almost all the alpha particles should not be deflected, but he expected a few to be slightly deflected by electrons. However, he observed that alpha particles emerged at all angles, even straight backwards. He described this as "... almost as incredible as if you fired a 15-inch shell at a piece of tissue paper and it came back and hit you." He suggested that the experiment could be understood if almost all of the mass of an atom was concentrated in a small, positively charged central nucleus. In this experiment, you will make observations similar to those of Professor Rutherford.

1. Set up this experiment by selecting *Rutherford Backscattering* on the clipboard of preset experiments.

   What source is used in this experiment? __*The alpha source*__

   What are alpha particles? __*Nuclei of He atoms (two neutrons and two protons)*__

   What detector is used in this experiment and what does it do? __*The phosphor screen detects alpha particles, and it glows momentarily at the positions where alpha particles impact the screen.*__

   What is the signal in the middle of the screen? __*The alpha particles that are not deflected*__

   What do other signals on the screen mean? __*Some of the alpha particles are deflected.*__

   Are most of the alpha particles undeflected or deflected? __*Undeflected*__

   According to the "plum pudding" model, what causes the slight deflection of some of the alpha particles? __*The electrons*__

2. Now move the phosphor screen to the front left of the optics table in order to detect backwards scattering.

   What causes alpha particles to deflect backwards? __*The small positive protons in the nuclei of the gold atoms cause backward deflection.*__

   How do the results of this experiment contradict the "plum pudding" atomic model? __*Backwards scattering could be caused by a concentrated positive charge in a centralized part of the nucleus, but not by a diffuse positive charge spread throughout the atom.*__

Are the atoms of the gold foil composed mostly of matter or empty space? __*Empty space*__

How does this experiment show that almost all the mass of an atom is concentrated in a small,

positively charged central nucleus? __*The majority of the alpha particles go though the gold foil*__

__*undeflected, and only a few encounter the small nucleus, which causes backwards scattering.*__

Rutherford Backscattering – 2

A key experiment in understanding the nature of atomic structure was completed by Ernest Rutherford in 1911. He set up an experiment that directed a beam of alpha particles (helium nuclei) through a gold foil and then onto a detector screen. He observed that alpha particles were not only emerging in the direction that he expected, but that he could detect alpha particles at all angles, even straight backwards. He described this as "... almost as incredible as if you fired a 15-inch shell at a piece of tissue paper and it came back and hit you." He suggested that the experiment could be understood if almost all of the mass of an atom was concentrated in a small, positively charged central nucleus. In this experiment, you will make observations similar to those of Professor Rutherford.

1. Set up the Rutherford experiment by placing the alpha-particle source on the optics table, pointed at the foil holder with a gold foil, and placing the phosphor screen behind the gold foil to detect the alpha particles coming through the foil.

2. Turn on both the alpha source and the phosphor screen.

   With the alpha-particle beam pointing directly through the foil and into the phosphor screen, draw a picture of what you see on the screen.

   What is the large signal in the middle of the screen?   __The alpha particles that are not deflected__

   What do other signals on the screen mean?   __Some of the alpha particles are deflected.__

   Why is the large signal in the middle so much more intense than the other signals?   __Most of the__ __alpha particles pass through the gold foil undeflected.__

3. Now change the detector to a different location. (If you don't see a signal for a position, you might have to turn on the persist button, and wait for a few minutes.)

   What differences do you see in the signal?   __There is no large signal in the middle of the screen,__ __and the other signals are not as frequent.__

How many distinct locations can you put the detector in? __*Seven*__

How does the signal depend on the angle formed by the source/foil/detector combination? __*The*__ __*greater the angle, the greater the signal*__

What two things cause the deflection of some of the alpha particles? __*The electrons and protons*__ __*in the gold foil*__

Why did Rutherford conclude that almost all the mass of an atom must be concentrated in a small, positively charged central nucleus? __*The majority of the alpha particles go though the gold foil*__ __*undeflected, and only a few encounter the small nucleus, which causes backwards scattering.*__

How do Rutherford's conclusions contradict the "plum pudding" atomic model? __*According to the*__ __*"plum pudding" atomic model, electrons float around in a cloud of positive charge. Based on this*__ __*model, only the electrons would cause the slight deflection of alpha particles in this experiment.*__

Rutherford Backscattering – 3

A key experiment in understanding the nature of atomic structure was completed by Ernest Rutherford in 1911. He set up an experiment that directed a beam of alpha particles (helium nuclei) through a gold foil and then onto a detector screen. He observed that alpha particles were not only emerging in the direction that he expected, but that he could detect alpha particles at all angles, even straight backwards. He described this as "... almost as incredible as if you fired a 15-inch shell at a piece of tissue paper and it came back and hit you." He suggested that the experiment could be understood if almost all of the mass of an atom was concentrated in a small, positively charged central nucleus. In this experiment, you will make observations similar to those of Professor Rutherford.

1. Set up the Rutherford experiment by placing the alpha-particle source on the optics table, pointed at the foil holder with a gold foil, and placing the phosphor screen behind the gold foil to detect the alpha particles coming through the foil.

2. Turn on both the alpha source and the phosphor screen. Observe the screen with the alpha-particle beam shining directly through the foil and into the phosphor screen.

    *What do the different signals on the screen mean?*___*The majority of the alpha particles pass*___

    ___*directly through the gold foil, but some of them are deflected.*___

3. Now change the detector to a different location. (If you don't see a signal for a position, you might have to turn on the persist button, and wait for a few minutes.)

    *What differences do you see in the signal?*___*There is no large signal in the middle of the screen,*___

    ___*and the other signals are not as frequent.*___

    *How many distinct locations can you put the detector in?*___*Seven*___

    *How does the signal depend on the angle formed by the source/foil/detector combination?*___*The*___

    ___*greater the angle, the greater the signal*___

4. Using the persist button, it is possible to estimate the number of particles that hit the screen as a function of angle. You can do this by counting the particles that hit the screen over a given length of time. Now graph this rate (in particle hits per second) as a function of angle.

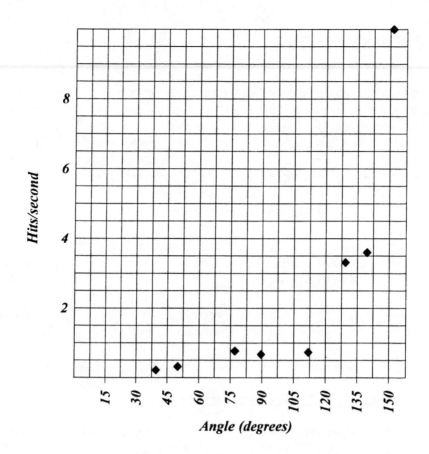

The alpha-particle source produces 100,000 particles per second in a beam that is 1 mm wide.

What percentage of the particles is being scattered backwards? __(0.06/100,000) × 100% = 0.00006%__

5. Assuming that scattering backwards means that the alpha particle hits a nuclei head on, and that the metal foil is 0.001 cm thick, estimate the diameter of a gold nucleus.

Note: The atomic diameter of a gold atom is about 2.88×10^{-10} m.

Calculations:

$$layers = \frac{0.00001}{2.88 \; x \; 10^{-10}};$$

$$\frac{A_{nucleus}}{A_{atom}} = \frac{(\# \, scattered \, / \, sec) \, / \, layers}{100,000};$$

$$d_{nucleus} = d_{atom} \sqrt{\frac{\# \, scattered \, / \, sec}{100,000 \; x \; layers}}.$$

*Gold nucleus diameter:*___**1.2 × 10⁻¹⁵ m**___

6. If R is the radius of an atomic nucleus, r_0 is the radius of a nucleon, and A is the atomic number, show how R can be approximated by $R = r_0 A^{1/3}$.

$$V_{nucleus} = \frac{4}{3}\pi R^3 \approx \left(\frac{4}{3}\pi r_0^{\,3}\right) A \,;$$

$$R^3 \approx r_0^{\,3} A \,;$$

$$R \approx r_0^{\,3} A^{\frac{1}{3}}.$$

7. Given that the value of r_0 is approximately 1.4 fm, calculate the size of the gold nucleus.

Expected size of gold nucleus: $\underline{\quad R = r_0 A^{1/3} = 6.0 \times 10^{-15} m \quad}$

How well does your previous calculation from your measurements agree with this expected value?

$\underline{\textbf{\textit{The previous calculation is the same order of magnitude, but is about five times smaller.}}}$

Why is your measured value not the same as the expected value? $\underline{\textbf{\textit{All the backwards scattering is}}}$

$\underline{\textbf{\textit{not taken into account since the measured value is less than the expected value.}}}$

Blackbody Radiation – 1

One of the critical factors in the development of quantum mechanics was the modeling of light emission by hot objects. We all know that if you heat a metal filament in a light bulb, it gives off light. Classical theory predicted that the intensity of light increased as the wavelength decreased for all wavelengths. However, classical predictions did not agree with the measured spectra. For this assignment, you will heat a tungsten metal foil and measure its spectrum.

1. Set up the optics table for this experiment by selecting *Blackbody Radiation* on the clipboard of preset experiments.

    Which metal foil is used in this experiment? __*Tungsten*__

    At what temperature is the metal foil being heated? __*3000 K*__

    What detector is used in this experiment and what does it measure? __*The spectrometer is used to*__ __*measure the intensity of light over a wide range of wavelengths.*__

    Does the spectrum show the same intensity of light at each wavelength? __*No*__

    Describe the spectrum: __*It has a spread out peak at about 965 nm, and it approaches zero*__ __*intensity at 0 nm and 5000 nm.*__

    How does this spectrum contradict classical predictions? __*Classical theory does not predict a*__ __*maximum in the spectrum, but instead predicts that the intensity increases at shorter and shorter*__ __*wavelengths.*__

2. Blackbody radiation consists of light emission in the ultraviolet, visible, and infrared regions of the electromagnetic spectrum. Scroll over the curve of the spectrum in order to zoom in.

    In what part of the electromagnetic spectrum is the peak of the spectrum? __*Infrared*__

3. Raise the temperature to 3600 K.

    How did the curve change? __*The peak shifted down to about 700 nm, and its intensity increased.*__

    Did the peak shift to a higher or lower wavelength? __*Lower wavelength*__

    Do shorter or longer wavelengths have more energy? __*Shorter wavelengths*__

Blackbody Radiation – 2

One of the critical factors in the development of quantum mechanics was the modeling of light emission by hot objects. We all know that if you heat a metal filament in a light bulb, it gives off light. Classical predictions of the intensity of light at each wavelength did not agree with the measured spectra. For this assignment, you will heat a tungsten metal foil and measure its spectrum.

1. Set up the optics table for blackbody radiation by placing a tungsten foil with a heater and the spectrometer on the table. Set the temperature of the foil to 3500 K.

    At what wavelength is the maximum intensity observed? (Use the hand to scroll over an area in order to zoom in and get better accuracy.) ___820 nm___

    Blackbody radiation consists of light emission in the ultraviolet, visible, and infrared regions of the electromagnetic spectrum.

    From what part of the electromagnetic spectrum is this wavelength? ___The infrared region___

    Draw the curve.

2. Lower the temperature to 3000 K.

    At what wavelength is the maximum intensity observed? ___965 nm___

    Draw the curve.

Quantum Assignments

3. Lower the temperature to 1000 K.

   At what wavelength is the maximum intensity observed? ___**2880 nm**___

   Draw the curve.

4. Lower the temperature to room temperature (300 K).

   At what wavelength is the maximum intensity observed? ___**The peak is off the chart.**___

   Draw the curve.

   What trends did you see? ___**The peak shifted to higher wavelengths and lower intensities as the temperature was decreased.**___

   What important ideas did Planck develop from this experiment? ___**Energy from electromagnetic radiation is proportional to the frequency of the radiation, but it is not continuous.**___

   What important equation did he derive? ___**$E = h\nu$**___

Blackbody Radiation – 3

One of the critical factors in the development of quantum mechanics was the modeling of light emission by hot objects. We all know that if you heat a metal filament in a light bulb, it gives off light. Classical predictions of the intensity of light at each wavelength did not agree with the measured spectra. For this assignment, you will heat a tungsten metal foil and measure its spectrum.

1. Set up the optics table for blackbody radiation by placing a tungsten foil with a heater and the spectrometer on the table. Set the temperature of the foil to 3000 K.

   What is the relation between the curve and the amount of radiation emitted? ___*The higher the*___

   ___*intensity of the curve, the greater amount of radiation emitted*___

   At what wavelength is the maximum intensity observed? (Use the hand to scroll over an area in order

   to zoom in and get better accuracy.) ___*~ 965 nm*___

   From what part of the electromagnetic spectrum is this wavelength? ___*The infrared region*___

   Draw the curve.

2. Switch the toggle on the spectrometer to show only the visible region of the electromagnetic spectrum.

   What happens to the curve when you lower or raise the temperature? ___*The curve shifts to lower*___

   ___*intensities at lower temperatures.*___

   At what temperature does tungsten melt? ___*3700 K*___

   Can you ever get the peak of the curve within the visible region? ___*No*___

   Blackbody radiation consists of light emission in the ultraviolet, visible, and infrared regions of the electromagnetic spectrum.

Which region has the longest wavelengths?   <u>**The infrared region**</u>

Which region has radiation of the highest energy?   <u>**The ultraviolet region**</u>

The Rayleigh-Jeans law, based on classical theory, is

$$I(\lambda, T) = \frac{2\pi c k_B T}{\lambda^4},$$

where I is the intensity of the radiation, c is the speed of light, k_B is Boltmann's constant, T is the temperature, and λ is the wavelength.

According to classical predictions, what would happen to the intensity as the wavelength approaches

zero?   <u>**The intensity would approach infinity.**</u>

Does the spectrum of tungsten at 3000 K agree with classical predictions?   <u>**No**</u>

Why or why not?   <u>**The intensity of the curve has a maximum at about 965 nm, and then it levels**</u>

<u>**off and approaches zero intensity with decreasing wavelength.**</u>

Photoelectric Effect – 1

Though Einstein is most famous for his work in describing relativity in mechanics, his Nobel Prize was for understanding a very simple experiment. It was long understood that if you directed light of a certain wavelength at a piece of metal, it would emit electrons. In classical theory, the energy of light was thought to be based on its intensity and not its frequency. However, the results of the photoelectric effect contradicted classical theory. These inconsistencies led Einstein to suggest that we need to think of light as being composed of particles and not just as waves. You will have a chance to recreate some of the measurements that led to Einstein's theory.

1. Set up this experiment by selecting *Photoelectric Effect (1)* on the clipboard of preset experiments.

    What source is used in this experiment and what does it do? __**The laser provides light at a single**__

    __**wavelength.**__

    At what intensity is the laser set? __**1 nW**__

    At what wavelength is the laser set? __**450 nm**__

    Which metal foil is used in this experiment? __**Sodium (Na)**__

    What detector is used in this experiment and what does it measure? __**The phosphor screen detects**__

    __**electrons, and it glows momentarily at the positions where the electrons impact the screen.**__

    What does the signal on the phosphor screen indicate about the laser light shining on the Na foil? _

    __**The laser light causes the emission of electrons from the surface of the Na metal foil.**__

2. Decrease the laser power to 1 photon/second.

    How does the signal change? __**The signal flickers on and off, and it is not as intense as before.**__

3. Increase the power to 1 kW.

    How does the signal change? __**The signal appears the same as when the power was at 1 nW.**__

4. Change the power back to 1 nW. Now increase the wavelength to 650 nm.

    What do you observe? __**The signal disappears.**__

    Does frequency of light increase or decrease as wavelength is increased? __**Decrease**__

    Does a lower frequency correspond to a lower or higher energy? __**Lower energy**__

5. Change the laser power to determine whether you can get the signal back to what it was before.

    Can you? __**No**__

What is the difference between wavelength and intensity?   ___*Wavelength corresponds to the energy*___

___*of the light emitted, whereas intensity is the amount of light emitted.*_____

Which matters in the formation of photoelectrons?   ___*Wavelength*_____

Photoelectric Effect – 2

Though Einstein is most famous for his work in describing relativity in mechanics, his Nobel Prize was for understanding a very simple experiment. It was long understood that if you directed light of certain wavelength at a piece of metal, it would emit electrons. Several inconsistencies in the results were known, which led Einstein to suggest that we need to think of light as being composed of particles and not just as waves. You will have a chance to recreate some of the measurements that led to Einstein's theory.

1. Set up this experiment by selecting *Photoelectric Effect (2)* on the clipboard of preset experiments.

   What source is used in this experiment and what does it do? __*The laser provides light at a single*__ __*wavelength.*__

   At what intensity is the laser set? __*1 nW*__

   At what wavelength is the laser set? __*400 nm*__

   Which metal foil is used in this experiment? __*Sodium (Na)*__

2. The detector used in this experiment is a bolometer. This instrument measures the kinetic energy of electrons emitted from the metal. You should see a peak on the bolometer detector screen. The intensity or height of the signal corresponds to the number of electrons being emitted from the metal. Zoom in on the area of the peak so that you can accurately read the kinetic energy of the electrons. Record this value.

   Kinetic energy of electrons: __*0.34 eV*__

3. Increase the power to 1 kW.

   What happens to the graph on the bolometer detector screen? __*The intensity of the peak*__ __*increases.*__

   Does the kinetic energy of the emitted electrons change? __*No*__

4. Decrease the wavelength to 300 nm.

   Does the kinetic energy of the emitted electrons change? __*Yes*__

   Does a shorter wavelength correspond to a lower or higher frequency? __*Higher frequency*__

   Does a higher frequency correspond to a lower or higher energy? __*Higher energy*__

   What characteristic of the laser light determines the kinetic energy of the electrons (wavelength or intensity)? __*Wavelength*__

Quantum Assignments

How does this experiment show that particles of light or photons have characteristic energies? ____

__Depending on the wavelength or frequency of light, different amounts of energy are transferred__

__to the electrons as the photons collide with them.__ _____

Photoelectric Effect – 3

Though Einstein is most famous for his work in describing relativity in mechanics, his Nobel Prize was for understanding a very simple experiment. It was long understood that if you directed light of certain wavelength at a piece of metal, it would emit electrons. Several inconsistencies in the results were known, which led Einstein to suggest that we need to think of light as being composed of particles and not just as waves. You will have a chance to recreate some of the measurements that led to Einstein's theory.

1. Set up the photoelectric effect experiment by placing the laser, a Sodium (Na) foil, and the phosphor screen detector on the table. You need to place them so that the laser and the phosphor screen are each at a 45-degree angle to the foil. Set the wavelength of the laser to 450 nm and the laser power to 1 nW, and turn on the phosphor screen. You should see a bright spot in the middle of the screen. These are the electrons that are emitted from the metal foil.

    How does the photoelectric effect show the particle-like nature of light? **Light consists of packets of energy that collide with electrons from the surface of the Na foil. If the packets of energy are great enough, then electrons are emitted from the foil.**

2. Decrease the laser power to 1 photon/second.

    Do you still see electrons being emitted? **Yes**

3. Increase the power progressively up to 1 kW.

    Are electrons still being emitted? **Yes**

    Explain what you see. **The intensity of the signal increased.**

4. Change the power back to 1 nW. Now increase the wavelength to 650 nm.

    What do you observe? **The signal disappeared.**

    Is wavelength proportional or inversely proportional to frequency and energy? **Wavelength is inversely proportional to both frequency and energy.**

5. Change the laser power to determine whether you can get the signal back to what it was before.

    Can you? **No**

    Does the wavelength or the intensity of light dictate the formation of photoelectrons? **The wavelength of light determines whether electrons will be emitted.**

Quantum Assignments

How does this experiment show that particles of light or photons have characteristic energies? ____

Only certain wavelengths of light have the required energy to eject electrons from the Na foil. ____

6. Change the power back to 1 nW. Change the wavelength until you can see the signal again.

What wavelength (to within 1 nm) is the largest that still gives a signal?   __450 nm__

We define the work function to be the minimum energy necessary to remove an electron from the metal.

In nm what is the work function of Na? __450 nm__

Photoelectric Effect – 4

Though Einstein is most famous for his work in describing relativity in mechanics, his Nobel Prize was for understanding a very simple experiment. It was long understood that if you directed light of certain wavelength at a piece of metal, it would emit electrons. Several inconsistencies in the results were known, which led Einstein to suggest that we need to think of light as being composed of particles and not just as waves. You will have a chance to recreate some of the measurements that led to Einstein's theory.

1. Set up the photoelectric effect experiment by placing the laser, a Sodium (Na) foil, and the bolometer on the table. The laser and the bolometer need to each be at about a 45-degree angle to the face of the metal foil. Turn on the laser, and set the power to 1 nW and the wavelength to 400 nm.

2. The bolometer measures the kinetic energy of electrons emitted from the metal. You should see a peak on the bolometer detector screen. Zoom in on the area of the peak so that you can accurately read the kinetic energy of the electrons. Record this value.

   Kinetic energy of electrons: ___**0.34 eV**_____

3. Increase the power progressively up to 1 kW. (Zoom out, if necessary, before increasing the power.)

   What happens to the graph on the bolometer detector screen? ___**The intensity of the peak**___

   ___**increases.**_____

   Does the kinetic energy of the emitted electrons depend on the intensity of light? ___**No**_____

   Why or why not? ___**The intensity of light does not correspond to the energy of the light emitted.**___

   ___**It only corresponds to the amount of light emitted.**_____

4. Decrease the power to 100 photons/sec.

   Why doesn't the bolometer show a signal? ___**The signal is too small to detect.**_____

   Would changing the wavelength help get the signal back? ___**No**_____

   Why or why not? ___**Changing the wavelength would only change the kinetic energy of the emitted**___

   ___**electrons. The signal would still be too small to detect.**_____

5. Increase the laser power in order to detect the signal again. Decrease the wavelength to 350 nm.

   With incident light of a shorter wavelength, what happens to the kinetic energy of the emitted

   electrons? ___**The kinetic energy of the emitted electrons increases.**_____

Why? Light of a shorter wavelength has a greater frequency and energy, so the photons transfer more energy to the electrons.

6. From the measured work function in the *Photoelectric Effect – 3* assignment, predict the wavelength in which the kinetic energy of the emitted electrons would approach zero.

Wavelength prediction: __450 nm__

Why would you predict this wavelength? __This is the highest wavelength (lowest frequency and energy) that will still eject electrons from the Na foil. Just enough energy is transferred to eject the electrons.__

What kinetic energy would the bolometer measure above this wavelength? __Electrons would no longer be ejected from the Na foil, so there would be no signal.__

What is the significance of this zero in the kinetic energy? __The photons transferred the exact amount of energy required to eject the electrons from the Na foil. No extra energy was transferred.__

Photoelectric Effect – 5

Though Einstein is most famous for his work in describing relativity in mechanics, his Nobel Prize was for understanding a very simple experiment. It was long understood that if you directed light of certain wavelength at a piece of metal, it would emit electrons. Several inconsistencies in the results were known, which led Einstein to suggest that we need to think of light as being composed of particles and not just as waves. You will have a chance to recreate some of the measurements that led to Einstein's theory.

1. Set up the photoelectric effect experiment by placing the laser, a Sodium (Na) foil, and the phosphor screen detector on the table. You need to place them so that the laser and the phosphor screen are each at about a 45-degree angle to the foil. Turn on the phosphor screen. Set the laser power to 1 nW and set the laser to the largest wavelength which still gives a signal.

    What wavelength (to within 1 nm) is the largest that still gives a signal?   ___**450 nm**___

    What is the equation that relates the wavelength of a photon to the energy of a photon?   ___**$E = hc/\lambda$**___

    _____

    We define the work function to be the minimum energy necessary to remove an electron from the metal.

    In nm what is the work function of Na? ___**450 nm**___

    What is it in eV? ___**2.76 eV**___

    Based on what you know about atoms, which would you predict has the smallest work function, Na,

    K, Rb, or Cs? ___**Cs**___

2. Measure the work functions for Na, K, Rb and Cs. Record the values in eV units.

    Na ___**2.76 eV**___   *K* ___**2.30 eV**___   *Rb* ___**2.16 eV**___   *Cs* ___**2.14 eV**___

    Do these values agree with your chemical intuition? ___**Yes. It takes less energy to eject electrons**___

    ___**from the bigger atoms, since the electrons are farther from the nucleus.**___

3. Predict the order of increasing work functions for Co, Ni, Cu and Zn, and then measure the work functions for these elements. Again, record the values in eV units.

    Ranking prediction: ___**Co < Ni < Cu < Zn**___

    Measured values for the work functions:

    Co ___**5.03 eV**___   *Ni* ___**5.17 eV**___   *Cu* ___**4.67 eV**___   *Zn* ___**4.34 eV**___

4. Make a graph of work function versus atomic number for every available metal foil.

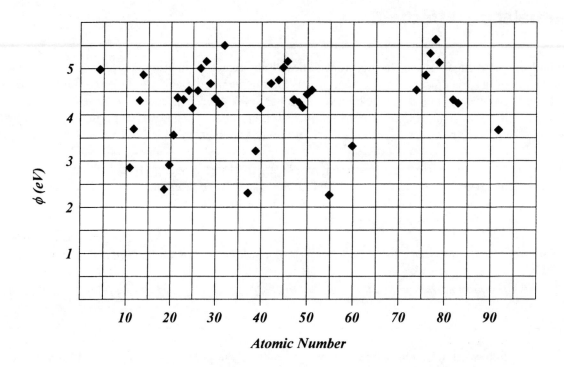

Describe the periodic trends in the results. __*In general, the work function decreases going down a group and increases across a period. However, the work function is less predictable for the transition elements.*__

Can you make any conclusions or generalizations about the trends you observed? __*The atomic radius increases going down a group and decreases across a period.*__

Photoelectric Effect – 6

Though Einstein is most famous for his work in describing relativity in mechanics, his Nobel Prize was for understanding a very simple experiment. It was long understood that if you directed light of certain wavelength at a piece of metal, it would emit electrons. Several inconsistencies in the results were known, which led Einstein to suggest that we need to think of light as being composed of particles and not just as waves. You will have a chance to recreate some of the measurements that led to Einstein's theory.

1. Set up the photoelectric effect experiment by placing the laser, a Sodium (Na) foil, and the bolometer on the table. The laser and the bolometer need to each be at a 45-degree angle to the face of the metal foil. Turn on the laser, and set the power to 1 nW and the wavelength to 400 nm.

2. The bolometer measures the kinetic energy of electrons emitted from the metal. You should see a peak on the bolometer detector screen. Zoom in on the area of the peak so that you can accurately read the kinetic energy of the electrons. Record this value.

    Kinetic energy of electrons: __*0.34 eV*__

3. Einstein suggested that the energy of the emitted electrons was the energy of a photon of light minus the work function of the metal, or the energy that binds the electrons to the metal. Calculate the work function (in units of eV) by taking the difference of the energy of a photon from the laser minus the kinetic energy of an electron.

    Work function for Na: __*2.76 eV*__

4. Measure the electron kinetic energy at five different wavelengths of light (less than 450 nm), and calculate the work function (ϕ) in units of eV.

λ	100	200	250	300	350
Energy of photon	*12.4 eV*	*6.2 eV*	*5.0 eV*	*4.1 eV*	*3.5 eV*
Kinetic energy of electron	*9.7 eV*	*3.4 eV*	*2.2 eV*	*1.4 eV*	*0.8 eV*
ϕ	*2.7 eV*	*2.8 eV*	*2.8 eV*	*2.7 eV*	*2.7 eV*

Is the work function independent of wavelength? __*Yes*__

Based on what you know about atoms, which would you predict would have the smallest work

function, Na, K, Rb or Cs? __*Cs*__

5. Measure the work functions for Na, K, Rb and Cs.

    Na __*2.76 eV*__   *K* __*2.30 eV*__   *Rb* __*2.16 eV*__ *Cs* __*2.14 eV*__

Quantum Assignments

Do these values agree with your chemical intuition? **Yes. It takes less energy to eject electrons from the bigger atoms, since the electrons are farther from the nucleus.**

6. Predict the order of increasing work functions for Co, Ni, Cu and Zn, and then measure the work functions for these elements.

Ranking prediction: **Co < Ni < Cu < Zn**

Measured values for the work functions:

Co **5.03 eV** Ni **5.17 eV** Cu **4.67 eV** Zn **4.34 eV**

7. Make a graph of work function versus atomic number for every available metal foil.

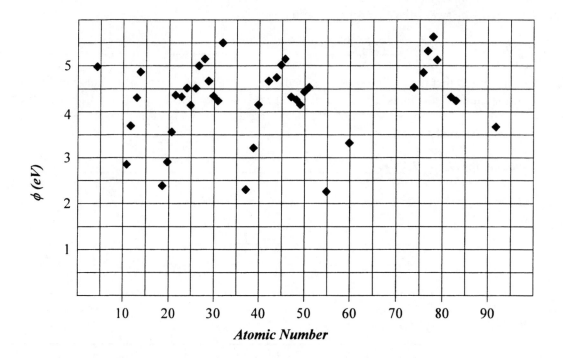

Describe the periodic trends in the results. **In general, the work function decreases going down a group and increases across a period. However, the work function is less predictable for the transition elements.**

Can you make any conclusions or generalizations about the trends you observed? **The atomic radius increases going down a group and decreases across a period.**

Millikan Oil Drop – 1

In the Thomson experiment, you discovered that you can use the deflection of an electron beam in electric and magnetic fields to measure the charge-to-mass ratio of an electron. If you then want to know either the charge or the mass of an electron, you need to have a way of measuring one or the other independently. Millikan and his student Harvey Fletcher showed that they could make very small oil drops and deposit small numbers of electrons on these drops (1 to 10 electrons). They would then measure the total charge on the oil drops. You will get a chance to repeat their experiments.

1. Set up this experiment by selecting *Millikan Oil Drop Experiment* on the clipboard of preset experiments.

   What source is used in this experiment? __*The electron gun*__

   How does this source affect the oil droplets in the oil mist chamber? __*As electrons from the*__

   __*electron gun pass through the oil mist, they are deposited on the oil droplets.*__

   The detector in this experiment is a video camera. In order to be able to detect the oil droplets, there is a telescopic eyepiece attached to the oil mist chamber.

   What do you observe from the video camera screen? __*Oil droplets are continuously falling down.*__

   Do all the oil drops fall at the same speed? __*No*__

   What force causes the drops to fall? __*The gravitational force*__

   The oil drops fall at their terminal velocities. The terminal velocity depends on the radius of the drops. By measuring the velocity of a droplet, the radius can be calculated. Then the mass of the drop can be calculated from its radius and the density of the oil.

   Why do the droplets fall at different velocities? __*The droplets are different sizes, and therefore they*__

   __*have different terminal velocities.*__

2. Turn on the electric field to 400 V.

   What do you observe on the detector screen? __*Some of the droplets are going upwards, but some*__

   __*are still falling down.*__

   What type of charge do the oil drops have? __*Negative*__

   The force exerted on an oil drop by the electric field depends on the amount of charge deposited on the drop, since the force on a charged particle is qE. Each drop has a certain number electrons attached to it, so the charge on each drop is an integral multiple of the charge of an electron, e. By calculating the charge on several droplets, the charge of an electron can be determined.

Besides the gravitational force, what other force affects the velocity of the charged oil drops?   **The**

force exerted on the electron by the electric field

Will this force have more or less of an effect if the oil drop has more deposited electrons?   **More**

Why?   **The force is equal to qE, and more electrons means a greater charge (q).**

Millikan Oil Drop – 2

In the Thomson experiment, you discovered that you can use the deflection of an electron beam in electric and magnetic fields to measure the charge-to-mass ratio of an electron. If you then want to know either the charge or the mass of an electron, you need to have a way of measuring one or the other independently. Millikan and his student Harvey Fletcher showed that they could make very small oil drops and deposit small numbers of electrons on these drops (1 to 10 electrons). They would then measure the total charge on the oil drops. You will get a chance to repeat their experiments.

1. Set up the Millikan-Fletcher experiment by placing the oil mist chamber in the center of the optics table, an electric field on it, the electron gun on the table to ionize the drops, and the video camera in position to look through the microscopy objective.

2. Turn on the video camera, but leave the electric field and the electron gun turned off. You should see drops falling from the top of the screen.

    What force causes the drops to fall? ___**The gravitational force**_____

    Do they all fall at the same speed? ___**No**_____

3. Use the stopwatch to measure the time it takes for 10 different drops to fall from the top of the screen to the bottom, and record these times. Calculate the velocity for each drop. (Note that you can press the slow-motion button to reduce the speed by a factor of five.)

Drop #	1	2	3	4	5	6	7	8	9	10
Time (s)	*12.9*	*15.6*	*9.1*	*15.2*	*7.9*	*11.1*	*28.8*	*22.8*	*9.4*	*14.5*
Velocity (m/s)	*7.8* $\times 10^{-5}$	*6.4* $\times 10^{-5}$	*1.1* $\times 10^{-4}$	*6.6* $\times 10^{-5}$	*1.3* $\times 10^{-5}$	*9.0* $\times 10^{-5}$	*3.5* $\times 10^{-5}$	*4.4* $\times 10^{-5}$	*1.1* $\times 10^{-4}$	*6.9* $\times 10^{-5}$

Why do some drops fall faster than others? ___**They fall at their terminal velocities. The terminal**___

___**velocity of a drop is proportional to the radius of the drop.**_____

_____

What range in velocities did you see? ___**1.27 $\times 10^{-5}$ m/s to 1.10 $\times 10^{-4}$ m/s**_____

The radius of the oil drop can be calculated from the terminal velocity.

What is terminal velocity? ___**The velocity at which the gravitational force is balanced by the**___

___**resistive force of air.**_____

In order to calculate the mass of the oil drops, what other information is needed besides the radii? _

___**The density of the oil**_____

4. Now turn on the electron gun to 1 nA and 100 eV.

What are you doing by shooting electrons at the oil drops? ___Depositing electrons on the oil drops___

Should this change the velocity at which the drops fall? ___No___

Why or why not? ___Without an electric field, there is no electric force acting on the charged oil drops.___

5. Turn on the electric field to 400 V.

What changes do you see? ___Some of the drops are still falling, but many of the oil drops are now rising and some are close to motionless.___

Now what other force is acting on the oil drops? ___An electric force___

Which way is the electric field aligned? ___Downward___

How can you tell? ___Negatively charged oil drops are rising upward.___

How is the electric field calculated from the voltage? ___$E = V/d_{plates}$ where d_{plates} is the distance between the voltage plates.___

6. Turn the voltage down to 200 V. Find a drop that is still rising on the screen. Decrease the voltage until this drop is stationary on the screen.

What two forces must be balanced in order for the drop to be stationary? ___The gravitational and electric forces must be balanced.___

How is the charge on each drop related to e, the electronic charge? ___Each drop has a charge that is an integer multiple of e.___

Millikan Oil Drop – 3

In the Thomson experiment, you discovered that you can use the deflection of an electron beam in electric and magnetic fields to measure the charge-to-mass ratio of an electron. If you then want to know either the charge or the mass of an electron, you need to have a way of measuring one or the other independently. Millikan and his student Harvey Fletcher showed that they could make very small oil drops and deposit small numbers of electrons on these drops (1 to 10 electrons). They would then measure the total charge on the oil drops. You will get a chance to repeat their experiments.

1. Set up the Millikan-Fletcher experiment by placing the oil mist chamber in the center of the optics table, an electric field on it, the electron gun on the table to ionize the drops, and the video camera in position to look through the microscopy objective.

   Why do some drops fall faster than others? _**The oil drops fall at their terminal velocities. The terminal velocity of a drop is proportional to the radius of the drop.**_

2. Now turn on the electron gun to 1 nA and 100 eV.

   Does this change the velocity at which the drops fall? Why or why not? _**No. Even though the oil drops are charged, there is no electric force acting on them.**_

3. Turn on the electric field to 300 V.

   What changes do you see? _**Some of the drops are still falling. However, many of the oil drops are now rising, and some are close to motionless.**_

   Are all of the drops still falling down? Why or why not? _**No. Some are rising since their charge is negative enough that the electric force upward is greater than the gravitational force downward.**_

4. Increase the voltage to 900 V.

   Are some drops still falling? Why? _**Yes. Even with a large electric field, their negative charge is not big enough for the electric force to be greater than the gravitational force.**_

   Are some rising faster than others? What makes the difference? _**Yes. The smaller the oil drops are and the more negative charge they have, the faster they rise.**_

5. Now turn the voltage down to 100 V. Find a drop that is only slightly moving. Adjust the voltage until this drop is stationary on the screen. Record the voltage for this drop. Now increase the voltage slowly until the drop rises to the top of the screen, and then turn off the electric field. Use the stopwatch to measure the time it takes for the drop to fall a certain distance. Use the slow-motion

button for more accurate time readings. Repeat this procedure with 10 other drops, choosing drops that require different voltages to suspend them. Record your data in the first three columns of the table below.

Drop #	Voltage (V)	Time (s)	Distance (m)	Terminal velocity (m/s)	Radius (m)	Mass (kg)	Charge (C)
1	75.8	17	0.00075	4.4×10^{-5}	5.6×10^{-7}	6.1×10^{-16}	7.9×10^{-19}
2	126	22	0.00075	3.4×10^{-5}	4.9×10^{-7}	4.0×10^{-16}	3.1×10^{-19}
3	251	11	0.00075	6.8×10^{-5}	7.1×10^{-7}	1.2×10^{-15}	4.8×10^{-19}
4	188	11	0.00075	6.8×10^{-5}	7.1×10^{-7}	3.1×10^{-15}	6.3×10^{-19}
5	503	7	0.00075	1.1×10^{-4}	9.0×10^{-7}	2.5×10^{-15}	4.8×10^{-19}
6	377	11	0.00075	6.8×10^{-5}	7.1×10^{-7}	1.2×10^{-15}	3.2×10^{-19}
7	755	7	0.00075	1.1×10^{-4}	9.0×10^{-7}	2.5×10^{-15}	3.2×10^{-19}
8	102	14	0.00075	5.4×10^{-5}	6.2×10^{-7}	8.3×10^{-16}	8.0×10^{-19}
9	635	8	0.00075	9.4×10^{-4}	8.4×10^{-7}	1.8×10^{-15}	3.1×10^{-19}
10	131	21.5	0.00075	3.5×10^{-5}	4.9×10^{-7}	4.1×10^{-16}	3.1×10^{-19}
11	128	14	0.00075	5.4×10^{-5}	6.2×10^{-7}	4.1×10^{-16}	6.4×10^{-19}

*Note that the time to fall from the top to the bottom of the screen is related to mass, and the voltage necessary to suspend them is related to charge.

6. Now fill out the remainder of the table and calculate the charge on each of these drops. Some of the information you will need to do this calculation is found in the *Quantum User Guide* or in the Help Menu (page 13 of *The Simulation*). What is the charge on the electron?

Calculations:

Approximate the radius by $r = \sqrt{\dfrac{9 \cdot \eta_{air} \cdot v_t}{2 \cdot g \cdot (\rho_{oil} - \rho_{air})}}$ **, then iterate** $r = \sqrt{\dfrac{9 \cdot \eta_{air} \cdot v_t}{2 \cdot g \cdot (\rho_{oil} - \rho_{air})} \cdot \left(\dfrac{1}{1 + b/pr}\right)^{1/2}}$,

where

v_t = terminal velocity;

g = 9.81 m·s^{-2}, acceleration due to gravity;

ρ_{oil} = density of oil = 821 kg·m^{-3} (an INI variable in *Video.ini*);

ρ_{air} = density of air = 1.22 kg·m^{-3} (an INI variable in *Video.ini*);

η_{air} = viscosity of air = 1.4607×10^{-5} kg·m^{-1}·s^{-1} (an INI variable in *Video.ini*);

b = correction for small drop size = 8.1184×10^{-8} m·atm;

p = atmospheric pressure in atm = 1 (an INI variable in *Video.ini*).

Then, $m = \dfrac{4\pi}{3} \cdot r^3 \cdot \rho_{oil}$**, and** $Q(n) \cdot C = \dfrac{d_{plates} \cdot m \cdot g}{V}$ **where**

q = total charge on the drop;

$Q(n)$ = number of electrons on the drop (an integer);

C = the fundamental charge of an electron;

d_{plates} = the distance between the voltage plates = 0.010 m (an INI variable in *Video.ini*);

V = voltage across the plates.

What is the charge on the electron? __1.61×10^{-19} C__

Diffraction of Light – 1

It has long been known that if you shine light through narrow slits that are spaced at small intervals, the light will form a diffraction pattern. For example, if you look carefully through sheer curtains at a light source, you can see a series of light and dark regions called a diffraction pattern. In this assignment, you will shine a laser through a device with two slits whose spacing can be adjusted and investigate the patterns that will be made at some distance from the slits.

1. Set up the diffraction by selecting *Two-Slit Diffraction - Photons* on the clipboard of preset experiments.

   What source is used in this experiment and for what reason? __*The laser since it provides light at a*__

   __*single wavelength*__

   What is the spacing of the two slits on the two-slit device? ___*3.0 μm*___

   Draw a picture of the pattern displayed on the video screen.

2. Change the power or intensity of the laser from 1 nW to 1 W.

   Does the intensity of the laser light affect the diffraction pattern? ___*No*___

   How does the laser function differently when the power is increased? __*More light is emitted.*__

3. Change the power back to 1 nW, and then change the wavelength of the laser light to 700 nm.

   How does the diffraction pattern change? __*There are fewer diffraction lines, and the color of the*__

   __*pattern has changed from green to red.*__

   What causes the light fringes to form? __*Constructive interference*__

   What causes the dark fringes to form? __*Destructive interference*__

Diffraction of Light – 2

It has long been known that if you shine light through narrow slits that are spaced at small intervals, the light will form a diffraction pattern. For example, if you look carefully through sheer curtains at a light source, you can see a series of light and dark regions called a diffraction pattern. In this assignment, you will shine a laser through a device with two slits whose spacing can be adjusted and investigate the patterns that will be made at some distance from the slits.

1. Set up the diffraction by placing the laser on the table, with the slits in the middle, and the video camera at the other end. Turn on the laser, and set the power to 1 nW and the wavelength to 500 nm. Set the slit spacing to 3 μm.

2. Turn on the video camera.

    Draw a picture of the pattern.

    What color is the pattern? Why? __It's green, since the light has a wavelength of 500 nm, which__

    __emits green light.__

    What causes the diffraction pattern? __The diffraction pattern is caused by constructive and__

    __destructive interferences of the light waves coming from the two slits.__

    Illustrate how two waves can interfere constructively.

Quantum Assignments

Illustrate how two waves can interfere destructively.

What would you expect to happen to the number of diffraction lines if you decreased the wavelength of the laser? Why? ___**The diffraction lines should increase as you decrease the wavelength, since a smaller wavelength creates more possibilities for constructive and destructive interferences.**___

3. Change the power or intensity of the laser from 1 nW to 1 mW.

   Does the diffraction pattern change? ___**No**___

   Should a change in power affect the diffraction pattern? ___**No**___

   Why or Why not? ___**Only changing the wavelength would change the diffraction pattern. The laser power only affects the amount of light emitted and not the wavelength.**___

Diffraction of Light – 3

It has long been known that if you shine light through narrow slits that are spaced at small intervals, the light will form a diffraction pattern. For example, if you look carefully through sheer curtains at a light source, you can see a series of light and dark regions called a diffraction pattern. In this assignment, you will shine a laser through a device with two slits whose spacing can be adjusted and investigate the patterns that will be made at some distance from the slits.

1. Set up the diffraction by placing the laser on the table, with the slits in the middle, and the video camera at the other end. Turn on the laser, and set the power to 1 nW and the wavelength to 700 nm. Set the slit spacing to 3 μm.

2. Turn on the video camera.

    Draw a picture of the pattern.

3. Change the power or intensity of the laser from 1 nW to 1 mW.

    Does the pattern change? Why or Why not? __*No. The laser power only affects the amount of light*__ __*emitted and not the wavelength. Only changing the wavelength would change the diffraction*__ __*pattern.*__

4. Adjust the spacing of the slits.

    How does the diffraction pattern change as you increase the spacing between the slits? __*The*__ __*number of diffraction lines increases.*__

    Why does the diffraction pattern change this way? __*As the spacing between slits increases, the*__ __*possibilities for constructive and destructive interferences also increase.*__

5. Change the power on the laser to 1000 photons/second (p/s). Turn on the persist mode on the video camera. You are now looking at individual photons coming through the slits.

   Is the pattern that builds up the same as the pattern from the continuous beam of photons? __***Yes***__

6. Change to 100 photons/second.

   Is the pattern still the same? __***Yes***__

   At these low laser intensities, there is never a time when two photons go through the slits at the same time.

   How can a single photon diffract? __***Although a photon is like a particle, it is also a wave. Thus, the***__

   __***wave of the photon goes through both slits.***__

   From this experiment, what conclusions can you make about the nature of light? __***Light has both a***__

   __***particle-like nature and a wave nature.***__

7. Change the wavelength on the laser from 700 nm to 400 nm, change the power back to 1 nW, and change the spacing of the slits back to 3 μm.

   Draw the pattern, and label any differences between this diffraction pattern and the first diffraction pattern. (For reference, the distance across the video screen is 7.5 cm.)

8. For each 50 nm wavelength across the visible spectrum, make a graph of wavelength on the *x*-axis versus number of diffraction lines on the *y*-axis.

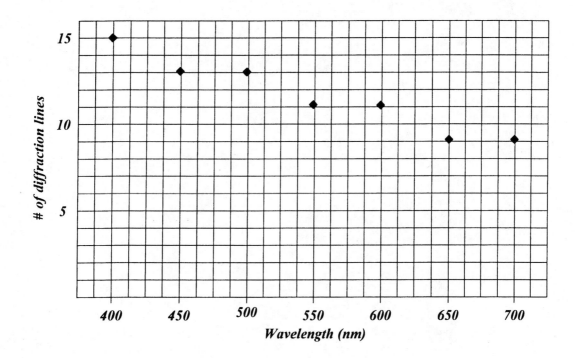

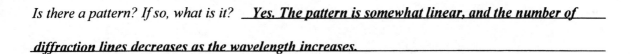

Is there a pattern? If so, what is it?   <u>*Yes. The pattern is somewhat linear, and the number of*</u>

<u>*diffraction lines decreases as the wavelength increases.*</u>

Diffraction of Particles – 1

De Broglie was the first person to suggest that particles could be considered as having wave properties. You have seen in the *Diffraction of Light* assignments that if we pass light through appropriately spaced slits, we get diffraction patterns that represent light waves interfering with each other. In this experiment, you will be able to observe a similar phenomenon with electrons.

1. Set up the diffraction by selecting *Two-Slit Diffraction - Electrons* on the clipboard of preset experiments.

   What source is used in this experiment and what does it do? __**The electron gun provides a**__

   __**collimated beam of electrons.**__

   What is the spacing of the two slits on the two-slit device? __**100 nm**__

   What detector is used in this experiment and what does it do? __**The phosphor screen detects**__

   __**electrons, and it glows momentarily at the positions where the electrons impact the screen.**__

   Draw a picture of the pattern displayed on the phosphor screen.

   What characteristic of light caused the diffraction pattern in the Diffraction of Light experiments? _

   __**The wave nature of light**__

   What characteristic of electrons causes the diffraction pattern in this experiment? __**The wave-like**__

   __**properties of electrons**__

2. Increase the current or intensity of the electron gun to 1 A.

   Does this change the diffraction pattern? __**No**__

3. Increase the energy on the electron gun from 4 meV to 24 meV.

   How does this affect the diffraction pattern? __**The number of diffraction lines increases.**__

Diffraction of Particles – 2

De Broglie was the first person to suggest that particles could be considered as having wave properties. You have seen in the *Diffraction of Light* assignments that if we pass light through appropriately spaced slits, we get diffraction patterns that represent light waves interfering with each other. In this experiment, you will be able to observe a similar phenomenon with electrons.

1. Set up a two-slit diffraction experiment using the electron gun, the two-slit device, and the phosphor screen. Set the current or intensity of the electron gun to 1 nA, the energy on the electron gun to 1.0 eV, and the slit spacing to 6 nm.

    Draw a picture of the diffraction pattern on the phosphor screen.

    What caused the diffraction pattern in the Diffraction of Light experiments? __*The wave nature of*__

    __*light*__

    What characteristic of electrons causes the diffraction pattern? __*The wave-like properties of*__

    __*electrons*__

2. Now increase the current on the electron gun to 1 μA.

    How does the electron gun function differently when the current is increased? __*The electron gun*__

    __*emits more electrons.*__

    Should the diffraction pattern change when the current is increased? Why or why not? __*No. The*__

    __*diffraction pattern is caused by the wave nature of electrons and does not depend on the*__

    __*number of electrons.*__

3. Decrease the current to 100 electrons/second. The pattern now builds up one electron at a time.

Draw the pattern after it has built up for at least 30 seconds.

Does the pattern look the same as before? __**Yes**__

Describe how the pattern builds up. __**The electrons hit the screen in many different places, and**__

__**collectively they form the same diffraction pattern as before.**__

4. Now put the phosphor screen in persist mode, and wait several minutes. At 1, 10, 100, or 1000 electrons/second, there is never a time when there are two electrons going through the slits at the same time.

Do you still see the same pattern as in the high-intensity experiment? __**Yes**__

What characteristic of an electron allows for it to diffract even if there is only one? __**The wave**__

__**properties of an electron**__

How is an electron different than a photon? __**An electron has mass, and a photon does not.**__

_____

How does this experiment show that an electron is similar to a photon? __**Both have the dual**__

__**particle and wave nature.**__

What conclusion about particles of matter can be made from this experiment? __**Just as photons**__

__**have wave properties, particles of matter can also exhibit wave properties.**__

_____

Diffraction of Particles – 3

De Broglie was the first person to suggest that particles could be considered as having wave properties. You have seen in *Diffraction of Light* assignments that if we pass light through appropriately spaced slits, we get diffraction patterns that represent light waves interfering with each other. In this experiment, you will be able to observe a similar phenomenon with electrons.

1. Set up a two-slit diffraction experiment using the electron gun, the two-slit device, and the phosphor screen. Set the current or intensity of the electron gun to 1 nA, the energy on the electron gun to 1.0 eV, and the slit spacing to 6 nm.

   Draw a picture of the diffraction pattern on the phosphor screen.

   How can an electron diffract?   ___***Electrons have wave properties, which create the diffraction***___

   ___***pattern.***___

2. Now increase the current on the electron gun to 1 mA.

   Does the pattern change? Why or why not?   ___***No. The diffraction pattern is caused by the wave***___

   ___***nature of electrons and does not depend on the number of electrons.***___

   *Would you expect a change in the diffraction pattern if you decreased or increased the energy of the electron gun? Why?*___***Yes. Changing the energy of the electrons will change the wavelength,***___

   ___***which affects the diffraction pattern.***___

3. Decrease the current to 10 electrons/second. The pattern now builds up one electron at a time. Now put the phosphor screen in persist mode and wait several minutes.

   Has the diffraction pattern changed? Why or why not?   ___***No. Even though the pattern builds***___

   ___***up one at a time, collectively they still form the same diffraction pattern.***___

   _____

   There is never a time when there are two electrons going through the slits at the same time.

Quantum Assignments

How can an electron diffract if there is only one? __Electrons have wave properties that cause the__ __diffraction pattern.__

What similarities do electrons and photons have in the two-slit diffraction experiment? __They both__ __exhibit their dual particle and wave nature.__

How is an electron different than a photon? __An electron has mass, and a photon does not.__

How did this experiment impact the development and interpretation of quantum mechanics? _____ __Particles of matter can exhibit wave properties just as photons of light.__

De Broglie – 1

De Broglie was the first person to suggest that particles could be considered as having wave properties. Specifically, he suggested that $\lambda = constant / p$ (wavelength is inversely proportional to momentum). In this assignment, you will calculate the constant that relates λ to p.

1. Set up the optics table to measure the diffraction of electrons with an energy of 2 meV using the electron gun, the two-slit device, and the phosphor screen. Set the current (intensity) of the electron gun to at least 1 nA.

   What is the kinetic energy of the electrons in Joules? __*3.20 J*__

2. Adjust the slit spacing, and observe how the diffraction pattern changes accordingly.

   How does the diffraction pattern change when you increase the spacing between the slits? __*The*__

   __*number of diffraction lines increases.*__

3. Find a slit spacing that gives 7 to 11 well-defined diffraction fringes.

   Draw a picture of the diffraction pattern.

   Slit spacing: __*130 nm*__

   What characteristic of the electron accounts for the diffraction pattern created by the two-slit

   experiment? __*Electrons have wave properties, which create the diffraction pattern.*__

4. Now, change the electron gun for the laser, and the phosphor screen for the camera. Set the intensity of the laser to at least 1 nW.

5. Keeping the slit spacing the same, find the wavelength of light that gives the same diffraction pattern.

   Wavelength: __*~ 27.2 nm*__

   How is this wavelength related to the wavelength of the electrons? __*It is approximately the same*__

   __*as the wavelength of the electrons.*__

6. Given that $E_{kinetic} = p^2/2m$, solve for p and then calculate the constant that relates p with λ.

Calculations:

$$p = \sqrt{2mE}$$

constant $= \lambda\sqrt{2mE}$

Constant = $\underline{\quad 6.6 \times 10^{-34}\ Js \quad}$

De Broglie – 2

De Broglie was the first person to suggest that particles could be considered as having wave properties. Specifically, he suggested that $\lambda = constant / p$ (wavelength is inversely proportional to momentum). In this assignment, you will calculate the constant that relates λ to p.

1. Set up the optics table to measure the diffraction of electrons using the electron gun, the two-slit device, and the phosphor screen. Set the current of the electron gun to at least 1 nA. Set the slit spacing to 100 nm.

2. Adjust the kinetic energy of the electrons.

   What happens to the diffraction pattern as you increase the energy of the electrons? ___***The number***___

   ___***of diffraction lines increases.***___

   Does this support De Broglie's equation? If so, how? ___***Yes. According to De Broglie's equation,***___

   ___***the wavelength decreases as the momentum increases. The momentum increases as the energy***___

   ___***increases, so the wavelength decreases, which results in more diffraction lines.***___

   Express the constant in De Broglie's equation as a function of kinetic energy, mass, and wavelength.

   Since $E_{kinetic} = p^2/2m$, ***then constant*** $= \lambda\sqrt{2mE}$.

3. Set the electron gun energy between 1 and 4 meV. Find a slit spacing that gives 7 to 11 well-defined diffraction fringes. Then, by using the laser and video camera, find the wavelength that gives this same diffraction pattern for this particular slit spacing. Repeat this procedure for two different kinetic energies, and record the values in the following table. Then calculate the constant that relates p with λ.

Electron Kinetic Energy	Slit Spacing	Diffraction Pattern	Wavelength	Constant
1.5 meV	*117 nm*	*7 fringes*	*31.9 nm*	*$6.67 \times 10^{-34} J \cdot s$*
2.5 meV	*115 nm*	*9 fringes*	*24.5 nm*	*$6.62 \times 10^{-34} J \cdot s$*
3.5 meV	*98 nm*	*9 fringes*	*21.3 nm*	*$6.65 \times 10^{-34} J \cdot s$*

   Averaged value for constant: ___***$6.65 \times 10^{-34} J \cdot s$***___

4. This constant that you have calculated is known as Planck's constant. Look up its actual value and compare it with your value.

   % deviation from Planck's constant: ___***$(6.65 \times 10^{-34} - 6.63 \times 10^{-34})/6.63 \times 10^{-34} \times 100\% = 0.3\%$***___

H₂ Gas Photoemission – 1

When a sample of gas is excited by passing an alternating electric current through it, it emits light at certain discreet wavelengths. The classical picture of atoms would allow electrons to be at any energy level, and thus the energy would be continuous over all wavelengths. This contradiction led Niels Bohr to propose that the energy levels of atoms are quantized, which led him to develop the first model of atoms that quantized the orbits of the electrons around the nucleus. This assignment illustrates the measurements that helped Bohr develop his quantum model. It also illustrates some practical uses for the science. Fluorescent lights are filled with mercury (Hg) gas and emit light when a current is passed through them. Most modern street lamps are filled with sodium (Na) gas, which emits visible light when a current is applied.

1. Set up the optics table for light emission by selecting *Photoemission – H₂* on the clipboard of preset experiments.

    *Which sample of gas is being used in this experiment?*___***Hydrogen***___

    *What voltage is being used to create an electric field?*___***300 V***___

    *What is the purpose of the electric field in this experiment?*___***To pass an electric current through***___

    ___***the gas in order to breakdown the H₂ gas molecules and to excite the hydrogen atoms***___

    *What detector is used in this experiment and what does it measure?*___***The spectrometer measures***___

    ___***the intensity of light at many wavelengths.***___

2. Switch the toggle on the spectrometer from *FULL* to *VISIBLE*.

    Draw the visible region of the H₂ gas spectrum.

    *How does this spectrum contradict classical ideas?*___***Only light at certain wavelengths or energies***___

    ___***is emitted. Thus, the electrons can only be at specific energies, which contradicts the classical***___

    ___***idea that electrons can be at any energy level.***___

    *What produces each line in the spectrum?*___***Excited atoms going back to their ground state***___

H₂ Gas Photoemission – 2

When a sample of gas is excited by passing an alternating electric current through it, it emits light at certain discreet wavelengths. The classical picture of atoms would allow electrons to be at any energy level, and thus the energy would be continuous over all wavelengths. This contradiction led Niels Bohr to propose that the energy levels of atoms are quantized, which led him to develop the first model of atoms that quantized the orbits of the electrons around the nucleus. This assignment illustrates the measurements that helped Bohr develop his quantum model. It also illustrates some practical uses for the science. Fluorescent lights are filled with mercury (Hg) gas and emit light when a current is passed through them. Most modern street lamps are filled with sodium (Na) gas, which emits visible light when a current is applied.

1. Set up the optics table for light emission by placing the gas cell filled with H₂ gas on the optics table with the electric field attached to it and the spectrometer pointed toward it.

2. Turn the voltage to 300 V AC to provide the electric field for the gas sample.

    What is the purpose of the electric field in this experiment? __*To pass an electric current through the gas in order to breakdown the H₂ gas molecules and to excite the hydrogen atoms*__

3. Turn on the spectrometer to see the emission spectrum.

    Draw the spectrum of H₂ gas.

    What produces each line in the spectrum? __*Excited electrons going back to their ground state*__

4. Increase the voltage.

    What happens? Why? __*The spectrum does not change. The voltage was already sufficient to breakdown the H₂ gas molecules and to excite the hydrogen atoms.*__

5. Decrease the voltage below 300 V.

What happens? Why? __*The lines in the spectrum disappear. The voltage is below the breakdown*__

__*voltage of the gas.*__

6. Set the voltage at 300 V again, and zoom into the visible region of the spectrum.

    What are the wavelengths of the peaks in this region? __*410.2925 nm, 434.1713 nm, 486.2725 nm*__

    __*and 656.4663 nm*__

7. Choose four other gases, and measure their spectra. Then write a short description of the spectra of each gas.

    Gas # 1 __*He gas–Many peaks, seven of which are in the visible region, and a high-intensity*__

    __*peak at 1083.3288*__

    Gas # 2 __*Hg gas–Blue gas, lots of peaks (many more than the He gas spectrum), over 30 peaks*__

    __*in the visible region, and several high-intensity peaks*__

    Gas # 3 __*HCl gas–Violet gas, many peaks that are mostly below 975 nm (the rest are above*__

    __*4900 nm), several high-intensity peaks, and 19 peaks (all are low intensity) in the visible region*__

    Gas # 4 __*H_2O gas–Voilet gas, many peaks, two sets of peaks below 325 nm and the rest of the*__

    __*peaks are above 655 nm), and only two peaks are in the visible region*__

    Do any of the gases emit the same spectrum? __*No.*__

    How can spectra be useful in chemical analysis? __*Line spectra may be used to learn more about*__

    __*atomic structure and to identify elements in samples of unknown substance.*__

H₂ Gas Photoemission – 3

When a sample of gas is excited by passing an alternating electric current through it, it emits light at certain discreet wavelengths. The classical picture of atoms would allow electrons to be at any energy level, and thus the energy would be continuous over all wavelengths. This contradiction led Niels Bohr to propose that the energy levels of atoms are quantized, which led him to develop the first model of atoms that quantized the orbits of the electrons around the nucleus. This assignment illustrates the measurements that helped Bohr develop his quantum model. It also illustrates some practical uses for the science. Fluorescent lights are filled with mercury (Hg) gas and emit light when a current is passed through them. Most modern street lamps are filled with sodium (Na) gas, which emits visible light when a current is applied.

1. Set up the optics table for light emission by placing the gas cell filled with H₂ gas on the optics table with the electric field attached to it and the spectrometer pointed toward it.

2. Turn the voltage to 300 V AC to provide the electric field for the gas sample.

3. Turn on the spectrometer to see the emission spectrum.

   Draw the spectrum of the H₂ gas.

4. Zoom into the section from 350 to 850 nm.

5. Identify the wavelengths for the peaks in the spectrum.

   Wavelengths: __*383.6475 nm, 389.0150 nm, 397.1200 nm, 410.2925 nm, 434.1713 nm,*__

   __*486.2725 nm, and 656.4663 nm*__

6. The peaks in the visible region are called the Balmer series. An early scientist, Rydberg, suggested that the peaks could be fit using the functional form
$$1/\lambda = R_H \left(1/n_f^2 - 1/n_i^2 \right),$$
   where R_H is the Rydberg constant, n_f is 2 for the Balmer series, n_i is the peak number, and λ is the wavelength corresponding to the n_i peak. Since $n_f = 2$ for the Balmer series, $n_i = 3, 4, 5$, and so forth.

   Would the lowest numbered peak be at the highest or lowest wavelength?   __*Highest*__

7. Plot $1/\lambda$ versus $\left(1/n_f^2 - 1/n_i^2 \right)$ in order to find R_H for H₂ gas.

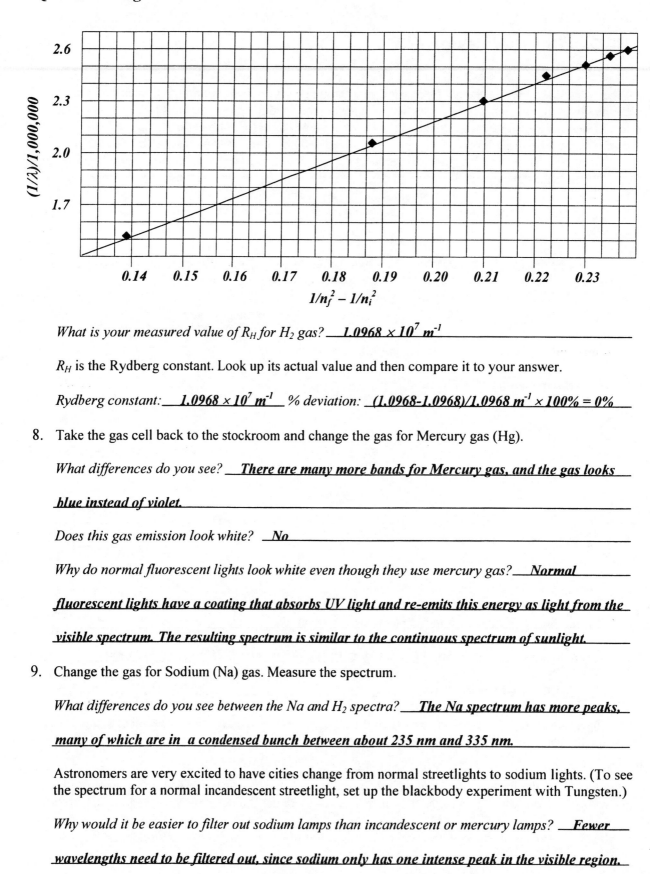

What is your measured value of R_H for H_2 gas? __**1.0968×10^7 m^{-1}**__

R_H is the Rydberg constant. Look up its actual value and then compare it to your answer.

Rydberg constant: __**1.0968×10^7 m^{-1}**__ *% deviation:* __**$(1.0968-1.0968)/1.0968$ m$^{-1} \times 100\% = 0\%$**__

8. Take the gas cell back to the stockroom and change the gas for Mercury gas (Hg).

    What differences do you see? __**There are many more bands for Mercury gas, and the gas looks**__

    __**blue instead of violet.**__

    Does this gas emission look white? __**No**__

    Why do normal fluorescent lights look white even though they use mercury gas? __**Normal**__

    __**fluorescent lights have a coating that absorbs UV light and re-emits this energy as light from the**__

    __**visible spectrum. The resulting spectrum is similar to the continuous spectrum of sunlight.**__

9. Change the gas for Sodium (Na) gas. Measure the spectrum.

    What differences do you see between the Na and H_2 spectra? __**The Na spectrum has more peaks,**__

    __**many of which are in a condensed bunch between about 235 nm and 335 nm.**__

    Astronomers are very excited to have cities change from normal streetlights to sodium lights. (To see the spectrum for a normal incandescent streetlight, set up the blackbody experiment with Tungsten.)

    Why would it be easier to filter out sodium lamps than incandescent or mercury lamps? __**Fewer**__

    __**wavelengths need to be filtered out, since sodium only has one intense peak in the visible region.**__

CO₂ Gas Photoemission

When a sample of gas is excited by passing an alternating electric current through it, it emits light at certain discreet wavelengths. The classical picture of atoms would allow electrons to be at any energy level, and thus the energy would be continuous over all wavelengths. This contradiction led Niels Bohr to propose that the energy levels of atoms are quantized, which led him to develop the first model of atoms that quantized the orbits of the electrons around the nucleus.

1. Set up the optics table for light emission by selecting *Photoemission – CO₂* on the clipboard of preset experiments.

    *Which sample of gas is being used in this experiment?*__ ***CO₂ gas***_____

    *What voltage is being used to create an electric field?*__ ***300 V***_____

    *What is the purpose of the electric field in this experiment?*__ ***To pass an electric current through***__

    __***the gas in order to breakdown the CO₂ gas molecules and to excite the atoms***_____

    *What detector is used in this experiment and what does it measure?*__ ***The spectrometer measures***__

    __***the intensity of light at many wavelengths.***_____

2. Switch the toggle on the spectrometer from *FULL* to *VISIBLE*.

    Draw a rough sketch of the visible region of the CO₂ gas spectrum.

    *How does this spectrum contradict classical ideas?*__ ***Only light at certain wavelengths or energies***__

    __***is emitted. Thus, the electrons can only be at specific energies, which contradicts the classical***__

    __***idea that electrons can be at any energy level.***_____

    Why would you expect the CO₂ gas emission spectrum to have more lines than the H₂ gas emission

    *spectrum?*__ ***There are more orbitals for the electrons to fill for the CO₂ molecules than for the***__

    __***H₂ molecules.***_____

HCl Gas Absorbance – 1

HCl gas does not absorb visible light, but it does absorb infrared light. When HCl absorbs one photon of infrared light to go from the ground vibrational state to the first excited vibrational state, it can also change rotational states. These rotations are also quantized, meaning that molecules can only rotate at certain frequencies. In this lab, you will measure the rotational energy changes that accompany vibrational changes.

1. Set up this experiment by selecting *Absorption in Gases – HCl* on the clipboard of preset experiments.

   What source is used in this experiment? ___***The super light bulb***___

   How is the light produced by this source different than the light produced by the laser? ___***The laser***___

   ___***emits light of only one wavelength, whereas the super bulb provides light at all wavelengths from***___

   ___***20 nm to 20,000 nm.***___

   Which sample of gas is being used in this experiment? ___***HCl gas***___

   What detector is used in this experiment and what does it measure? ___***The spectrometer measures***___

   ___***the intensity of light over many wavelengths.***___

2. Zoom in on the two large sets of peaks.

   Draw a rough sketch of what you see.

   From which region of the electromagnetic spectrum does HCl gas absorb? Infrared, visible, or ultraviolet? ___***Infrared***___

   What type of energy changes results from absorption of light from this region? ___***Changes in the***___ ___***vibrational energy state***___

   Rank the infrared, visible, and ultraviolet regions of the electromagnetic spectrum in order of increasing energy. ___***Infrared, visible, ultraviolet***___

227

Quantum Assignments

The two large sets of peaks that you sketched are from hydrogen atoms. Hydrogen has two different isotopes (different nuclear weights). We label these H (for hydrogen), which has a mass of 1 amu (atomic mass unit), and D (for deuterium), which has a mass of 2 amu.

Which isotope is more abundant? Hydrogen or deuterium? __**Hydrogen**__

Which set of peaks is larger? The set of peaks at lower or higher wavelengths? __**The set of peaks**__

__**at lower wavelengths.**__

Predict which set of peaks is due to hydrogen and which set is due to deuterium. __**Based on the**__

__**intensities of the peaks, the set of peaks at lower wavelengths is due to hydrogen, and the high-**__

__**frequency peaks are due to deuterium.**__

HCl Gas Absorbance – 2

HCl gas does not absorb visible light, but it does absorb infrared light. When HCl absorbs one photon of infrared light to go from the ground vibrational state to the first excited vibrational state, it can also change rotational states. These rotations are also quantized, meaning that molecules can only rotate at certain frequencies. In this lab, you will measure the rotational energy changes that accompany vibrational changes.

1. Go to the stockroom, and check out the super light bulb, the gas cell with HCl gas, and the spectrometer. Set up the experiment with the light directed through the gas and into the spectrometer. Turn on the spectrometer, and set the units to frequency.

    Draw a picture of what you see.

    What causes the peaks to form?   ___**Vibrational and rotational energy changes**___

Hydrogen comes in two different isotopes (different nuclear weights). We label these H (for hydrogen), which has a mass of 1 amu (atomic mass unit), and D (for deuterium), which has a mass of 2 amu. Chlorine atoms also come in two isotopes with masses of 35 and 37 amu. In the spectrum are two sets of peaks with different relative intensities.

If you have both isotopes of hydrogen and of chlorine, how many different molecules are you

measuring? ___**Four**___

What are they? ___**$^1H^{35}Cl$, $^1H^{37}Cl$, $^2H^{35}Cl$, and $^2H^{37}Cl$**___

The energy spacing between successive absorption peaks is inversely proportional to I, the moment of inertia. $I = \mu r^2$ where μ is the reduced mass and r is the internuclear spacing. For a diatomic molecule, the reduced mass is $m_1 m_2/(m_1 + m_2)$, where m_1 and m_2 are the masses of the two atoms.

Calculate μ for each molecule being measured. ___**$^1H^{35}Cl$: 0.972, $^1H^{37}Cl$: 0.974, $^2H^{35}Cl$: 1.892, and**___

___**$^2H^{37}Cl$: 1.897**___

As you can see, the isotopes of hydrogen affect the reduced mass significantly more than the isotopes of chlorine. The two large sets of peaks that you drew are due to the two isotopes of hydrogen.

Which isotope of hydrogen has smaller energy spacings between successive absorption peaks? ____

Deuterium that has a mass of 2 amu, since its reduced mass is greater than that of hydrogen.

Which isotope of hydrogen causes the higher frequency set of peaks? ___***Deuterium***___

2. Select either set of peaks. By zooming in sufficiently, you will notice that each main peak is a doublet.

    Draw a picture of what you see.

    What do you suspect causes the doublets to form? ___***The two isotopes of chlorine – ^{35}Cl and ^{37}Cl.***___

    Why would one of the peaks of the doublet be smaller than the other? ___***One isotope of chlorine is***___

    more abundant than the other.

HCl Gas Absorbance – 3

HCl gas does not absorb visible light, but it does absorb infrared light. When it absorbs one photon of infrared light to go from the ground vibrational state to the first excited vibrational state, it can also change rotational states. These rotations are also quantized, meaning that molecules can only rotate at certain frequencies. In this lab, you will measure the rotational energy changes that accompany vibrational changes.

1. Go to the stockroom, and check out the super light bulb, the gas cell with HCl gas, and the spectrometer. Set up the experiment with the light shining through the gas and into the spectrometer. Turn on the spectrometer, and set the units to frequency.

    Draw a picture of what you see.

    There are two large sets of peaks due to the hydrogen atoms. Hydrogen has two different isotopes (different nuclear weights). We label these H (for hydrogen), which has a mass of 1 amu (atomic mass unit), and D (for deuterium), which has a mass of 2 amu.

    Which one would you expect to absorb at the lower frequency and why?   ___Hydrogen, since it has a___

    ___larger reduced mass and the energy spacing between absorption peaks is smaller for the lower___

    ___frequency peaks. (Energy spacing is inversely proportional to reduced mass.) In addition,___

    ___hydrogen is more abundant than deuterium, and the lower frequency peaks are more intense.___

    Which isotope is more abundant?   ___Hydrogen___

    Do the relative intensities of the two sets of peaks correlate to their natural abundances? Why or why

    not?   ___No. The intensities of the two sets of peaks are too similar. The natural abundance of___

    ___deuterium is less than 0.02% of all hydrogen atoms. DCl must have been added to the sample.___

    _____

2. Zoom in on the lower frequency peaks.

Quantum Assignments

Draw a picture of what you see.

Chlorine atoms also come in two isotopes with masses of 35 and 37 amu. By zooming in sufficiently, you will notice that each main peak is a doublet.

Predict which peaks of the doublets belong to ^{35}Cl and which to ^{37}Cl. ___**The smaller peaks belong to**___

___^{37}Cl **and the larger peaks belong to** ^{35}Cl.___

Which is more abundant? ___^{35}Cl___

Does this agree with the mass for chlorine that you see on a periodic table (which is an average mass

based on natural abundances)? ___**Yes. The periodic table gives chlorine a mass of 35.45 amu, which**___

___**is in between the two isotopic masses, yet closer to the mass of the more abundant isotope.**___

Both large sets of peaks have two branches of peaks. The branch of lower frequency peaks have a change from a higher rotational state in the ground vibrational state to a lower one in the first excited vibrational state, and the higher frequency peaks have a change from a lower rotational state in the ground vibrational state to a higher one in the first excited vibrational.

Which branch of peaks is more intense? ___**The higher frequency peaks**___

Why? ___**The intensity of the peaks depends on the number of molecules in the various vibrational**___

___**and rotational states. Since the majority of atoms are in the ground rotational state, the higher**___

___**branch will be more intense. (The transitions causing the lower frequency branch of peaks start**___

___**from above the ground rotational state.)**___

I$_2$ Gas Absorbance – 1

I$_2$ gas is interesting because it absorbs visible light, which causes an electron to move between two electronic energy levels. At the same time, the molecule can change vibrational energy. Because the vibrations are quantized (the molecule can only vibrate at certain frequencies), the spectrum is not continuous, but instead has peaks where the vibrations change from one energy level to another.

1. Set up this experiment by selecting *Absorption in Gases – I$_2$* on the clipboard of preset experiments.

    What source is used in this experiment? **The super light bulb**

    How is the light produced by this source different than the light produced by the laser? **The laser emits light of only one wavelength, whereas the super bulb provides light at all wavelengths from 20 nm to 20,000 nm.**

    Which sample of gas is being used in this experiment? **I$_2$ gas**

    What detector is used in this experiment and what does it measure? **The spectrometer measures the intensity of light over many wavelengths.**

2. On the spectrometer screen, switch the toggles from *FULL* to *VISIBLE* and from *WAVELENGTH* to *FREQUENCY*.

    Draw a rough sketch of what you see.

    What types of energy changes cause these absorption peaks? **Changes in the electronic and vibrational energy states**

    Why is the spectrum not continuous, but instead has peaks? **Molecules can only be at certain electronic and vibrational energy states, since these energy levels are quantized.**

Notice that there are three distinctive bumps of peaks in the spectrum. These bumps correlate to electronic energy transitions starting from the lowest three vibrational states of the ground electronic state. The lowest vibrational state is the most occupied state.

Which of the three bumps of peaks is largest?   __*The bump of peaks at the highest frequency*__

Which of the three bumps of peaks correlates to transitions starting from the lowest vibrational state?

__*The bump of peaks at the highest frequency*__

I₂ Gas Absorbance – 2

I_2 gas is interesting because it absorbs visible light, which causes an electron to move between two electronic energy levels. At the same time, the molecule can change vibrational energy. Because the vibrations are quantized (the molecule can only vibrate at certain frequencies), the spectrum is not continuous, but instead has peaks where the vibrations change from one energy level to another.

1. Go to the stockroom, and bring out the super light bulb, the gas cell with I_2 gas, and the spectrometer. Set up the experiment with the light directed through the gas and into the spectrometer.

2. Carefully zoom in on the spectrum.

    Draw the basic structure that you see.

    What causes the peaks to form? __***Changes in the electronic and vibrational energy states***__

3. Change into frequency units, and zoom in on the visible region of the spectrum. Notice that there are three distinctive bumps of peaks in the spectrum. These bumps correlate to electronic energy transitions starting from the lowest three vibrational states of the ground electronic state.

    Which of the three bumps of peaks correlates to transitions starting from the lowest vibrational state?

    __***The bump of peaks at the highest frequency***__

    Why is the highest frequency peak the biggest peak? __***The lowest vibrational state is the most***__

    __***occupied, and transitions from the lowest vibrational state cost the most energy (higher energy,***__

    __***higher frequency).***__

4. Zoom in further to where the most light is absorbed (where the transmittance is the lowest). Focus on the first few well-resolved peaks of the highest frequency.

    Does the spacing between adjacent peaks decrease or increase at higher frequencies? __***The spacing***__

    __***decreases at higher frequencies.***__

Why?   *Successive vibrational energy levels are closer together at higher energies. Eventually,*

they become continuous at the energy in which the molecule dissociates.

I₂ Gas Absorbance – 3

I_2 gas is interesting because it absorbs visible light, which causes an electron to move between two electronic energy levels. At the same time, the molecule can change vibrational energy. Because the vibrations are quantized (the molecule can only vibrate at certain frequencies), the spectrum is not continuous, but instead has peaks where the vibrations change from one energy level to another.

1. Go to the stockroom and bring out the super light bulb, the gas cell with I_2 gas, and the spectrometer. Set up the experiment with the light shining through the gas and into the spectrometer.

2. Carefully zoom in on the spectrum.

   Draw the basic structure that you see.

3. Increase the power of the super light bulb.

   Does the spectrum change? Why or why not?   __*No. Although there are more photons, the same*__

   __*ratio of different types of electronic and vibrational energy transitions will occur, which results*__

   __*in the same spectrum.*__

4. Change into frequency units, and zoom in on the area of the spectrum near where it absorbs the most light (where the transmittance is the lowest). You should see a series of peaks. Using the cursor and the *x-y* scale, measure the difference in frequency between neighboring peaks for the first 10 well-resolved peaks (highest energy peaks). Numbering the peaks from 1 to 10, plot the differences in frequency against peak number.

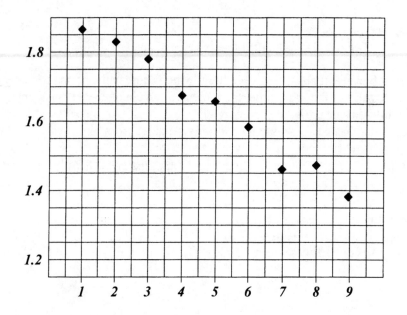

What does the function look like? __**Linear**__

What happens to the difference in frequency between neighboring peaks at higher frequency peaks?

__**The difference decreases.**__

What happens to the energy difference between neighboring peaks at higher frequency peaks? __**It**__

__**decreases.**__

What does this tell you about vibrational modes within an electronic state? __**Successive vibrational**__

__**energy levels are closer together at higher energies, and they will eventually become continuous**__

__**(at the dissociation energy).**__

238

Water Absorption

Water absorbs light in the infrared region of the electromagnetic spectrum. Absorption spectroscopy in the infrared region is called infrared (IR) spectroscopy. Infrared radiation causes the bonds within molecules to vibrate. For this reason, IR spectroscopy is sometimes called vibrational spectroscopy. The atoms within molecules are always moving. The bonds between atoms will absorb light if the light is at the same frequency as the frequency of the vibration of the bond. Thus, bonds act like springs, and just the right amount of energy must be added to make them vibrate. The absorption of this energy makes the vibration have greater amplitude, yet the vibration remains at the same frequency and wavelength. A certain functional group will always absorb within the same general region of the spectrum. For example, the O—H group gives a strong absorption peak around 2778 nm to 3125 nm.

1. Set up the optics table for this experiment by selecting *Absorption in Liquids – Water* on the clipboard of preset experiments.

   What source is used in this experiment?   __**The super light bulb**__

   How is the light produced by this source different than the light produced by the laser?   __**The super**__

   __**light bulb emits light at all wavelengths from 20 nm to 20,000 nm, whereas the laser produces**__

   __**light at only one wavelength.**__

   Which liquid sample is being used in this experiment?   __**Water**__

   What detector is used in this experiment and what does it measure?   __**The spectrometer measures**__

   __**the intensity of light over many wavelengths.**__

   Draw a rough sketch of the spectrum.

   Between what wavelengths is the first wide absorption peak?   __**2600 nm – 3700 nm**__

   What causes this absorption peak?   __**The O—H bond**__

2. On the spectrometer screen, switch the toggle from *FULL* to *VISIBLE*.

What do you observe? __*There is no absorption in this region.*__

Would you expect water to absorb light in the visible region? Why or why not? __*No. Water is*__

__*transparent and should not absorb nor reflect light in the visible region.*__

Benzene Absorption

Like other organic compounds, benzene absorbs light in the infrared region of the electromagnetic spectrum. Absorption spectroscopy in the infrared region is called infrared (IR) spectroscopy. Infrared radiation causes the bonds within molecules to vibrate. For this reason, IR spectroscopy is sometimes called vibrational spectroscopy. The atoms within molecules are always moving. The bonds between atoms will absorb light if the light is at the same frequency as the frequency of the vibration of the bond. Thus, bonds act like springs and just the right amount of energy must be added to make them vibrate. The absorption of this energy makes the vibration have greater amplitude, yet the vibration remains at the same frequency and wavelength. The region between 6000 nm and 10000 nm is often called the fingerprint region, since this region is unique for a particular compound. Slight differences in structure give different spectra especially within the fingerprint region, which acts as a molecular fingerprint for compounds.

1. Set up the optics table for this experiment by selecting *Absorption in Liquids – Benzene* on the clipboard of preset experiments.

   What source is used in this experiment?   **The super light bulb**

   How is the light produced by this source different than the light produced by the laser?   **The super light bulb emits light at all wavelengths from 20 nm to 20,000 nm, whereas the laser produces light at only one wavelength.**

   · *Which liquid sample is being used in this experiment?*   **Benzene**

   What detector is used in this experiment and what does it measure?   **The spectrometer measures the intensity of light over many wavelengths.**

   What causes the absorption peaks in this spectrum?   **The bonds between atoms absorb light at certain frequencies, which causes the absorption peaks.**

2. On the spectrometer screen, scroll over the region between 6000 nm and 10000 nm in order to zoom in on this area.

   Draw the spectrum in this region.

Why is this region referred to as the "fingerprint region"?   *This region is unique for each compound, so this region can be used for identification.*

Raman Scattering - 1

The vibrational modes of a molecule are quantized, which means that molecules can only vibrate at certain frequencies. In normal light absorbance spectroscopy, absorbance peaks are observed at frequencies of light that have the correct amount of energy to make molecules vibrate one step faster. C. V. Raman, a scientist from India, was the first person to demonstrate another type of spectroscopy, and so it is named after him. In this measurement, you send laser light in the visible region through a sample. Most of the photons in the beam travel through the sample, but a small number interact with the sample and are scattered in different directions. An even smaller number (less than one in a million) interact with the sample and during the process either absorb one vibrational energy quantum from a molecule (leading to photons with a bit more energy) or give one quantum of energy to a molecule (leading to photons with a bit less energy). In the Raman spectra, make sure to zoom in to the spectra in the wings around the central peak to see the other peaks. These satellite peaks are very small.

1. Set up this experiment by selecting *Raman Scattering – Benzene* on the clipboard of preset experiments.

    What source is used in this experiment and what does it do? __*The laser provides light at a single*__

    __*wavelength.*__

    Which liquid sample is being used in this experiment? __*Benzene*__

    What detector is used in this experiment and what does it measure? __*The spectrometer measures*__

    __*the intensity of light over many wavelengths.*__

2. Scroll over a thin layer across the bottom of the spectrum in order to maximize the satellite peaks.

    Draw a picture of what you see.

    What causes the central peak? __*Photons that are scattered by the sample, but are not involved in*__

    __*any energy transfer*__

3. On the spectrometer screen, switch the toggle from *WAVELENGTH* to *FREQUENCY*.

Quantum Assignments

There are peaks both to the left and to the right of the central peak. Which peaks are caused by the photons absorbing one vibrational energy quantum from the sample?   ***The peaks to the right***

Which peaks are caused by the photons giving one vibrational energy quantum to the sample?   ***The peaks to the left***

Raman Scattering - 2

The vibrational modes of a molecule are quantized, which means that molecules can only vibrate at certain frequencies. In normal light absorbance spectroscopy, absorbance peaks are observed at frequencies of light that have the correct amount of energy to make molecules vibrate one step faster. C. V. Raman, a scientist from India, was the first person to demonstrate another type of spectroscopy, and so it is named after him. In this measurement, you send laser light in the visible region through a sample. Most of the photons in the beam travel through the sample, but a small number interact with the sample and are scattered in different directions. An even smaller number (less than one in a million) interact with the sample and during the process either absorb one vibrational energy quantum from a molecule (leading to photons with a bit more energy) or give one quantum of energy to a molecule (leading to photons with a bit less energy). In the Raman spectra, make sure to zoom in to the spectra in the wings around the central peak to see the other peaks. These satellite peaks are very small.

1. Go to the stockroom; bring out the laser, the gas cell filled with HCl, and the spectrometer; and arrange them on the table with the laser directed into the gas cell, and the laser and spectrometer at a 90-degree angle from each other.

2. Set the laser power to 1 nW and the wavelength to 620 nm. Turn on the spectrometer.

   Draw a picture of what you see.

   What causes the central peak? __*Photons that are scattered by the sample, but are not involved in*__

   __*any energy transfer.*__

3. With the spectrometer set for wavelength, measure the difference between the main peak and the satellite peaks using laser wavelengths of 620, 570, 520, 470 and 420 nm.

Laser Wavelength	620	570	520	470	420
Peak 1 (diff. in λ)	*94.1 nm*	*80.5 nm*	*67.9 nm*	*56.1 nm*	*45.4 nm*
Peak 2 (diff. in λ)	*135.1 nm*	*112.2 nm*	*91.8 nm*	*73.8 nm*	*57.9 nm*

   Is the difference the same at different laser wavelengths? __*No*__

4. Set the spectrometer to frequency units.

245

Quantum Assignments

Draw a picture of what you see.

Which peak has the lowest energy and which has the highest energy? ___**The peak to the left has the**

lowest energy, and the peak to the right has the highest energy.___

What causes the lower frequency peak? ___**Photons that have given a vibrational energy quantum**

to an HCl molecule___

What causes the higher frequency peak? ___**Photons that have absorbed a vibrational energy**

quantum from an HCl molecule___

5. With the spectrometer set for frequency, measure the difference between the main peak and the satellite peaks in terahertz (THz) using the same laser wavelengths as before (620, 570, 520, 470, and 420 nm).

Laser Wavelength	620	570	520	470	420
Peak 1 (diff. in ν)	*86.6 THz*	*86.6 THz*	*86.6 THz*	*86.6 THz*	*86.6 THz*
Peak 2 (diff. in ν)	*86.6 THz*	*86.6 THz*	*86.6 THz*	*86.6 THz*	*86.6 THz*

Is this difference constant? ___**Yes**___

6. Perform the same experiment with CO_2 gas. Only measure the satellite peak to the left of the main peak.

Laser Wavelength	620	570	520	470	420
Difference (in λ)	*47.6 nm*	*40.5 nm*	*33.9 nm*	*27.9 nm*	*22.4 nm*
Difference (in ν)	*40.2 THz*	*40.2 THz*	*40.2 THz*	*40.2 THz*	*40.2 THz*

How do these results compare to the previous results with HCl gas? ___**The difference still varies**

when measured in wavelength units, and the difference still remains constant when measured in

frequency units.___

For CO_2, what is the difference in the Raman spectrum in THz? ___**40.2 THz**___

Now we will do some similar measurements with liquids.

7. Return the gas cell to the stockroom, and replace it with the liquid cell. Fill the cell with Benzene (C_6H_6), and return it to the laboratory. Set up the experiment again for a Raman experiment using a laser wavelength of 620 nm.

    Draw a picture of the spectrum.

8. Look at the spectrum of each of the liquids, and count the sets of satellite peaks for each one.

    Which has the most peaks?   __*C_6H_{10} – Cyclohexene*__

    Which has the least?   __*H_2O – Water*__

    What are the differences between liquids and gases in a Raman spectrum? __

    __*Besides water, the liquids have many more satellite peaks than the gases.*__

	# of satellite peaks
C_6H_6	*11*
H_2O	*0*
CCl_4	*7*
C_6H_{12}	*14*
THF	*23*
MeOH	*17*
CH_3CN	*15*
C_6H_{10}	*29*

Raman Scattering – 3

The vibrational modes of a molecule are quantized, which means that molecules can only vibrate at certain frequencies. In normal light absorbance spectroscopy, absorbance peaks are observed at frequencies of light that have the correct amount of energy to make molecules vibrate one step faster. C. V. Raman, a scientist from India, was the first person to demonstrate another type of spectroscopy, and so it is named after him. In this measurement, you send laser light in the visible region through a sample. Most of the photons in the beam travel through the sample, but a small number interact with the sample and are scattered in different directions. An even smaller number (less than one in a million) interact with the sample and during the process either absorb one vibrational energy quantum from a molecule (leading to photons with a bit more energy) or give one quantum of energy to a molecule (leading to photons with a bit less energy). In the Raman spectra, make sure to zoom in to the spectra in the wings around the central peak to see the other peaks. These satellite peaks are very small.

1. Go to the stockroom; bring out the laser, the gas cell filled with HCl, and the spectrometer; and arrange them on the table with the laser directed into the gas cell, and the laser and spectrometer at a 90-degree angle from each other.

2. Set the laser power to 1 nW and the wavelength to 620 nm. Turn on the spectrometer.

   Draw a picture of what you see.

   What causes each peak? ___*Photons that have given a vibrational energy quantum to an HCl*___

   ___*molecule cause the peak to the right. Photons that have absorbed a vibrational energy quantum*___

   ___*cause the peak to the left. The main peak is formed by photons that are scattered by the sample,*___

   ___*but have not given or absorbed a vibrational quantum energy.*___

3. Increase the power of the laser.

   Does this change the spectrum? Why or why not? ___*No. Although there are more photons, the same*___

   ___*proportion is still absorbing or giving a vibrational quantum energy as before.*___

4. Now change the wavelength of the laser.

Does this change the spectrum? If so, how? __Yes. All peaks shift to higher wavelengths as you__

__increase the wavelength of the laser and to the left as you decrease the wavelength of the laser.__

5. With the spectrometer set for wavelength, measure the difference between the main peak and the satellite peaks using laser wavelengths of 620, 570, 520, 470 and 420 nm. Only measure the satellite peak to the left.

Laser Wavelength	620	570	520	470	420
Difference (in λ)	*94.1 nm*	*80.5 nm*	*67.9 nm*	*56.1 nm*	*45.4 nm*

Is the difference the same at different laser wavelengths? __No__

6. Make a plot of wavelength versus the difference.

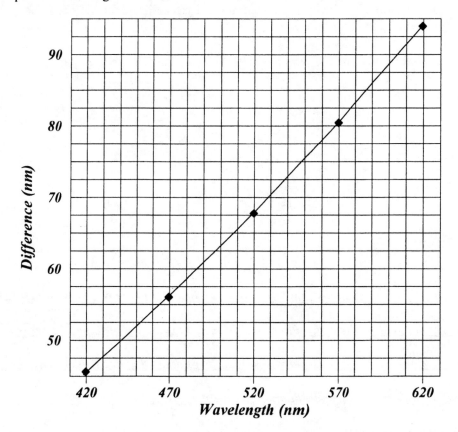

Is the function linear? __No__

How is wavelength related to energy? __Wavelength is inversely proportional to energy: E = hc/v.__

7. With the spectrometer set for frequency, measure the difference between the main peak and the satellite peaks in terahertz (THz) using the same laser wavelengths as before (620, 570, 520, 470, and

420 nm). Again, only measure the satellite peak to the left.

Laser Wavelength	620	570	520	470	420
Difference (in v)	*86.6 THz*	*86.6 THz*	*86.6 THz*	*86.6 THz*	*86.6 THz*

Is this difference constant? Why should this be expected?   __Yes. Whatever the starting wavelength__

__and frequency, the photons absorb or give the same amount of energy.__

What is the difference in the Raman spectrum in THz?   __86.6 THz__

What wavelength of light has this frequency?   __3462 nm__

8. Exchange the laser with the super light bulb, and measure the absorbance spectrum by placing the spectrometer in line with the super light bulb and the sample.

   Do you see an absorbance peak at the wavelength that you specified earlier?   __No__

   Why or why not?   __The selection rules for Raman absorption allow for the transition from one__

   __vibrational state to the next without a change in the rotational state. However, this transition is not__

   __allowed in infrared spectroscopy, as the vibrational transition must be accompanied by a__

   __rotational transition.__

9. Switch the super light bulb for the laser again. Set the wavelength of the laser 100 nm below that of your specified wavelength. Set the intensity of the laser to at least 1 nW. Then exchange the spectrometer for the photodiode. Turn on the photodiode, and keep it in line with the laser and sample.

   What is the function of the photodiode?   __The photodiode measures the integrated intensity of light__

   __over many wavelengths and plots this intensity as a function of time.__

10. Slowly increase the wavelength of the laser 200 nm.

    What do you observe?   __The intensity drops and rises.__

    What causes the differences in intensity?   __Absorption peaks in the infrared region cause the__

    __differences in intensity. Vibrational transitions accompanied by rotational transitions cause the__

    __absorption peaks.__

    Now we will do some measurements with liquids.

11. Return the gas cell and photodiode to the stockroom, and replace it with the liquid cell and

spectrometer, respectively. Fill the cell with Benzene (C_6H_6), and return both to the laboratory. Set up the experiment again for a Raman experiment using a laser wavelength of 620 nm.

Draw a picture of the spectrum.

12. Measure the difference in frequency between each satellite peak in the spectrum and the main peak (the frequency of the laser beam).

Main peak frequency: ___**483.5 THz**___

Satellite peak number	ν	ν of symmetrical peak	Difference between main and satellite ν's
1	*465.7 THz*	*502.1 THz*	*18.2 THz*
2	*458.4 THz*	*509.4 THz*	*25.5 THz*
3	*454.1 THz*	*513.6 THz*	*29.8 THz*
4	*448.6 THz*	*519.2 THz*	*35.3 THz*
5	*436.3 THz*	*531.4 THz*	*47.6 THz*
6	*435.7 THz*	*532.1 THz*	*48.2 THz*
7	*415 THz*	*552.7 THz*	*68.9 THz*
8	*410.1 THz*	*557.6 THz*	*73.8 THz*
9	*407.5 THz*	*560.2 THz*	*76.4 THz*
10	*395.4 THz*	*572.3 THz*	*88.5 THz*
11	*392 THz*	*575.7 THz*	*91.9 THz*

13. Look at the spectrum of each of the liquids, and count the number of satellite peaks for each one.

Which has the most peaks? ___**C_6H_{10} – Cyclohexene**___

Which has the least? ___**H_2O – Water**___

What are the differences between liquids and gases in a Raman spectrum? __

Besides water, these liquids have many more satellite peaks than the gases.

_____

Why? ___**These liquids have more atoms in each molecule than the gases, so**

they have more vibrational modes. However, all of the vibrational modes in water are IR active,

so they are inactive in Raman spectroscopy.___

	# of satellite peaks
C_6H_6	11
H_2O	0
CCl_4	7
C_6H_{12}	14
THF	23
MeOH	17
CH_3CN	15
C_6H_{10}	29

Inorganic User's Guide

Overview

Welcome to *Virtual ChemLab: Inorganic*, a realistic and complete simulation of inorganic qualitative analysis. In this virtual laboratory, students are free to make the choices and decisions that they would confront in an actual qualitative experiment and, in turn, experience the resulting consequences. The general features of the simulation include 26 cations that can be added to test tubes in any combination, 11 reagents that can be added to the test tubes in any sequence and any number of times, necessary laboratory manipulations, a lab book for recording results and observations, and a stockroom for creating test tubes with known mixtures, generating practice unknowns, or retrieving instructor assigned unknowns. The simulation uses over 2500 actual pictures to show the results of reactions and over 220 videos to show the different flame tests. With 26 cations that can be combined in any order or combination and 11 reagents that can be added in any order, there are in excess of 10^{16} possible outcomes in the simulation.

Quick Start

After launching the program, you will be brought to the general chemistry laboratory (shown in Figure 1) where you will find five different laboratory benches that represent five different general chemistry laboratories. Mousing over each of these laboratory benches pops up the name of the selected experiment. To access the inorganic qualitative analysis laboratory, click on the Inorganic laboratory bench at the far left.

Figure 1. The general chemistry laboratory. Each general chemistry experiment is accessed by clicking on the appropriate lab bench.

Once inside the inorganic laboratory, go to the stockroom counter by clicking on the stockroom window. Inside the stockroom, known solutions can be made by clicking and dragging a test tube from the box of test tubes, dropping it on the holder, and then adding cations by clicking on the bottles. Practice unknowns can be created by clicking on the "Unknowns" sign underneath the small test tube rack. Test tubes are returned to the laboratory by clicking on the *Return to Lab* arrow or by clicking on the *Done* button underneath the test tube in the test tube holder.

In the laboratory, up to 12 test tubes can be stored in the test tube rack on the lab bench. To add reagents to a test tube, click and drag a test tube from the rack and place it in the test tube holder. Once a test tube is in the holder, reagents can be added by clicking a reagent bottle once. Changes in the test tube will be shown in the display window with an appropriate picture. Laboratory manipulations such as centrifuging, decanting, pH, and heat are performed by clicking buttons at the bottom of the laboratory. Test tubes are disposed of by dragging them to the disposal bucket.

Other important items in the laboratory include the pull-down TV in the upper left corner, where the contents of test tubes containing known solutions are displayed. Help is also accessed through the pull-down TV. The electronic lab book is accessed by clicking the laboratory notebook laying on the lab bench. The notebook is used to record procedures and observations and to report the results of practice unknowns and assignments. The general chemistry laboratory is accessed by clicking the door.

The Simulation

The primary purpose of the simulation is to teach the thinking processes that are the foundation of an inorganic qualitative analysis laboratory. To achieve this, the simulation is designed to allow a student to enter a virtual inorganic qualitative analysis instructional laboratory, where they are free to make the choices and decisions that they would confront in an actual laboratory environment and, in turn, experience the resulting consequences.

To achieve this goal and to keep the simulation at a manageable size and complexity, a few assumptions and restrictions have been applied:

(1)   The cations are the nitrates and are dissolved in water to form a 0.02 M solution except for NH_4^+, which is a 1 M solution.

(2)   Additional cations cannot be added once the test tube is in the laboratory.

(3)   The reagents have concentrations of 3 M for HNO_3, NaOH, and NH_3, 0.1 M for the Na_2S, 3% H_2O_2, and 1 M for the NaCl, Na_2SO_4, and Na_2CO_3 solutions.

(4)   The pH 4, pH 7, and pH 10 solutions are inert buffers and are added in sufficient quantity to set the pH of the solution to the indicated value.

(5)   Reagents are added in excess.

(6)   After decanting, precipitates are rinsed with an appropriate solution so the precipitate does not dissolve.

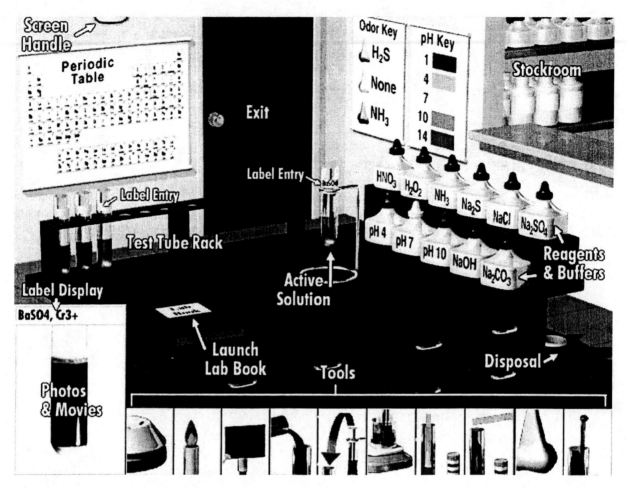

Figure 2. The virtual inorganic chemistry laboratory.

Laboratory

The essential features of the laboratory (shown in Figure 2) are described subsequently starting from the upper left hand corner of the lab and proceeding clockwise.

- *Pull-Down TV.* In the upper left-hand corner of the laboratory above the periodic table is a small handle which, when clicked, pulls down a TV and can display information in two different modes. In tutorial mode, the TV lists the chemical formulas of the relevant species for the active solution in the test tube holder. The TV will also show the contents of test tubes in the rack when they are moused over. Tutorial mode is automatically turned off for practice unknowns and assignments. In help mode, the TV lists the help menu for the laboratory.

- *Periodic Table.* A periodic table is provided for use in the virtual laboratory. Mousing over an individual element in the table provides an enlarged image of the table entry for that element showing the element abbreviation, atomic number, and molecular weight.

- *Door.* Clicking the door exits the inorganic laboratory and returns the user to the general chemistry laboratory.

- *Charts.* Hanging on the wall to the right of the door are two charts for an Odor Key and a pH Key. The odor key provides an interpretation of color for the different noses when a solution is smelled. The pH key is used to interpret the color of the pH paper.

- *Stockroom.* Clicking the stockroom window brings the user to the stockroom counter. While at the stockroom counter, test tubes containing known mixtures of cations can be made, practice unknowns can be created, and assignments can be accepted. All of these test tubes can be returned to the laboratory for further laboratory work.

- *Disposal Bucket.* To the right of the lab bench is a disposal bucket for discarding test tubes that are no longer needed in the laboratory. All test tubes in the laboratory can be cleared at once by clicking the disposal bucket.

- *Buttons.* At the bottom of the laboratory are 10 buttons used for performing different laboratory manipulations.

- *Picture Window.* The picture window is used to display real pictures depicting the contents of the various test tubes. The picture window is also used to show videos of the flame tests.

- *Test Tube Holder.* The test tube holder is used to hold the active test tube for which reagents can be added and laboratory manipulations can be performed.

- *Reagents.* To the right of the test tube holder are 11 reagents that can be added to the active test tube in any order and any combination. Reagents are added by clicking the selected bottle once.

- *Test Tube Rack.* On the back of the lab bench are two test tube racks that can store up to 12 test tubes. Test tubes are moved from the rack to the holder or to the disposal bucket by clicking and dragging.

- *Lab Book.* The lab book is used to record procedures and observations while doing experiments in the virtual laboratory. Assignments are also submitted through the lab book for automatic grading.

Test Tubes

Test tubes in the virtual laboratory are used and generally manipulated as they would be in an actual laboratory. The test tube rack is used for storing test tubes and the holder is used for adding reagents and performing other laboratory manipulations. As an added feature in the virtual laboratory, test tubes that are dragged from the rack and dropped over an existing test tube in the holder, or *vise versa*, automatically switch positions. Test tubes that are brought from the stockroom take the first available slot to the left in the rack.

Test tubes that are created in the stockroom or in the laboratory (by decanting or dividing) are not automatically labeled. Test tubes can be labeled by clicking on the label area and typing an appropriate description. The label is stored by pressing *Enter*. The first five or six letters of the label are displayed on the test tube, but the full label is displayed above the picture window.

Pictures

The test tubes that are manipulated in the virtual laboratory are given colors that show the approximate color of the contents. For the current test tube in the holder, an actual picture of the contents is shown in the picture window. Pictures of the test tubes in the rack can also be seen by mousing over the test tube of interest. Flame tests are also shown in the same picture window using 10 second video clips.

Reagents

The available reagents that can be added to the active test tube in the holder are on the right of the lab bench. Reagents are added by clicking the appropriate bottle and are always added in excess. The reagents have concentrations of 3 M for HNO_3, $NaOH$, and NH_3, 0.1 M for the Na_2S, 3% H_2O_2, and 1 M for the $NaCl$, Na_2SO_4, and Na_2CO_3 solutions. When the pH 4, 7, or 10 reagents are selected, the pH of the solution is set to the indicated value. Depending on the speed of your computer or the number of cations in the test tube, it may take up to several seconds to determine the results of adding a particular reagent. Some patience might be required.

Buttons

The bottom row of buttons are used for performing various laboratory manipulations on the test tube in the holder. Starting from left to right, these buttons perform the following functions:

(1)   Centrifuges the contents of the active solution.

(2)   Plays a 10 second video showing a flame test of the active solution.

(3)   Plays a 10 second video showing a flame test of the active solution using a cobalt filter. (The cobalt filter is usually necessary to filter out masking colors from other cations, usually Na^+, that interfere with the K^+ color.)

(4)   Decants the solution from the active test tube into a new test tube leaving any precipitate behind. (The new test tube is placed in the first available slot from the left in the test tube rack and is not labeled. If the rack is full, decanting is not possible.)

(5)   Divides or makes a copy of the active test tube and, again, the copy is placed in the first available slot from the left.

(6)   Heats the solution. (The presence of the hot plate on the lab bench is equivalent to placing the test tube in a beaker of boiling water.)

(7)   Measures the pH of the solution using pH paper. (The color of the pH paper indicates the pH of the solution. A pH Color Key is hanging on the wall in the virtual laboratory.)

(8)   Measures the pH of the vapor above the test tube in a manner similar to the pH of the solution.

(9)   Smells the contents of the test tube with the color of the nose indicating the smell. (A blue nose smells like NH_3, a red nose smells like H_2S or rotten egg gas, and a neutral nose has no smell.)

(10)   Stirs the contents of the test tube.

Disposal Bucket

Unwanted test tubes can be disposed of by dragging and dropping the test tube in the disposal bucket. All the test tubes in the laboratory can be disposed of at once by clicking on the disposal bucket. As in an actual laboratory, there is no way to undispose an already disposed test tube.

Pull-Down TV

Located above the chalkboard is a small handle that, when clicked, pulls down a television. The television has two different display modes, each of which is described subsequently.

- *Tutorial.* The tutorial mode is used to display the list of cations in the active test tube. This list reflects the changes to the cations as various reagents are added to the test tube or other laboratory manipulations are performed. The cation list is the main tutorial or learning tool when exploring the chemistry of the cations. The cation tutorial is not active for assignments or practice unknowns.

- *Help.* In help mode, the table of contents for the laboratory help is listed on the TV. Clicking a subject listed in the table of contents brings up the help window.

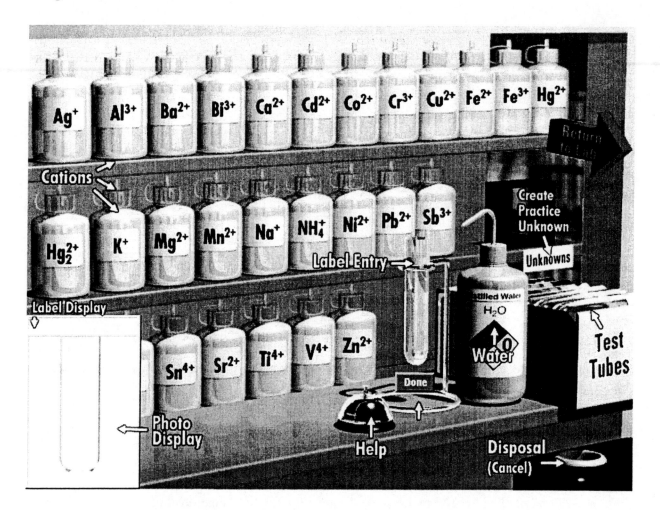

Figure 3. A view of the inorganic stockroom.

Stockroom

The stockroom (shown in Figure 3) is used to prepare test tubes containing known combinations of cations and to make practice unknowns. The essential features of the stockroom are described as follows:

- *Bottles.* The bottles on the shelves contain the indicated cation at a concentration of 0.02 M except NH_4^+, which has a concentration of 1.0 M. Cations are added to a test tube by clicking once on the bottle.

- *Unknown Rack.* To the right of the bottles on the middle shelf is a small two-test tube rack where test tubes containing unknowns are placed. The left slot is used for instructor assignments and the right slot is used for practice unknowns.

- *"Unknowns" Sign.* The "Unknowns" sign underneath the unknown rack is used to access the practice unknown dialog screen. The practice unknown screen is used to define randomized unknowns for practicing and self-testing.

- *Test Tube Box.* The test tube box contains empty test tubes for making known solutions. To get a new test tube, click the test tube box, and drag the test tube to the holder on the stockroom counter.

- *Test Tube Holder.* The test tube holder is used to hold test tubes when cations are added to make known solutions. The holder is also used for placement of unknowns obtained from the unknown rack. The label area on the test tube can be clicked to label the test tube. A *Done* button appears underneath the test tube and is used to return the test tube to the laboratory.

- *Water Bottle.* The water bottle is used to add water to a test tube. The water bottle is not active if cations are already present in the test tube, and adding cations after water has been added is the same as adding the cations to the test tube directly.

- *Picture Window.* The picture window is used to show an actual picture depicting the solution in the holder. The picture window also shows pictures of the unknowns in the unknown rack when they are moused over.

- *Disposal Bucket.* The disposal bucket is used to discard test tubes that are in the holder. Discarding a practice unknown generates a new random unknown and places the unknown in the unknown rack. Discarding an assigned unknown places the unknown back in the unknown rack.

- *Bell.* As in most stockrooms, the bell is used to access Help for the stockroom.

- *Return to Lab Arrow.* Clicking the *Return to Lab* arrow returns the user to the laboratory. If a test tube is in the holder at the time the arrow is pressed, then that test tube is also returned to the laboratory. Remember, test tubes that are returned to the laboratory are placed in the first available position to the left in the test tube rack.

Known Solutions

Known combinations of cations are created by grabbing a test tube from the test tube box and placing it in the holder. Cations are added by clicking the bottles on the stockroom shelves. Water can be added by clicking the water bottle. An actual picture of the contents of the test tube is shown in the picture window as cations are added. As in an actual laboratory, cations may not be removed from the test tube once added, but a test tube may be discarded by dragging it to the disposal bucket. Once a test tube has been prepared, it can be labeled and then taken to the laboratory by clicking *Done* or by clicking on the *Return to Lab* arrow. Clicking *Done* allows more solutions to be made.

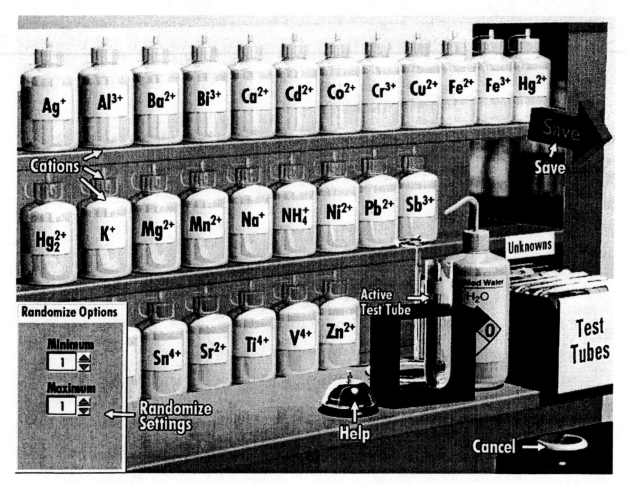

Figure 4. The practice unknown screen..

Practice Unknowns

The practice unknown screen (shown in Figure 4) is accessed by clicking on the "Unknowns" label underneath the unknown rack. A practice unknown is then created by selecting or defining a set of cations from which a certain number of cations will be randomly selected. The number of cations that will be selected from the defined set is also randomly determined as defined by the specified minimum and maximum limits. The minimum limit defines the minimum number of cations that can be selected from the set and the maximum defines the maximum number.

- *Selecting the Cation Set.* To define the set of cations, simply click the corresponding bottles on the shelves. A cation can be removed from the set by clicking the bottle again. Note that the number of cations in the set must be at least equal to the number specified in the *Minimum* setting.

- *Setting **Maximum**.* To set the maximum number of cations that can be included in the unknown, use the arrow keys to the right of the ***Maximum*** box. The up arrow adds 1 to the current number, and the down arrow subtracts 1. Note that *Maximum* cannot be set to less than 1. Note also that *Maximum* cannot be greater than the number of cations in the set. However, the number of cations in the set may exceed *Maximum*.

- *Setting* **Minimum.** To set the minimum number of cations that can be included in the unknown, use the arrow keys to the right of the **Minimum** box. The up arrow adds 1 to the current number, and the down arrow subtracts 1. Note that if *Minimum* is set to zero, then water (or no cations) can be assigned as a possible unknown. Note also that *Minimum* can be equal to but cannot exceed *Maximum*.

- *Saving the Unknown.* To exit the *Practice Unknown* screen and generate random practice unknowns, click on the green *Save* arrow, which replaced the *Return to Lab* arrow that was in the stockroom. The first practice unknown will be placed in the right slot of the unknown rack in the stockroom.

- *Cancel.* To cancel making a practice unknown and return to the stockroom, click the disposal bucket.

Quantum User's Guide

Overview

Welcome to *Virtual ChemLab: Quantum,* a set of simulated physical chemistry experiments that demonstrate many of the concepts and ideas that led to the development of atomic theory and quantum mechanics. The level of these experiments can be very basic or very sophisticated, depending on the level of the class and the purpose for performing the experiments. A partial list of some of these experiments includes Thomson's measurement of the charge-to-mass ratio of the electron, Rutherford's backscattering experiment, Planck's blackbody radiation, Millikan's oil drop experiment, the photoelectric effect, emission spectra of gases, two-slit diffraction, plus many others.

The purpose of the quantum laboratory is to allow students to explore and better understand the foundational experiments that led to the development of quantum mechanics. Because of the very sophisticated nature of most of these experiments, the quantum laboratory is the most "virtual" of the *Virtual ChemLab* laboratory simulations. In general, the laboratory consists of an optics table where a source, sample, modifier, and detector combination can be placed to perform different experiments. These devices are located in the stockroom and can be taken out of the stockroom and placed in various locations on the optics table. The emphasis here is to teach students to probe a sample (e.g., a gas, metal foil, two-slit screen, etc.) with a source (e.g., a laser, electron gun, alpha-particle source, etc.) and detect the outcome with a specific detector (e.g., a phosphor screen, spectrometer, etc.). Heat, electric fields, or magnetic fields can also be applied to modify an aspect of the experiment. As in all *Virtual ChemLab* laboratories, the focus is to allow students the ability to explore and discover, in a safe and level-appropriate setting, the concepts that are important in the various areas of chemistry.

Because these physical chemistry experiments can be complex and not intuitive to set up properly, a set of 15 preset experiments have been defined and are accessible through the clipboard in the stockroom. Complete details on the quantum laboratory, its use and limitations, and the scope of the simulations will be described in this section.

Quick Start

After launching the program, you will be brought to the general chemistry laboratory (shown in Figure 1) where you will find five different laboratory benches that represent five different general chemistry laboratories. Mousing over each of these laboratory benches pops up the name of the selected laboratory. To access the quantum laboratory, click the optics table located at the far right.

Figure 1. The general chemistry laboratory. The general chemistry laboratory contains five different laboratories, each of which is accessed by clicking on the appropriate lab bench.

Once inside the quantum laboratory, go to the stockroom counter by clicking the stockroom window. Located inside the stockroom are shelves containing the various sources, samples, detectors and modifiers. An experiment is setup or defined by selecting any combination of a source, sample, and detector with any necessary modifiers and dragging the selected devices individually to the stockroom counter. Clicking the *Return to Lab* arrow returns the user to the main laboratory where these devices can then be placed on the optics table by clicking and dragging the devices from the stockroom counter onto the table. There are only certain allowed locations on the optics table for the sources, samples, detectors, and the modifiers. For each device, these locations are identified with spotlights as each device is dragged to the table. At this point, the source and detector can be turned on and the various LCD control boxes adjusted in order to perform an experiment. Any results from the experiment will be shown in the detector window. Individual devices on the optics table can be returned to the stockroom as needed and replaced with different pieces of equipment. Clicking the *Reset Lab* button will return all the equipment on the optics table to the stockroom.

The difficulty in these experiments is knowing what combinations of instruments to use for a desired investigation, where to place these instruments on the optics table, what settings to use, and how to interpret the results shown on the detectors. In order to make experiments in the quantum laboratory more accessible, instructors can allow students to utilize a set of 15 experiments that have already been defined. These preset experiments are accessed by clicking the clipboard while at the stockroom window. Clicking the desired experiment automatically brings the necessary equipment to the stockroom counter, and clicking the *Return to Lab* arrow will setup the equipment on the optics table.

Other important items in the laboratory include the pull-down TV in the upper left corner where Help is accessed and the spectrum chart hanging on the wall that can be enlarged into its own window by clicking the chart. This chart is used solely as a reference for identifying the different regions in the electromagnetic spectrum. The electronic lab book is accessed by clicking the laboratory notebook laying on the table. The notebook is used to record procedures, observations, and conclusions. Output from the detectors can be saved to the lab book. The general chemistry laboratory is accessed by clicking the exit sign.

The Simulation

Overview

The primary purpose of the quantum simulation is to teach the concepts and fundamental principles that led to the development of atomic theory and eventually quantum mechanics. As is usually the case, these concepts and principles were discovered or elucidated by a series of experiments that were developed and carried out over a period of many years by some of the great minds of the 19th and 20th centuries. These experiments most often require extremely sophisticated equipment whose setup and operation is well beyond the scope of the *Virtual ChemLab* simulations.

In *Virtual ChemLab: Quantum*, these classic experiments (plus several others) are reproduced in a framework consistent with the other *Virtual ChemLab* simulations; that is, the student is put into a virtual environment where they are free to choose their equipment and build a *conceptual* experiment of their own design and then experience the resulting consequences. The focus in the quantum simulation is not how to use lasers, spectrometers, diodes, electron sources, and other pieces of equipment, but the focus is how each foundational experiment was *conceptually* conceived and realized and how the outcomes of these experiments were observed in the laboratory. The interpretation of these experiments and outcomes is the ultimate goal of these simulations and ties the concepts taught in the classroom with the great experimental work of the past.

In general, the simulated experiments in *Virtual ChemLab: Quantum* are based on the concept that a sample is probed with a source and then a detector of some kind is used to measure or detect any changes caused by the probe. In addition to the source, sample, and detector combination, a modifier can also be used to modify either the sample or the source. Not every experiment requires a source, a sample, or a modifier, but a detector must be used to detect a result or make an observation. The relative positions of the source, sample, and detector with each other is also an important component of the experimental design.

Given in the sections that follow are descriptions of the available sources, samples, detectors, and modifiers. Details on adjusting the settings on these devices and placing them on the optics table are given in the "Laboratory" section. Most of these devices have been highly idealized in order to simplify the simulation to within the general scope of the *Virtual ChemLab* series. A description of the degree of idealization for each device is also given.

Sources

Source	*Description*	*Idealization*
Alpha Particles	This source provides a collimated beam of alpha particles (^{4}He nuclei) with an energy of 5.4 MeV and an intensity of 10^5 particles per second. The source is turned on and off by opening and closing the cover.	The alpha particles are assumed to come from an ^{241}Am source with a small aperture in front of the sample to collimate the beam. Experiments involving alpha particles should take place in a vacuum, but this is not shown in the simulation.
Super Light Bulb	This source provides light at all wavelengths from 20 nm up to as high as 20,000 nm with a uniform intensity. The intensity of the light can be selected at values of 1 nW, 1 μW, 1 mW, 1 W, 1 kW, and 1 MW. The super light bulb is turned on and off by clicking the green and red buttons.	Light sources do exist that provide light over a wide spectrum, but these sources cannot cover such a wide region of the electromagnetic spectrum nor do they provide light at a uniform intensity, thus the name for this source and the "virtual" look.
Electron Gun	This source provides a collimated beam of electrons with selectable energies from 1 meV up to 50 keV and selectable intensities of 1 electron per second (e/s), 10 e/s, 100 e/s, 1000 e/s, 1 nA, 1 μA, 1 mA, and 1 A. The electron gun is turned on and off by clicking the green and red buttons.	An electron source does not exist that can produce a collimated beam of electrons over this range of energies and with a range of intensities from electrons per second up to amps. In addition, an actual laboratory experiment would require that these electrons be contained in a vacuum; otherwise, the electrons would ionize the air at high

Source	Description	Idealization
		intensities and energies or collide with the air molecules at low intensities and be adsorbed.

Laser

This source provides laser light at a single, selectable wavelength from 20 nm up to as long as 1 m with selectable intensities of 1 photon per second (p/s), 10 p/s, 100 p/s, 1000 p/s, 1 nW, 1 µW, 1 mW, 1 W, 1 kW, and 1 MW. The laser is turned on and off by clicking the green and red button.

Lasers do exist that can produce light over a range of wavelengths, but not even close to the range that this "virtual" laser can produce. The range of intensities covered by this laser is also significantly wider than what can be produced by a real laser. It should be noted, however, that the image used for this laser was modeled after an actual laser. The insides of this laser can be seen by mousing over the laser while it is on the optics table and turned off.

Samples

Sample	Description	Idealization

Oil Mist

This is a conceptual oil mist chamber. Oil mist is provided by the atomizer outside the box, and the oil mist is allowed to fall through a small hole between the two plates. Another small hole (not shown) allows electrons to pass through the mist depositing electrons on the droplets. A telescopic eye piece is provided to see the oil droplets.

This oil mist chamber is only meant to be a conceptual image of the key features necessary for the Millikan oil drop experiment. There are several actual self-contained Millikan oil drop experiments that can be purchased and look significantly different from what is depicted here. The key ideas to remember here are that this chamber provides oil drops than can be viewed, allows electrons to be deposited on these drops, and allows an electric field to be applied.

Sample	Description	Idealization
 Liquids	This is a cuvette used for holding liquid samples. Eight different liquids can be added by selecting from the bottles on the top shelf in the stockroom.	There is no significant idealization done here except for the cuvette holder graphic. This graphic is an artist's rendition of a cuvette holder that is consistent with the other graphic elements used in the simulation.
 Metal Foils	This is a device used for holding metal foils. The metal foils used in the simulation are 1 μm thick, and there are 41 metals that can be selected from the metals box on the top shelf in the stockroom.	It is assumed in the simulation that all the metals can be rolled out into foils of 1 μm thick and in sufficient quantities to account for the size indicated in the graphic. Of course, many of the metals that can be selected in the simulation are (a) too reactive in air and cannot exist as shown on the optics table, (b) too rare and cannot be provided in quantities large enough to make the foils shown, or (c) too brittle and cannot be rolled out into foils.
 Gases	This is a cell used for holding gas samples. Ten different gases can be added by selecting from the gas cylinders on the top shelf in the stockroom.	There is no significant idealization done here except for the cell holder graphic. This graphic is an artist's rendition of a cell holder that is consistent with the other graphic elements used in the simulation.
 Two Slit Device	This is a device used for adjusting the spacing of two infinitely narrow slits spaced as narrow as 1 nm wide up to 1 cm wide.	This device is fictional and does not exist in reality. An infinitely narrow slit is a limiting case with respect to the wavelength of the particle, and a device cannot be constructed that would adjust the slit spacings over such a wide range of values.

Detectors

The detectors used in the simulation are all fictional devices conceptually patterned after actual laboratory instruments. These *types* of detectors are actually used in the laboratory, but in this simulation they have been greatly simplified and idealized in order to focus on what they are detecting instead of how they are detecting it. The correct interpretation of a detector's output is the primary concern.

Brief descriptions of what each detector can measure and where they are useful are given in the following table. The graphic of each detector represents the detector on the optics table. Each detector is turned on and off in the simulation by clicking the red or green buttons. When a detector is turned on, a detector window is brought up that shows the detector output. Details on these detector windows are given in the *Laboratory* section.

Detector	*Description*
 Phosphor Screen	A phosphor screen is used to detect high-energy particles such as electrons or alpha particles. When a high-energy particle impacts the phosphor screen, the phosphor momentarily glows as a small spot at the position of impact. The brightness of a spot or area on the phosphor screen is a qualitative measure of the number of particles or intensity of the beam at that location. An actual phosphor screen is not an electronic device, but in the simulation it is treated as such in order to be consistent with the other detectors.
 Spectrometer	A spectrometer is used to measure the intensity of light over a wide range of wavelengths. The spectrometer used here can operate at any necessary wavelength and plots the intensity of the detected light as a function of wavelength. The plotted intensity is expressed as a relative intensity from 0 to 1. The "relative" nature of the intensity changes depending on the experiment being performed. The spectrometer cannot measure single photon events.
 Video Camera	An "everyday" video camera detects the wavelength and spatial location of photons as they strike the detector. In the simulation, of course, the video camera has been idealized to be able to detect photons of all wavelengths inside or outside the visible region. Essentially, the video camera and phosphor screen are similar in that they both detect the spatial locations of particles as they strike the detector except a phosphor screen detects electrons and alpha particles and a video camera detects photons. Both detectors indicate the intensity using brightness. The video camera can also measure the energy of photons in the visible region (the frequency) using color.

Detector	Description
 Photodiode	A photodiode detects the integrated intensity of light over all wavelengths. That is, a photodiode is not wavelength specific but integrates the intensity of light over all wavelengths it can detect. In the simulation, the photodiode measures this intensity as a function of time. As with the spectrometer, the intensity is displayed as a relative intensity from 0 to 1.
 Bolometer	A bolometer is used to measure the energy and intensity of particles over a wide range of energies. The energies of these particles are measured in eV or in joules. The bolometer used here can detect electrons or alpha particles and plots the intensity of these particles as a function of energy. The plotted intensity is expressed as a relative intensity from 0 to 1. The "relative" nature of the intensity changes depending on the experiment being performed. The bolometer cannot measure single particle events. In most ways, the bolometer is equivalent to the spectrometer except it detects particles instead of photons.

Modifiers

The modifiers are used to apply electric or magnetic fields to the sample, used to heat up a sample, or placed before a detector to bend a particle beam. Again, the idea is to conceptually apply an electric field, or a magnetic field, or apply heat in order to observe a change with the detector. How these things are actually carried out in the laboratory is beyond the scope of this simulation. The following are descriptions of these modifiers.

Modifier	Description
 Electric Field	An electric field can be applied to a sample, or it can be placed on the optics table separate from the sample. How this will change the output on the detector will depend on the experiment. In nearly all cases, a DC field will be applied except in the case of a gas sample where an AC field is used. The type of field used is indicated on the LCD controller. The electric field can be placed in combination with a magnetic field. The maximum voltage that can be applied is 5000 V.
  Magnetic Field	A magnetic field can be applied to a sample, or it can be placed on the optics table separate from the sample. How this will change the output on the detector will depend on the experiment. A uniform magnetic field is applied in all cases. The maximum field that can be applied is 100 T.

Modifier	Description
  Heat	The heat modifier will heat a sample to a maximum temperature of 4000 K. If the sample temperature is raised too high, then appropriate outcomes will occur. The heat modifier can only be applied to a sample.

Other Idealizations

In the course of performing some of the experiments in *Virtual ChemLab: Quantum*, several other important idealizations or assumptions are made. The following is a list of some of the most important:

1. Most experiments involving light, especially in the visible region, require the room to be dark or the apparatus to be enclosed in order to avoid contamination from extraneous light sources. These types of precautions have not been taken in the simulation.

2. Experiments involving alpha particles and electrons, especially high energy and high intensity electrons require the experiment to be contained in a vacuum. This requirement is not shown in the simulation.

3. In the photoelectric and reverse photoelectric experiments, light or electrons strike a metal surface at an angle and give off electrons and photons, respectively. For the sake of simplicity, these electrons and photons come off the metal in a direction perpendicular to the incident beam and are collimated.

4. The emission spectra for HCl was generated by adding the individual atomic emission spectra for H and Cl. All other emission spectra were either measured or obtained from the NIST database.

Important Experimental Parameters

In order to quantitatively measure the charge-to-mass ratio of an electron (Thomson's experiment) and the charge on an electron (Millikan's oil drop experiment), several experimental parameters must be known that cannot be readily measured or determined in the simulation. These parameters and their values are given subsequently. Please keep in mind that the values for these parameters can be changed by the instructor. The values given are the default values specified at installation.

Thomson's Experiment

d = the spacing between the electric plates. The default setting is 5 cm.

l = the path length of the applied electric and magnetic fields. The default setting is 5 cm.

b = the distance from the end of the electric and magnetic field to the phosphor screen. The default setting is 76.2 cm.

Millikan's Oil Drop Experiment

ρ_{oil} = density of oil = 821 kg·m^{-3}

ρ_{air} = density of air = 1.22 kg·m^{-3}

η_{air} = viscosity of air = 1.4607×10^{-5} kg·m^{-1}·s^{-1}

b = correction for small drop size = 8.1184×10^{-8} m·atm

p = atmospheric pressure = 1 atm

d_{plates} = the distance between the voltage plates = 1 cm

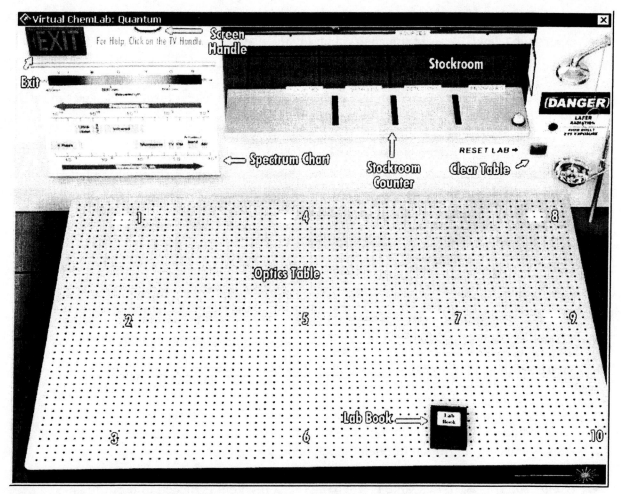

Figure 2. The virtual quantum laboratory. Each of the different parts of the main laboratory are labeled. The numbers represent where the sources, samples, detectors, and modifiers are allowed to be placed. See *Laboratory* section for more details.

Laboratory

The essential features of the laboratory (shown in Figure 2) are described as follows starting from the upper left hand corner of the lab and proceeding clockwise.

- *Exit.* Clicking the exit sign exits the quantum laboratory and returns the user to the general chemistry laboratory.

- *Pull-Down TV.* In the upper left-hand corner of the laboratory above the spectrum chart is a small handle that, when clicked, pulls down a TV that can display information in two different modes. In assignment mode, the TV displays the assignment text for the currently accepted assignment. This is intended to allow easy reference to the assignment while performing the work in the virtual laboratory. When an assignment has not been accepted, the assignment mode is left blank. In help mode, the TV lists the help menu for the laboratory.

- *Spectrum Chart.* A spectrum chart depicting the different regions of the electromagnetic spectrum is provided as a reference in the virtual laboratory. Clicking the chart will bring up an expanded view in a separate window. When the laser is out in the laboratory and turned on, arrows will be displayed on the chart showing the wavelength set on the laser in relation to the rest of the electromagnetic spectrum.

- *Stockroom.* Clicking the stockroom window brings the user to the stockroom counter. While at the stockroom counter, various pieces of experimental equipment in the stockroom can be brought down to the stockroom counter for later use in the laboratory. The clipboard hanging in the stockroom can also be clicked to select preset experiments or accept an assignment.

- *Stockroom Counter.* Equipment that was brought down to the stockroom counter while in the stockroom stays on the counter when returning to the laboratory. From the laboratory, this equipment can be clicked and dragged from the counter and placed on selected locations on the optics table to perform an experiment. It is up to the user to design the experiment, arrange the equipment appropriately, and set the correct values on the instruments.

- *Reset Lab.* Clicking the *Reset Lab* button will automatically clear the laboratory and return any equipment back to their appropriate locations on the stockroom shelves.

- *Lab Book.* The lab book is used to record procedures and observations while performing experiments in the virtual laboratory. Detector output can also be saved to the lab book, and assignments are submitted through the lab book for grading.

- *Optics Table.* The optics table is where all the equipment is placed to perform an experiment. In an actual laboratory, an optics table is used to isolate the experiment from the vibrations of the building.

Optics Table

The optics table is where the equipment is placed to perform an experiment. In an actual laboratory, an optics table is used to isolate the experiment from the vibrations of the building. Shown in Figure 2 are ten spotlights where a selected piece of equipment is allowed to be placed on the table. As each piece of equipment is selected from the stockroom counter (while in the main laboratory), the spotlights will show where the selected item can be placed. Sources can be placed in positions 1, 2, or 3; samples can only be placed in position 5; detectors can be placed in positions 1, 3, 4, 6, 8, 9, or 10; the electric and magnetic field modifiers can be placed together or individually in position 5 (when a sample is present) or in position 7 (alone); and the heat modifier can only be placed at position 5 when a sample is present. Be aware that the instructor has the capability to turn off the spotlights to add difficulty to the laboratory simulation.

LCD Controllers

Many of the instruments used in the simulation have LCD (Liquid Crystal Display) controllers that are used to operate these instruments. These controllers can be divided into two types: (1) Intensity Controllers and (2) Setting Controllers.

Intensity Controllers. The super light bulb, electron gun, and laser sources all have controllers that allow the intensity of the output to be set. The intensities of these sources cannot be continuously adjusted, but are restricted to certain allowed values. Shown to the right is the intensity controller for the laser. The intensity controllers for the electron gun and super light bulb are similar except with their own set of allowed intensities. The LCD screen is used to display the current intensity, clicking the button above the screen advances to the next highest intensity, and clicking the button below the screen advances to the next lowest intensity.

Setting Controllers. The electron gun, laser, two slit device, magnetic field, electric field, and heater all use controllers to adjust the specific settings for these devices. The setting that is actually set on these devices using the controller is unique to each device, but the use and operation of a setting controller is uniform for all devices. As an example, the setting controller for the electric field modifier is shown in the accompanying illustration. The key areas on the controller are the LCD screen and the buttons above and below the screen. Shown on the LCD screen, from left to right, is (a) the sign of the setting (only present if the setting can be positive or negative), (b) the three-digit number representing the setting, (c) the decimal place, and (d) the units and scaling factor. The sign of the setting (if present) can be changed by clicking on the + or – sign, and the decimal place can be moved by clicking on the location between the digits where the decimal should be placed. Each of the digits of the setting can be changed by clicking the button above or below the digit, and the scaling factor is changed by clicking the button above or below the units. Note that in some of these controllers, the letter "u" is used to represent the symbol "μ" in the units.

Detectors

Most of the theory, concepts, and background information about the detectors used in this simulation were given in "The Simulation" section previously. In this section, examples of the five detector screens will be given along with a description of the buttons, switches, and other features associated with each detector screen. All of the detectors are turned on by clicking the red and green buttons on the detector on the optics table. The detectors are turned off by clicking the red and green buttons again or by clicking the on/off button on the detector screen. The detectors are passive in that they do not affect the outcome of an experiment but instead only detect or measure certain physical phenomena. The interpretation of this output from each detector forms the fundamental learning objective of these simulations.

Phosphor Screen. A phosphor screen (Figure 3) is used to detect high-energy particles such as electrons or alpha particles. When a high-energy particle impacts the phosphor screen, the phosphor momentarily glows as a small spot at the position of impact. The brightness of a spot or area on the phosphor screen is a qualitative measure of the number of particles or intensity of the beam at that location. An actual phosphor screen is not an electronic device, but in the simulation it is treated as such in order to be consistent with the other detectors.

The four buttons on the phosphor screen include (1) *Record,* which saves the current detector output to the lab book; (2) *Clear Screen,* which clears or cleans the phosphor screen; (3) *Persist Mode,* which puts the phosphor screen into a mode where the individual impacts of particles are saved and do not disappear; and (4) *Grid,* which overlays a grid on the phosphor screen in order to measure the positions of spots on the screen.

Spectrometer. A spectrometer is used to measure the intensity of light over a wide range of wavelengths. The spectrometer used here can operate at any necessary wavelength and plots the intensity of the detected light as a function of wavelength. The plotted intensity is expressed as a relative intensity from 0 to 1. (See Figure 4.) The "relative" nature of the intensity changes depending

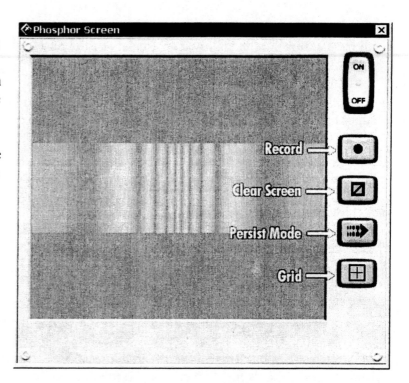

Figure 3. The phosphor detector screen. The experiment depicted here is two-slit diffraction involving electrons.

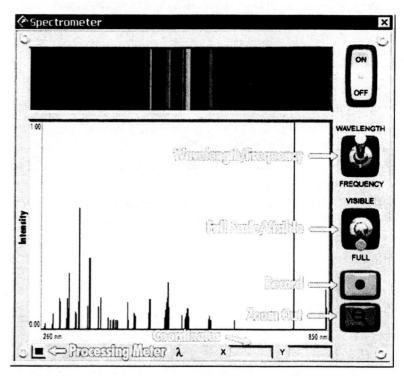

Figure 4. The spectrometer detector screen. The output depicted here is for photoemission of CO_2 gas.

on the experiment being performed. The spectrometer cannot measure single photon events.

An important feature of the spectrometer is the ability to zoom in on selected portions of the spectrum. This is done by clicking and then dragging the cursor over a selected region of the spectrum causing an orange box to outline the selected region. Releasing the mouse will enlarge the selected region in the viewing window. This process can be repeated in order to achieve the necessary resolution.

The buttons and switches on the spectrometer include (1) the *Wavelength/Frequency* switch, which allows the spectra to be plotted as a function of wavelength or frequency; (2) the *Full/Visible* switch, which plots either the full spectrum or just the portion in the visible region; (3) the *Record* button, which saves the current detector output to the lab book; and (4) the *Zoom Out* button, which zooms out to the previous level of detail. Other import elements of the spectrometer window are the *x, y* coordinate boxes, which show the current *x, y* coordinates of the cursor in the units specified on the graph, and the processing meter, which indicates when the spectrometer is processing data.

Video Camera. An "everyday" video camera detects the wavelength and spatial location of photons as they strike the detector. In the simulation, of course, the video camera (Figure 5) has been idealized to be able to detect photons of all wavelengths inside or outside the visible region. Essentially, the video camera and phosphor screen are similar in that they both detect the spatial locations of particles as they strike the detector except a phosphor screen detects electrons and alpha particles and a video camera detects photons. Both detectors indicate the intensity using brightness. The video camera can also measure the energy of photons in the visible region (the frequency) using color.

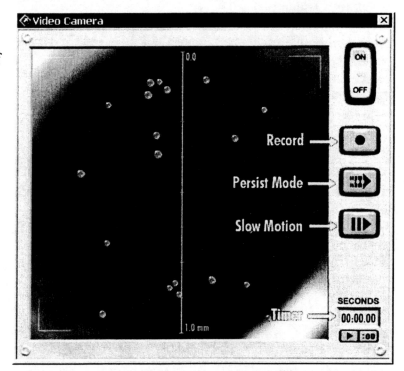

Figure 5. The video camera detector screen. The output shown here is for the Millikan Oil Drop experiment.

The video camera is essentially the "eyes" of the laboratory. When the video camera is placed on the optics table it will "take a picture" of what it sees at the sample position. In certain experiments, such as the Millikan oil drop experiment and two-slit diffraction with photons, the video camera view will be magnified or changed as appropriate for the experiment, but in most cases the video camera will show an image of what is happening at the sample position even if that involves explosions, metals melting, or smoke.

The buttons on the video camera include (1) *Record,* which saves the current detector output to the lab book; (2) *Persist Mode,* which puts the video camera into a mode where the individual impacts of photons are saved and do not disappear (this is not a freeze frame mode); and (3) *Slow Motion,* which puts the video camera into slow-motion mode. (This is only available during the Millikan oil drop experiment.) During the Millikan oil drop experiment, there is also a Timer available, which allows the velocity of the oil drops to be measured even in slow motion. The *Arrow* button is used to start the timer, pressing the button again pauses the timer, and the *:00* button resets the timer.

Photodiode. A photodiode detects the integrated intensity of light over all wavelengths. That is, a photodiode is not wavelength specific but integrates the intensity of light over all wavelengths it can detect. In the simulation, the photodiode (Figure 6) measures this intensity as a function of time. As with the spectrometer, the intensity is displayed as a relative intensity from 0 to 1.

The buttons on the photodiode include (1) *Record,* which is a toggle button on this detector and records the entire time trace while the button is toggled, and (2) *Clear Screen,* which resets the time trace back to zero.

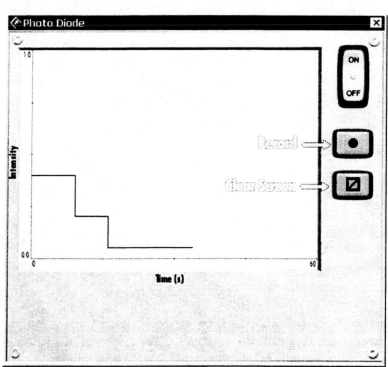

Figure 6. The photodiode detector screen. The photodiode measures the integrated intensity of light as a function of time.

Bolometer. A bolometer is used to measure the energy and intensity of particles over a wide range of energies. The energies of these particles are measured in eV or in joules. The bolometer used here can detect electrons or alpha particles and plots the intensity of these particles as a function of energy or plots the integrated intensity as a function of time. The plotted intensity is expressed as a relative intensity from 0 to 1. (See Figure 7.) The "relative" nature of the intensity changes depending on the experiment being performed. The bolometer cannot measure single particle events. In most ways, the bolometer is equivalent to the spectrometer and photodiode except it detects particles instead of photons.

An important feature of the bolometer is the ability to zoom in on selected portions of the energy spectrum. This is done by clicking and then dragging the cursor over a selected region of the spectrum causing an orange box to outline the selected region. Releasing the mouse will enlarge the selected region in the viewing window. This process can be repeated in order to achieve the necessary resolution.

The buttons and switches on the bolometer include (1) the *Energy Units* switch, which allows the energy to be plotted in eV or joules; (2) the *Mode* switch, which sets the detector in either the Energy Resolved mode or Integrated mode; (3) the *Record* button, which saves the current detector output to the lab book; (4) the *Clear Screen* button, which resets the time trace to zero in the Integrated mode; and (5) the *Zoom Out* button, which zooms out to the previous level of detail. Other import elements of the bolometer window are the *x*, *y* coordinate boxes, which show the current *x*, *y* coordinates of the cursor in the units specified on the graph, and the processing meter which indicates when the bolometer is processing data.

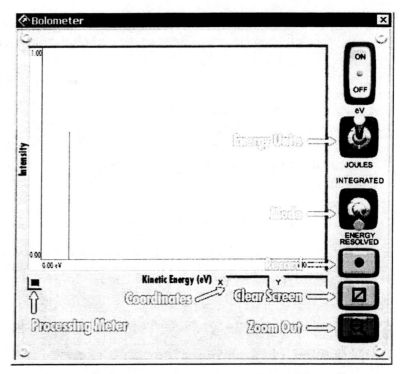

Figure 7. The bolometer detector screen. The output shown here is for the photoelectric effect.

Stockroom Window

Clicking the stockroom window brings the user to the stockroom counter. While at the stockroom counter, various pieces of experimental equipment in the stockroom can be brought down to the stockroom counter for later use in the laboratory. The clipboard hanging in the stockroom can also be clicked to select preset experiments. Equipment that was brought down to the stockroom counter stays on the counter when returning to the laboratory. From the laboratory, this equipment can be clicked and dragged from the counter and placed on selected locations on the optics table to perform an experiment. It is up to the user to design the experiment, arrange the equipment appropriately, and set the correct values on the instruments.

Pull-Down TV

In the upper left-hand corner of the laboratory above the spectrum chart is a small handle, which when clicked, pulls down a TV and can display information in two different modes:

- *Assignments.* Assignments cannot be accepted in the student version of the software.

- ***Help.*** In help mode, the table of contents for the laboratory help is listed on the TV. Clicking a subject listed in the table of contents brings up the help window.

Spectrum Chart

A spectrum chart depicting the different regions of the electromagnetic spectrum is provided as a reference in the virtual laboratory. Clicking the chart will bring up an expanded view in a separate window. When the laser is out in the laboratory and turned on, arrows will be displayed on the chart showing the wavelength set on the laser in relation to the rest of the electromagnetic spectrum.

Reset Button

Clicking the *Reset Lab* button will automatically clear the laboratory and return any equipment back to its appropriate location on the stockroom shelves. The laboratory can also be cleared by dragging the individual pieces of equipment back to the stockroom. Note that the laboratory does not have to be cleared to modify or start a new experiment. Individual pieces of equipment can be brought to the stockroom and exchanged for different items, or samples can be changed.

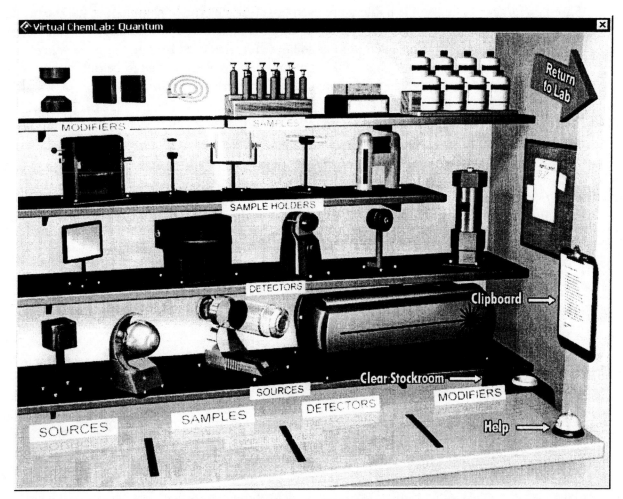

Figure 8. The quantum stockroom. The equipment used for performing various experiments in the laboratory is divided into sources, detectors, samples, and modifiers. A piece of equipment is selected by clicking and dragging the equipment down to the stockroom counter.

Stockroom

The stockroom (shown in Figure 8) is used to select the equipment for a particular experiment that will be carried out on the optics table in the laboratory. The essential features of the stockroom are described in the following list.

- *Sources.* The available sources include an alpha-particle source, super light bulb, electron gun, and laser. Details on these sources were given in the *Simulation* section. Only one source can be out in the laboratory; however, a source is not always necessary for an experiment.

- *Detectors.* The available detectors include a phosphor screen, spectrometer, video camera, photodiode, and bolometer. Details on these detectors are given in the *Simulation* section and in the "Laboratory" section. Only one detector can be out in the laboratory.

- *Sample Holders.* The sample holders are used to select the type of sample that will be probed with the source or modifier. These include an oil mist chamber, a cuvette used for liquids, a metal foil holder, a gas sample cell, and an idealized device used for adjusting the separation between two infinitely narrow slits. Only one sample holder is allowed to be out in the laboratory; however, a sample is not always necessary for an experiment.

- *Samples.* When a liquid, gas sample holder, or metal foil has been selected, the actual sample that will be used in the experiment is selected by clicking the liquid bottles, gas cylinders, or box of foils, respectively.

- *Modifiers.* Samples can be modified by applying an electric field, a magnetic field, or by applying heat to raise the temperature. The electric and magnetic field modifiers can also be placed in front of a detector to bend a particle beam.

- *Clipboard.* Clicking the clipboard gives access to 15 fundamental experiments that are already predefined and ready to run. Be aware that access to these preset experiments can be turned off by the instructor. The clipboard also gives access to assignments given by the instructor.

- *Disposal Bucket.* Clicking the disposal bucket will clear the stockroom of any equipment that may be on the stockroom counter. It is meant to be a fast way to clean up.

- *Bell.* As in most stockrooms, the bell is used to access Help for the stockroom.

- *Return to Lab Arrow.* Clicking the *Return to Lab* arrow returns the user to the laboratory. Any equipment that is on the stockroom counter will be available in the laboratory to be placed on the optics table. Equipment on the stockroom counter does not necessarily have to be placed on the optics table. Instead, the stockroom counter can be used as a temporary storage location while investigating different experimental configurations.

Selecting Equipment

The various pieces of equipment in the stockroom are selected by either (a) clicking and then dragging the item to its allotted location on the stockroom counter or (b) double-clicking on the item. Similarly, an item can be returned to the shelf by clicking and dragging or by double-clicking. If a source, sample, or detector is already on the stockroom counter or out in the laboratory, then another source, sample, or detector cannot be selected. Modifiers are handled somewhat differently since the electric and magnetic field modifiers can be combined, but the heater can only be out in the laboratory by itself without an electric or magnetic field modifier.

A liquid, metal foil, or gas sample is added to its corresponding holder by (a) clicking on the respective liquid bottles, box of foils, or gas cylinders (which brings up an enlarged view of the containers) and then (b) clicking on the appropriate sample. There are 8 available liquids, 41 metal foils, and 10 gases. Mousing over the sample holder while the holder is on the stockroom counter or out in the laboratory will generate a pop-up identifying the current sample in the holder.

While in the stockroom, a sample can be removed from a sample holder in several ways: (1) the sample is automatically removed when the sample holder is dragged back to the shelf, (2) double clicking on the sample holder while on the stockroom counter removes the sample but keeps the holder in place on the counter, or (3) the sample holder can be dragged and then dropped on the disposal bucket in the stockroom.

Preset Experiments

When allowed by the instructor, the clipboard gives access to a list of 15 fundamental experiments that are predefined and ready to run. To select one of these experiments, click the clipboard and then click the desired experiment. The necessary equipment will be automatically selected and placed on the stockroom counter. Clicking the *Return to Lab* arrow will then automatically place the equipment on the optics table in the laboratory and start the experiment. If, after having selected the preset experiment from the clipboard, the equipment on the stockroom counter is touched before returning to the laboratory, the preset nature of the experiment will be turned off and the equipment will have to be placed manually in the laboratory.

The following point should be kept in mind: The 15 preset experiments that are included with the installation cover most of the fundamental experiments that lead to the development of atomic theory and quantum mechanics. These preset experiments are only a small set of the large number of experiments that can be designed and implemented in this simulation.

Electronic Lab Book

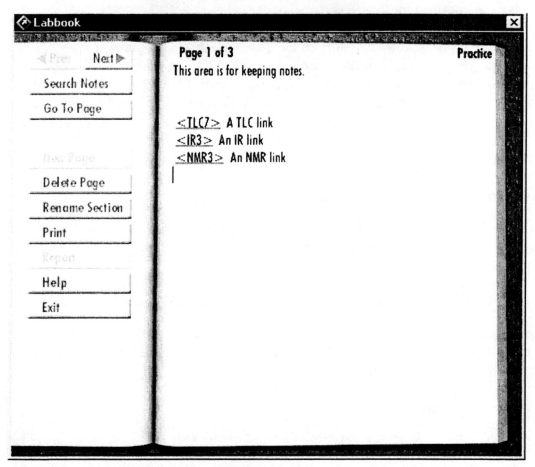

Figure 1. The electronic lab book used by the student to record notes.

Overview

The laboratory notebook (shown in Figure 1) is used to write and save experimental procedures and observations for each student. In addition, detector output from the quantum laboratory can also be saved in the lab book as well. The notebook is organized by sections and pages. The section name and current page number for the section are listed at the top of the page. New pages can be created as needed for each section. The default section is labeled *Practice* and is always the section that is available to the student with a student version of the program.

Typing/Editing Notes and Inserting Links

To start recording notes on the current page, click the page until a cursor appears. Notes can be typed as normal until the bottom of the page. New pages are not automatically created. Text can be inserted past the end of the page (and accessed using the arrow keys), but text that extends beyond the end of the page is *not* accessible to the instructor during grading. Text is always inserted when typed, and text can be deleted with both the forward and backward delete keys. Blocks of text can be marked using conventional methods, which in turn, can be cut, copied, and pasted using Ctrl-x, Ctrl-c, and Ctrl-v, respectively, for PC computers or Cmd-x, Cmd-c, and Cmd-v for Macintosh. Mouse clicks or arrow keys are used to move around on the page. No other keys are defined for the lab book.

When you generate detector output from the quantum laboratory, you can save these results to the lab book by pressing the *Save* or *Record* button on the appropriate window. Each detector output saved in the lab book is saved as a link (in blue or red) with a unique label and is placed on the last line of the current page. Clicking a link displays the saved item as it was originally shown in the laboratory. Links can be deleted from the lab book by deleting the *entire* link label, and links can be moved by adding or deleting text around a link. Links cannot be moved using cut (or copy) and paste commands.

Navigation

Moving around inside the lab book from page to page and section to section is accomplished using the four buttons grouped at the top of the left page of the lab book. The functionality for each of these buttons is described in the sections that follow.

◄ Prev   Next ►   **Prev/Next**

The *Previous* and *Next* buttons are used to go to the previous or next page in the current section. If a page in either the downward or the upward direction is not available in the section, the button is grayed out and not active.

Search Notes   **Search Notes**

The *Search Notes* button is used to specify a word or an exact phrase that can be searched for in the current section or in the entire lab book. Shown on the right is the Search dialog area that is placed on the left page of the lab book when the *Search Notes* button has been pressed. The text box is used to enter the word or words that will be searched for. The *Search* button initiates the search for the word or words typed in the text box. If a match is found, the page with the match will be shown on the right page of the lab book with the match highlighted. Pressing the *Search* button again will search for the next occurrence. After a match has been found, pressing the *OK* button will close the Search dialog and switch the lab book to the new page. Pressing the *Cancel* button closes the Search dialog and keeps the lab book on the old page. The *Current Section* and *All Sections* radio buttons specify whether the search is to be made on the current section or over all sections in the lab book, respectively.

Go To Page   **Go To Page**

The *Go To Page* button is used to jump to any page in any of the sections in the lab book. Shown in the accompanying figure is the dialog box that is displayed when the *Go To Page* button is pressed. The first box lists the available sections in the lab book by name. Clicking one of these will then list the available pages for the highlighted section in the second box. Clicking one of the pages will switch the lab book to the indicated page and section. Pressing the *Cancel* button keeps the lab book on the old page.

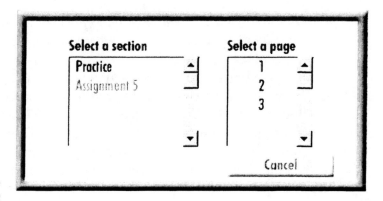

Functions

Grouped below the navigation buttons is a set of buttons that perform various functions in the lab book. These functions are described in the sections that follow.

New Page

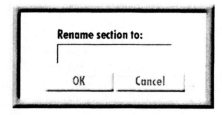

This button creates a new page at the end of the current section. The button is only active when you are on the last page of the section. Pages cannot be inserted elsewhere in the section.

Delete Page

This button deletes the current page in the currently selected section. A warning is given before the deletion occurs.

Rename Section

This buttons brings up a dialog box that allows the name of the current section to be changed. By default, the first section in the lab book is given the name *Practice*, and other sections that are added to the lab book for each assignment are given the name *Assignment n* where *n* represents the assignment number. The practice section is for keeping notes when exploring and learning in the laboratory, and the assignment sections are used for keeping notes during assignments and are eventually graded by the instructor. The *Rename Section* function allows these default names to be changed.

Print

This button brings up a dialog box that allows either the current page or the current section to be printed to a user-selected printer. IR and NMR spectra and TLC images cannot be printed.

Report

This button allows the current assignment that is out in the laboratory to be submitted to the instructor for grading and is only active when an assignment is out in the laboratory. Upon submitting an assignment for grading, further modifications to the assignment section are locked out and an extra page is added to the end of the section containing grading information specific to the assignment. The exception to this is when an Inorganic practice unknown is submitted which only reveals the actual contents of the unknown and no grading is performed.

- *Inorganic Assignments.* Pressing the *Report* button for an inorganic assignment brings up a report window (shown in Figure 2) where the possible cations in the unknown are listed. To report the contents of the unknown, click the appropriate tiles corresponding to the cations present in the unknown. For assigned unknowns, these selections can be saved by pressing the *Save* button allowing the user to return to the lab for further work on the unknown. The *Save* button is disabled for practice unknowns. When the assigned or practice unknown is ready for grading, click the *Submit* button, which in turn, brings up a warning box stating that no further modifications can be made to the assignment. Clicking *OK* submits the unknown and then marks each cation in the unknown as correct (green) or incorrect (red). For assigned unknowns, the score is also posted, and the entire grading report is written on the last page of the assignment section.

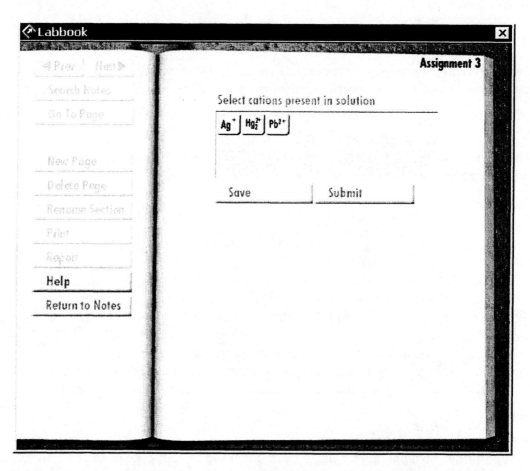

Figure 2. The report window for reporting inorganic assignments. Use the *Return to Notes* button to cancel the submission process.

- *Quantum Assignments.* Pressing the *Report* button for a quantum assignment brings up a text box warning the student that submitting an assignment prevents further modification of the assignment section. Selecting *OK* brings up a second warning box which, when *OK* is selected again, submits the assignment, closes the lab book, and clears the laboratory. Grading information is placed on the last page of the section.

Instructor Utilities

Figure 1. The stockroom main screen. The upper two drawers of the filing cabinet access class management functions, the bottom drawer accesses database backup and restore functions as well as other utilities, and the stack of lab books access grading functions. Click the bell for help.

Overview

The stockroom (Figure 1), as entered via the stockroom door in the hallway, is the laboratory management side of *Virtual ChemLab* and is used by an instructor to establish classes, make assignments, and view the results, grades, and lab books of the students. Access to this part of the stockroom (or *Instructor Utilities*) is allowed only to those individuals with administrative rights. The stockroom is divided into three main areas or functions:

(1) Class Management;

(2) Grading;

(3) Utilities.

Brief descriptions of these areas are given.

Class Management

Class Management functions are accessed by clicking one of the top two drawers of the filing cabinet. Some of the functions available in these drawers include creating classes, managing access privileges, defining assignments for the different labs, and viewing scores and lab books.

Grading

The grading of a specific assignment for an entire class is accessed by clicking the stack of lab books on the desk. Depending on the type of assignment being graded, various options are available to make the assignment of scores as painless as possible.

Utilities

Since the class lists, assignments, scores, and lab books are stored in a centralized database, basic backup and restore functions are available to protect against accidental or intentional corruption of the database. These functions are accessed by clicking the bottom drawer of the filing cabinet. Other functions include broadcasting messages to a class or set of classes and enabling Web connectivity.

Database

The database that contains the classes, students, assignments, scores, and lab books is kept in the *Data* directory inside the main installed *Virtual ChemLab* directory. The database is stored as encrypted text files and cannot be accessed or modified without the encryption key. All login information is stored in a separate file, and student lists, assignments, and scores are stored in files for each individual class. A separate subdirectory is created for each student inside the *Data* directory and contains the data for each student's lab book. Because the database is centralized and contains important grading information, simple backup and restore functionality has been added to protect against accidental or intentional corruption of the database. The backup and restore functions are not intended to protect against hardware failures.

Note: Multiple instances of the *Instructor Utilities* can be open at any given time. However, during grading, adding classes and students, and making assignments it is highly recommended that only one instance of *Instructor Utilities* is open at a time. This will insure that all updated database information has been recorded correctly.

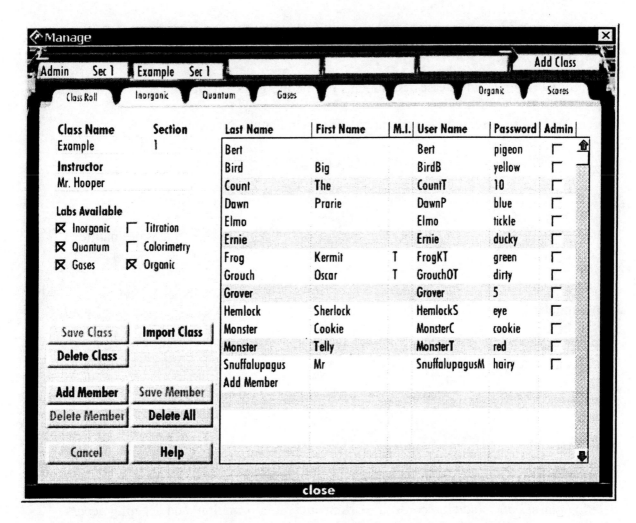

Figure 2. The Class Management drawer showing the Class Roll manila folder.

Class Management

Class management functions are accessed by clicking one of the top two drawers of the filing cabinet. Inside the drawer, there are several green hanging folders and eight manila folders within the hanging folders. Each hanging folder represents a class (a collection of students), and each manila folder represents a management function for the selected class. The class management drawer is closed by clicking the bottom of the drawer where it is labeled *close*. Closing the drawer brings the instructor back to the main stockroom.

Classes are selected by clicking the hanging folder label for the indicated class (which brings that label forward). The green arrows to the left and right of the hanging folders cycle through the list of classes five classes at a time. A new class is created by clicking the *Add Class* hanging folder. Details on adding and managing classes follow.

The eight manila folders in each hanging folder perform specific class management functions. A brief description of each folder is given. Details are found in their respective help sections.

Class Roll. Add and delete classes; add, delete, and import students; specify access IDs; assign administrative privileges (stockroom access).

Inorganic. Define and release assignments for the inorganic qualitative analysis laboratory.

Quantum. Define and release assignments for the quantum experiments.

Gases. * Define and release assignments for the gases experiments.

Titration. * Define and release assignments for the titration experiments.

Calorimetry. * Define and release assignments for the calorimetry or thermodynamic experiments.

Organic. Define and release assignments for organic synthesis and organic qualitative analysis experiments.

Scores. View scores assigned to each student for each assignment, export scores, view lab books, and determine availability of lab books for grading.

*Features available in future releases.

Class Roll

Overview
The class roll folder contains class and student information as well as functions for adding and deleting classes and student records, importing student information, and defining access privileges. (See Figure 2.) The folder is divided into three areas:

   (1) class information,

   (2) function buttons, and

   (3) a spreadsheet view of student records.

Details on the three areas of the folder are given in their respective sections which follow. An overview of the routine or common functions performed in the class roll folder is described here.

Adding a Class. A new class is added by clicking the hanging folder labeled *Add Class* followed by filling in the Class Name, Section, and Instructor text boxes. Pressing *Tab* or *Enter* automatically advances to the next text box. Pressing *Tab* or *Enter* in the Instructor text box saves the class information. The laboratories that will be accessed by this class must also be selected.

Adding Students. Students can be added individually by clicking the *Add Member* button or by clicking the *Add Member* listed at the end of the spreadsheet. Students can also be imported from a tab-delimited text file.

Deleting a Class. The currently selected class can be deleted by clicking the *Delete Class* button.

Deleting Students. The currently highlighted member can be deleted by clicking the *Delete Member* button.

Modifying Information. Class information or member information can be modified by clicking the appropriate text box and typing the correction. The *Save Class* or *Save Member* button, respectively, must be pressed to save the modified information.

Note on Organizing Classes. Since only a few individuals require access to the stockroom to make assignments and grade lab books, it is suggested that a separate administrative class be created for those who require access to the stockroom. Selecting the *Admin* box next to an individual listed in the spreadsheet grants access to the stockroom.

Class Information

The class information area shows the class name, section number, instructor name, and the selected (and available) laboratory experiments for the selected hanging folder. (See Figure 2.) The class name, section number, and instructor can be modified by clicking the appropriate text box. Pressing *Tab* or *Enter* advances the cursor to the next text box except after the instructor box which, instead, saves the class information to the database. Pressing the *Save Class* button also saves the class information to the database. It is not necessary to perform a *Save Class* when selecting the experiments that will be available to the class. These changes are saved automatically.

Function Buttons

These buttons perform most of the class roll functionality and are shown in Figure 2. A detailed description of these buttons is given.

Save Class. This button is active when text is being entered or modified in the class information text boxes. Pressing this button saves the currently entered information in all three text boxes.

Import Class. This button is used to import members into the currently selected class using a tab-delimited text file. Clicking the button brings up a dialog box which allows the import file to be located and selected. If errors are found during the import process, an error file is created (and placed in the installed *Virtual ChemLab* directory) and an appropriate error message is displayed. The format of the import file is as follows:

Last		First		MI	Username		Password
Frog	[Tab]	Kermit	[Tab]	T	[Tab]	[Tab]	green
Bird	[Tab]	Big	[Tab]		[Tab]	[Tab]	yellow
Grouch	[Tab]	Oscar	[Tab]	T	[Tab]	[Tab]	dirty
Ernie	[Tab]		[Tab]		[Tab]	[Tab]	ducky
Bert	[Tab]		[Tab]		[Tab]	[Tab]	pigeon
Etc.							

Only the last name and password are required with four [Tab]s on each line. Class members that are imported are always given student access rights. An import file can easily be created by importing a class list into a spreadsheet program, editing the list to the preceding format, and saving the list as a tab-delimited text file.

Delete Class. This button deletes the currently selected class. A warning is given before the deletion occurs.

Add Member. This button adds a member to the currently selected class. Text entry starts on the left with the last name and proceeds to the right by pressing *Tab* or *Enter*. The mouse can also be used to advance to the next field. Pressing *Tab* or *Enter* after the ID has been entered, saves the member automatically to the database. Pressing the *Save Member* button will also save the member.

Save Member. When a new member is being added to a class or member information is being modified, this button saves the current entries to the database.

Delete Member. This button deletes the currently selected member. A warning is given before the deletion occurs.

Delete All. This button deletes all the members in the currently selected class without deleting class information. A warning is given before the deletion occurs.

Cancel. This button cancels text entry in any of the class information or member information text boxes.

Help. This button accesses the help screen for class rolls.

Student Records

The list of members for the class is given in the spreadsheet. Listed for each member is the last name, first name, middle initial, username, password (usually the student ID), and administrative privileges. A member can be added by clicking the *Add Member* at the end of the spreadsheet (which may not be visible if the list is long) or by pressing the *Add Member* button. The last name and password (or ID) are required for each member. The first name and middle initial are optional. The username is generated automatically, but it can also be specified. The password is used by the member to gain access to the different laboratories in *Virtual ChemLab* and must be unique to each member. Clicking the *Admin* box for a member gives that person administrative privileges, which means they can enter the stockroom and create, modify, and delete classes, students, and assignments.

When adding a member, text entry is started on the left with the last name and proceeds to the right by pressing *Tab* or *Enter*. The mouse can also be used to advance to the next field. Pressing *Tab* or *Enter* after the password has been entered saves the member automatically to the database. Pressing the *Save Member* button will also save the member. The information for a member can be modified by clicking the appropriate text box and pressing *Tab* or *Enter* until the password is saved or by pressing the *Save Member* button. Scrolling through the member list is accomplished using the scroll bar.

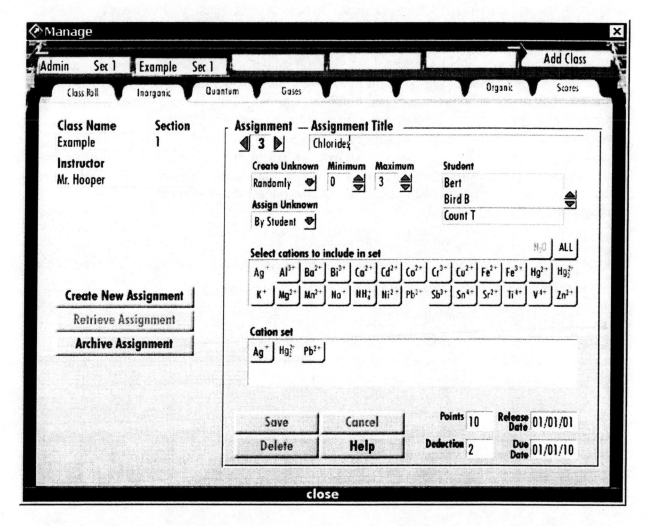

Figure 3. The Inorganic Assignment folder showing a *Random/By Student* assignment.

Inorganic Assignments

Overview

The inorganic assignment folder allows the instructor to define and release inorganic qualitative analysis unknowns to the class in the inorganic laboratory. These unknowns (or assignments) are given to the students in the left slot of the unknown rack in the inorganic stockroom, and the student's work on these assignments is recorded (by the student) in the lab book. A new section is created in the lab book for each assignment accepted by the student. A student reports their unknown by pressing the *Report* button in the lab book and then selecting the cations they determined to be present based on their analysis. After submitting their results, a score is automatically computed by subtracting points for each incorrect positive or negative result. This score can be changed at a later time if necessary.

Each unknown is made up of a set of cations that has been selected by the instructor and constitutes the cations the students will be trying to separate and identify. The instructor can assign unknowns to the students in four different ways, but the different types of unknowns only differ by how the actual cations are assigned to the students. These four unknown types are *Random/By Class*, *Random/By Student*, *Manual/By Class*, and *Manual/By Student* where *Random* means the cations are assigned to the students randomly based on certain criterion, *Manual* means the cations are assigned manually by the instructor, *By Student* means a different unknown (but from the same set of cations) is assigned to each student, and *By Class* means each student in the class receives the same unknown. As part of the assignment, the instructor must also specify the total points possible, the number of points deducted per wrong answer, the date the assignment will be available to the students (the release date), and the date when the assignment is due.

The inorganic assignment folder is shown in Figure 3 and can be divided into three general areas: (a) class information, (b) assignment/archive buttons, and (c) the assignment area. The following details are on these three areas.

Class Information
In the upper-left of the inorganic assignment folder is the class information area where information on the currently selected class is given, followed by three buttons that are used to create, retrieve, or archive inorganic assignments. Class information cannot be modified in this folder.

Assignment/Archive Buttons
Create New Assignment. This button creates a blank assignment, which can be defined by the instructor and then released to the class. Details on defining an inorganic assignment are given in the *Assignments* section.

Retrieve Assignment. This button retrieves an inorganic assignment from a set of assignments that have been previously archived. Details on archiving and retrieving inorganic assignments are given in the *Archiving and Retrieving Assignments* section.

Archive Assignment. This button saves or archives the currently selected or defined inorganic assignment. Details on archiving and retrieving inorganic assignments are given in the *Archiving and Retrieving Assignments* section.

Assignments
The general procedure for creating an assignment includes the following steps:

1. Create a blank assignment using the *Create New Assignment* button. (This is not necessary if it is the first assignment.)

2. Enter a title for the assignment.

3. Specify the assignment as *Random/By Class*, *Random/By Student*, *Manual/By Class*, or *Manual/By Student*.

4. Define the cation set.

5. Assign the unknowns as appropriate for the assignment type. (See #3.)

6. Assign the points possible, points for deductions, the release date, and the due date.

The assignment area can be divided into the following parts: (a) Assignment Number, (b) Assignment Title, (c) Assignment Type, (d) Student List, (e) Cation Set, (f) Function Buttons, and (g) Points, Deductions, Release Date, and Due Date. Each of these are described in the following list:

(a) *Assignment Number.* The number of the current assignment is shown in the assignment number box. Assignments that have already been created can be accessed using the left and right arrows next to the box. It can take several seconds to update the assignment information as each assignment is accessed. Rapidly advancing through the assignments bypasses the assignment update for each intermediate assignment. The assignment number only reflects the order in which they were created. The release date determines when they are accessible to the students.

(b) *Assignment Title.* Each assignment must be given a title. The title is intended as an aid to identify the type of unknown that has been assigned, and it is also used as the default name when archiving the assignment. (See *Archiving and Retrieving Assignments* for details.) Assignment titles are entered by clicking the text box and typing the appropriate text.

(c) *Assignment Type.* The type of assignment is selected by clicking the **Create Unknown** and **Assign Unknown** drop-down menus. The **Create Unknown** menu allows the unknown to be assigned *Randomly* or *Manually*, and the **Assign Unknown** menu allows the unknown to be assigned *By Student* or *By Class*. The combination of these two drop-down menus yields the four different types of unknowns: *Random/By Class*, *Random/By Student*, *Manual/By Class*, or *Manual/By Student*.

(1) *Random Assignment.* In a *Random* assignment, the cations that have been selected for the cation set (see *Cation Set* below) are assigned randomly based on the *Minimum* and *Maximum* parameters. (See Figure 3.) The *Minimum* and *Maximum* parameters only appear on the folder when a *Random* unknown has been selected. The *Minimum* parameter defines the minimum number of cations that can be assigned from the cation set. A "1" would indicate that no fewer than one cation would be present in the unknown out of the cations in the cation set, a "2" would mean that no fewer than two cations would be in the unknown, and so on. A special case of "0" (zero) is allowed and indicates that no cations or a water unknown could be assigned. Similar to the *Minimum* parameter, the *Maximum* parameter defines the maximum number of cations that can be assigned as an unknown from the cation set. Some restrictions to these parameters include (i)

299

Maximum cannot be greater than the number of cations in the set and (ii) *Minimum* cannot be greater than *Maximum*. The *Minimum* and *Maximum* parameters are adjusted by clicking the up and down arrows next to each parameter.

(2) *Manual Assignment*. In a *Manual* assignment, an unknown is assigned by selecting the cations for each unknown manually from the cations in the cation set. (See *Cation Set.*) Cations are selected from the cation set by clicking the cation tiles in the Cation Set box.

(3) *By Class*. When an assignment is given by class, then every student in the class will receive the same unknown. For a *Random* assignment, the unknown is randomly selected from the cation set, and for a *Manual* assignment, the cations in the unknown are selected manually.

(4) *By Student*. When an assignment is given by student, then every student in the class will receive a unique unknown. For a *Random* assignment, each unknown is randomly selected from the cation set, and for a *Manual* assignment, the cations in each unknown are selected manually for each student.

(d) *Student List*. A student list (see Figure 3) is provided for *By Student* assignments, for making *Manual* (or individual) assignments and to show the unknowns that have been assigned to each student. The list shows three students. The middle student in the box is the currently selected student, and there is a student before and after. Student names in red indicate an assignment has not been given, whereas student names in blue indicate an assignment has been given. The up and down arrows are used to scroll through the list. When an assignment has been made (name in blue), the cations that have been assigned to that student are highlighted in the Cation Set box. Changes in the assignments can be made up until the release date.

(e) *Cation Set*. Before an unknown can be given to the students in the class, a cation set must be defined. This is done by selecting cations from the Cation List and placing them in the Cation Set box. Cations are selected by either (i) clicking and dragging a cation tile from the list to the Cation Set box or (ii) clicking the cation tile in the Cation List. Cations can be removed from the Cation Set box and returned to the list by clicking and dragging from the Cation Set to the Cation List or by double-clicking the desired tile in the set. For *Manual* assignments, cations are assigned from the Cation Set box by clicking once on the desired cation tiles. For a *By Class* assignment, this cation selection process is only done once. For a *By Student* assignment, the cation selection process must be done for each student. Pressing *Save* saves the assignment for the indicated student (see *Student List*) and automatically advances the student list to the next student. For a *Random* assignment, cations in the Cation Set box cannot be selected manually, but once the assignment has been saved, the depressed tiles in the Cation Set box indicate the cations that have been assigned to the class or to the indicated student.

(f) *Function Buttons*. The four function buttons are *Save*, *Cancel*, *Delete*, and *Help*. The *Save* button saves the current assignment. For *Random* assignments, pressing the *Save* button actually assigns the unknowns to the class (*By Class*) or to each student (*By Student*). The

Cancel button resets the current assignment to a blank assignment if it has not yet been saved; otherwise, it restores the assignment to its last saved state. The *Delete* button deletes an assignment that has not been released, and the *Help* button opens the help window for inorganic assignments.

(g) *Points, Deductions, Release Date, and Due Date.* The points, deductions, release date, and due date for the assignment are specified in these text boxes. The points are the total numbers of points assigned for the assignment, and the deductions are the numbers of points to be deducted for each wrong answer by the student (either a false positive or false negative). The minimum score possible is zero. By default, text entry starts in the title box and pressing *Tab* or *Enter* advances the cursor to the points box, then the deductions box, then the release date, and then the due date. Pressing *Tab* or *Enter* in the due date box automatically saves the assignment. The release date is the date (starting at midnight) the assignment will be available to the students, and the due date is the last day the assignment will be available (ending at midnight). The format for the entered dates must correspond to *MM/DD/YY* where *MM* is a two-digit month, *DD* is a two-digit day, and *YY* is a two-digit year. An assignment cannot be modified once it has been released to the students, but it is possible to change the release date or due date. Changing the release date allows a previously released assignment to be modified, but unpredictable consequences may occur if students have started accepting assignments.

Archiving and Retrieving Assignments

Defining an inorganic qualitative analysis unknown can be a time-consuming and laborious process, especially if there are several unknowns and there are several classes for which these unknowns need to be defined. To make this process less time consuming, inorganic assignments can be archived, or saved, and then retrieved using the *Archive Assignment* and *Retrieve Assignment* buttons.

To archive an assignment, define an inorganic assignment following the steps and procedures that were described in the *Assignments* section. Pressing the *Archive Assignment* button will save the cation set, the assignment type, the assignment title, the points, and the deductions. A dialog box will come up asking for a name for the archive and where to save it. The assignment archive can be stored anywhere, but the default location is the *Assignment /Inorganic* directory located where the database is stored. Any number of archives can be stored with any combination of unknowns.

To retrieve an assignment, an inorganic assignment must first be created. Pressing the *Retrieve Assignment* button will bring up a dialog box where the instructor may select from any of the available archives. Selecting an archive will automatically define the assignment based on the information that was saved during the archive. At this point, the release date and due date for the assignment must still be specified, and the actual unknowns must be assigned to the students by saving the assignment (pressing the *Save* button) for a *Random* assignment or by selecting the cations from the cation set for a *Manual* assignment.

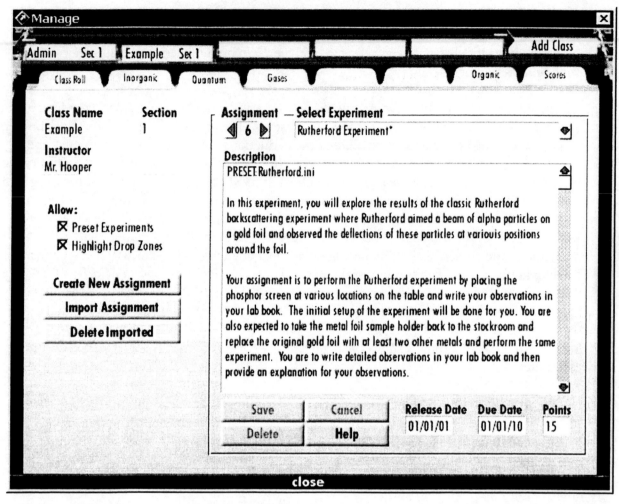

Figure 4. The Quantum Assignments folder.

Quantum Assignments

Overview

The quantum assignment folder allows the instructor to define and release text-based instructions (or assignments) for performing a number of simulated experiments that demonstrate many of the concepts and ideas that led to the development of quantum mechanics. The level of these experiments can be very basic or very sophisticated, depending on the level of the class and the purpose for performing the experiments. These assignments are given to the students using the clipboard in the quantum stockroom, and the student's work on these assignments is recorded (by the student) in the lab book. A new section is created in the lab book for each assignment accepted by the student.

The purpose of the quantum laboratory is to allow a student to explore and better understand the foundational experiments that led up to the development of quantum mechanics. Because of the very sophisticated nature of most of these experiments, the quantum laboratory is the most "virtual" of the *Virtual ChemLab* laboratory simulations. In general, the laboratory consists of an optics table where various sources, samples, modifiers, and detectors can be placed to perform different experiments. These devices are located in the stockroom and can be taken out of the stockroom and placed on the optics table. The emphasis here is to teach the students to probe a sample (e.g., a gas, metal foil, two-slit screen, etc.) with a source (e.g., a laser, electron gun, alpha-particle source, etc.) and detect the outcome with a specific detector (a phosphor screen, spectrometer, etc.). Heat, electric fields, or magnetic fields can also be applied to modify an aspect of the experiment. As in all *Virtual ChemLab* laboratories, the focus is to allow students the ability to explore and discover, in a safe and level-appropriate setting, the concepts that are important in the various areas of chemistry. Complete details on the quantum laboratory, its use and limitations, and the scope of the simulations can be found in the *Quantum User's Guide*.

Because these physical chemistry experiments can be complex and not necessarily intuitive to set up properly, a set of 15 preset experiments has been defined and is accessible to the student through the clipboard in the stockroom. These preset experiments are defined using a set of INI variables that describe the various aspects of each experiment. Details on how to change the preset experiments are found in Appendix A. These preset experiments can also be turned off as will be described later.

Assignments in the quantum laboratory consist of a set of instructions outlining what is required of the students to complete the assignment. These assignments are text based, and when a student accepts the assignment it is displayed on the clipboard. If the student decides to proceed, the assignment is displayed in the laboratory TV for reference during the experiment. As installed, *Virtual ChemLab: Quantum* comes with a set of predefined assignments with varying levels of difficulty. However, the number and difficulty of experiments that can be performed in the quantum laboratory is enormous; therefore, the ability to import custom assignments and add them to the database of assignments has also been provided. These custom assignments can also include custom preset experiments.

Shown in Figure 4 is an example of a quantum assignment folder. The folder can be divided into two general areas: (1) laboratory setup and (2) assignments. Details on these two areas of the folder are given in their respective sections.

Laboratory Setup

The laboratory setup area of the quantum assignment folder consists of a class information area for the currently selected class at the top, followed by the laboratory setup options, followed by three buttons that are used to create a new assignment, import a custom assignment, and delete a custom assignment. Class information cannot be modified in this folder.

Preset Experiments. The clipboard in the quantum stockroom contains a list of 15 preset experiments that the student can select to automatically set up experiments out in the laboratory. Deselecting this option will turn off access to these preset experiments. Details on modifying the preset experiments available to the students are found in Appendix A. This setting can be changed at any time.

Highlight Drop Zones. When individual items of equipment are brought from the stockroom counter to the optics table, there are specific positions that are allowed for each type of equipment. To help the student see where these allowed drop zones are located, spotlights appear on the optics table indicating the allowed positions as each item is dragged from the stockroom counter and dropped on the optics table. Deselecting this setting turns off the spotlights. This setting can be changed at any time.

Create New Assignment. This button creates a blank assignment that can be defined by the instructor and then released to the class. Details on defining assignments are given in the *Assignments* section.

Import Assignment. Virtual ChemLab: Quantum comes with a set of predefined assignments with varying levels of difficulty that demonstrate the concepts and ideas that led up to the development of quantum mechanics (and beyond). However, it is recognized that the types of experiments and their level of difficulty will most often need to be custom tailored for the level of the class, the level of the students, and the individual teaching style of the instructor. This button allows a custom assignment to be imported into the quantum assignment database. Pressing the button brings up a dialog box, which allows the instructor to locate the new assignment file and then bring it into the quantum assignment database. Once the file has been successfully imported, it is not necessary to keep the original file. This import file must be a text- (or ASCII-) based file with the following format:

[Assignment with a preset experiment]

1 Assignment Title
2
3 PRESET:preset_file.ini
4
5 Descriptive text of assignment without hard-returns except at paragraphs.

[Assignment without a preset experiment]

1 Assignment Title
2
3 Descriptive text of assignment without hard-returns except at paragraphs.

The first line is the assignment title and will be used to identify the assignment in the assignment list (see Figure 4) and on the clipboard in the stockroom. The second line must be blank. The third line is an optional line. If the word "PRESET:" is present on the third line followed by a preset experiment file, then, when the assignment is accepted by the student, the preset experiment will be set up automatically in the laboratory after exiting the stockroom. An assignment does not necessarily have to have a preset assignment. It is only meant as an option that allows different levels of experiments to be assigned to the students. If the PRESET: line is missing then the third line in the text file is assumed to be the beginning of the assignment description. If the PRESET: line is wrong or an invalid or missing file is found, the third line is also interpreted as the beginning of the assignment description. Preset experiments for assignments **must** be located in the *Assignment/Quantum* directory located in the installed *Virtual ChemLab* directory and must have the extension ".ini". Note also that there should be no space between the "PRESET:" and the file name. Details on defining preset experiments are found in Appendix A, although several have been included with the software.

Delete Imported. This button will delete the currently selected assignment (displayed in the assignment list) from the quantum assignment database *if* the selected assignment is an imported assignment. Imported assignments are identified with an "*" after the title. A warning will be given before the deletion is allowed to proceed.

Assignments
The general procedure for creating an assignment includes the following steps:

1. If the desired assignment is not present in the quantum assignment database, write the assignment using the format described and import the assignment.

2. Create a blank assignment using the *Create New Assignment* button. (This is not necessary if it is the first assignment.)

3. Select the desired experiment using the Select Experiment drop-down list.

4. Assign the points possible, the release date, and the due date.

Shown in Figure 4 is the assignment area for a quantum assignment. The parts of the assignment area are the following: (a) Assignment Number, (b) Select Experiment, (c) Description Box, (d) Function Buttons, and (e) Points, Release Date, and Due Date. Each of these is described in the following list:

(a) *Assignment Number.* The number of the current assignment is shown in the assignment number box. Assignments that have already been created can be accessed using the left and right arrows next to the box. It can take several seconds to update the assignment information as each assignment is accessed. Rapidly advancing through the assignments bypasses the assignment update for each intermediate assignment. The assignment number only reflects the order in which they were created. The release date determines when they are accessible to the students.

(b) *Select Experiment.* The list of available experiments in the quantum assignment database is contained in the Select Experiment drop-down list. Experiments are listed by title and sorted alphabetically. Experiments with an "*" at the end are imported assignments and can be deleted using the *Delete Imported* button. Experiments are selected by clicking the desired experiment. Currently selected experiments can be replaced by clicking a new experiment.

(c) *Description Box.* The description box contains the text of the actual experiment for review. No editing of the experiment description can be done in this box. If a preset experiment is indicated as part of the experiment, it will also be listed here, but not shown to the student.

(d) *Function Buttons.* The four function buttons are *Save, Cancel, Delete,* and *Help.* The *Save* button saves the current assignment. The *Cancel* button resets the current assignment to a blank assignment if it has not yet been saved; otherwise, it restores the assignment to its last saved state. The *Delete* button deletes an assignment that has not been released, and the *Help* button opens the help window for quantum assignments.

(e) *Points, Release Date, and Due Date.* The points, release date, and due date for the assignment are specified in these text boxes. By default, text entry starts in the release date box and pressing *Tab* or *Enter* advances the cursor to the due date and then the points box. Pressing *Tab* or *Enter* in the points box automatically saves the assignment. The release date is the date (starting at midnight) the assignment will be available to the students, and the due date is the last day the assignment will be available (ending at midnight). The format for the entered dates must correspond to *MM/DD/YY* where *MM* is a two-digit month, *DD* is a two-digit day, and *YY* is a two-digit year. An assignment cannot be modified once it has been released to the student, but it is possible to change the release date or due date. Changing the release date allows a previously released assignment to be modified, but unpredictable consequences may occur if students have started accepting assignments.

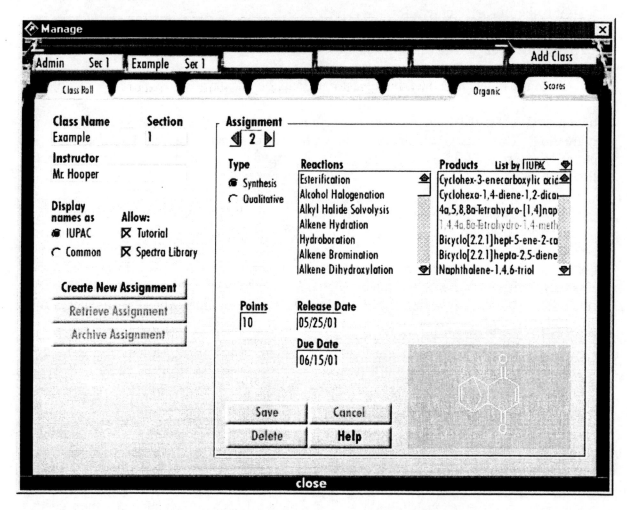

Figure 5. The Organic Assignment folder showing a synthesis assignment.

Organic Assignments

Overview

The organic assignment folder allows the instructor to define and release organic synthesis and organic qualitative analysis assignments to the class in the organic laboratory. These assignments are given to the students using the clipboard in the organic stockroom, and the student's work on these assignments is recorded (by the student) in the lab book. A new section is created in the lab book for each assignment accepted by the student.

In the organic laboratory, the instructor has the option to specify whether (a) compound names are listed as IUPAC names or common names, (b) if the TV tutorial is available to the student during practice sessions, and (c) if the spectra library is available to the students. These settings are independent of the assignments and can be changed at any time.

The instructor can assign to the students of a class any number of synthesis or qualitative analysis experiments. For either type of assignment, the instructor specifies the total points possible, the date the assignment will be available to the students (the release date), and the date

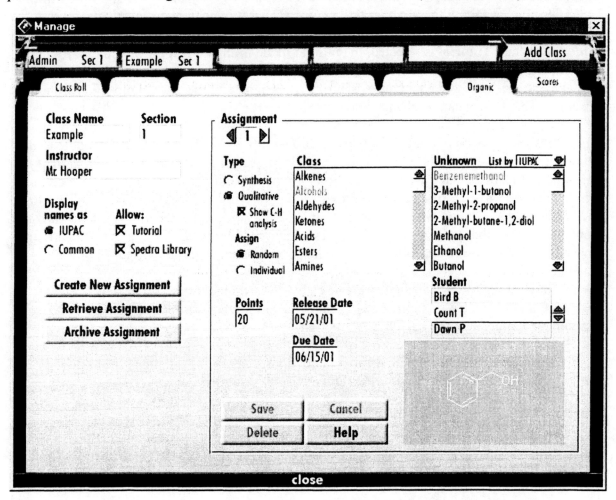

Figure 6. The Organic Assignment folder showing a qualitative analysis experiment.

when the assignment is due. A synthesis assignment involves selecting one of 17 different reactions, which defines a set of available starting materials, and a product that each student in the class will make, purify, and characterize. An organic qualitative analysis assignment involves assigning unknowns (compounds with an unknown structure) to each student either randomly or individually, and the student, in turn, will use the analytical techniques and functional group tests in the laboratory to determine the structure of the unknown. The organic assignment folder is divided into two areas: (1) laboratory setup and (2) assignments. Details on these two areas of the folder are given in their respective sections below.

Laboratory Setup

Shown in Figure 5 and Figure 6 is the laboratory setup area of the organic assignment folder. Information on the currently selected class is given at the top, followed by the laboratory setup options, followed by three buttons that are used to create assignments and retrieve or archive qualitative analysis assignments. Class information cannot be modified in this folder.

Display Names As. In various parts of the organic laboratory, the names of compounds are displayed either as pop-ups, on the chalkboard, or on the TV. Selecting **IUPAC** or **Common** specifies in what format these names will appear. This setting can be changed at any time.

Tutorial. When **Tutorial** is selected, the tutorial mode is enabled on the laboratory TV and the student has the ability to see the contents of different solutions on the lab bench when an assignment *is not* out in the laboratory. During an assignment, the tutorial mode is automatically disabled. This setting can be changed at any time.

Spectra Library. A library of approximately 700 FTIR and NMR spectra are available to the student through the spectra library option on the laboratory TV. Selecting **Spectra Library** allows the students to have access to this library in the laboratory and to save these spectra in their lab books. When a spectra is saved in the lab book from the spectra library, the spectra is clearly labeled as coming from the library. Note that the spectra for the qualitative unknowns are contained in the library; therefore, it is suggested that the library be disabled while qualitative analysis assignments are available to the students. This setting can be changed at any time.

Create New Assignment. This button creates a blank assignment that can be defined by the instructor and then released to the class. Details on defining a synthesis or qualitative analysis assignment are given in the *Assignments* section.

Retrieve Assignment. This button retrieves a qualitative analysis assignment from a set of assignments that have been previously archived. Details on archiving and retrieving qualitative analysis assignments are given in the *Archiving and Retrieving Assignments* section.

Archive Assignment. This button saves or archives the currently selected qualitative analysis assignment. Details on archiving and retrieving qualitative analysis assignments are given in the *Archiving and Retrieving Assignments* section.

Assignments

The general procedure for creating an assignment includes the following steps:

1. Create a blank assignment using the *Create New Assignment* button. (This is not necessary if it is the first assignment.)

2. Specify the type of the assignment as Synthesis or Qualitative Analysis.

3. For synthesis assignments, choose the reaction and product to be made by the students.

4. For qualitative analysis experiments, choose the set of unknowns (or retrieve an archive) and assign them to the students.

5. Assign the points possible, the release date, and the due date.

Shown in Figure 6 is the assignment area for a qualitative analysis assignment. A synthesis assignment screen is similar (shown in Figure 5) except for the contents of the two scroll boxes and the absence of the student list (described subsequently). The parts of the assignment area are the following: (a) Assignment Number; (b) Assignment Type; (c) Reactions/Class Scroll Box; (d) Products/Unknown Scroll Box; (e) Points, Release Date, and Due Date; (f) Student List; (g) Structure Display Box; and (h) Function Buttons. Each of these is described in the following list:

(a) *Assignment Number.* The number of the current assignment is shown in the assignment number box. Assignments that have already been created can be accessed using the left and right arrows next to the box. It can take several seconds to update the assignment information as each assignment is accessed. Rapidly advancing through the assignments bypasses the assignment update for each intermediate assignment. The assignment number only reflects the order in which they were created. The release date determines when they are accessible to the students.

(b) *Assignment Type.* The type of assignment is selected by clicking the Synthesis or Qualitative radio buttons. For a qualitative analysis assignment, additional information defining the assignment is also listed. **Show C–H Analysis** specifies whether a C–H analysis of the unknowns will be available to the student for this assignment. Qualitative analysis unknowns can be assigned randomly or individually. In a random assignment, a set of unknowns is defined by the instructor and then randomly assigned to each student in the class. In an individual assignment, an unknown can be selected for each student in the list.

(c) *Reactions Scroll Box.* For a synthesis assignment, the first scroll box is labeled as "Reactions" and lists 17 named reactions. These same reactions are listed on the clipboard in the organic stockroom. Selecting a reaction on the clipboard defines a set of starting materials from which the student is free to choose to perform a reaction. Although the starting materials were chosen to demonstrate the chemistry of the named reaction, the student is not forced to perform that reaction, but instead, can choose any of the 15 reagents in the laboratory to perform any other viable reaction. Thus, any named reaction (or starting material set) is capable of producing a number of products in addition to the products of the named reaction. Selecting a named reaction in the reactions scroll box defines a list of products (shown in the products scroll box) that can be assigned to the class to make from the starting material set. A reaction is chosen by clicking the appropriate reaction.

Class Scroll Box. For a qualitative analysis assignment, the first scroll box is labeled as "Class" and lists 11 classes of unknowns grouped by functional group. Selecting a functional group in the class scroll box defines a list of unknowns containing that functional group (shown in the unknown scroll box) that can be assigned to the students. A functional group is chosen by clicking the appropriate group.

(d) *Products Scroll Box.* Once a reaction has been selected, a list of the products that can be made from the starting material set for the reaction is listed in the products scroll box. (See Appendix B for a complete list.) The products that are listed first are products that correspond to the selected named reaction. Other products are also listed that demonstrate different reactions or selectivity, but can be made from the same selected starting materials using other reagents and reaction conditions. Clicking a product selects that product, but does not save the assignment. Above the products scroll box is a drop-down menu, which allows the products to be listed by IUPAC name or Common name.

Unknown Scroll Box. Once a class or functional group has been selected, a list of unknowns containing that functional group is listed in the unknown scroll box. (See Appendix C for a complete list of unknowns.) Within a class, unknowns are generally listed with single functional groups first followed by multiple functional group unknowns and from less difficult to more difficult. Above the unknown scroll box is a drop-down menu, which allows the products to be listed by IUPAC name or Common name. Unlike a synthesis assignment, where there is only one product that can be assigned, for a random assignment it is typical to select a set of unknowns, which, in turn, will be assigned randomly to the students. Sets of unknowns do not have to be restricted to one functional group, but can extend to other functional groups as well. A single unknown is selected by clicking the name. Multiple unknowns are selected by <u>Ctrl</u>-click (both for the Mac and PC) and ranges of unknowns are selected by <u>Shift</u>-click. For individual assignments, an unknown is assigned to each student by selecting a class (functional group) and a single unknown. After the unknown is selected, the assignment is automatically saved and the student list is advanced to the next student. This process should proceed until each student has an unknown.

(e) *Points, Release Date, and Due Date.* The points, release date, and due date for the assignment are specified in these text boxes. By default, text entry starts in the points box, and pressing *Tab* or *Enter* advances the cursor to the release date, and then the due date. Pressing *Tab* or *Enter* in the due date box automatically saves the assignment. The release date is the date (starting at midnight) the assignment will be available to the students, and the due date is the last day the assignment will be available (ending at midnight). The format for the entered dates must correspond to *MM/DD/YY,* where *MM* is a two-digit month, *DD* is a two-digit day, and *YY* is a two-digit year. An assignment cannot be modified once it has been released to the student, but it is possible to change the release date or due date. Changing the release date allows a previously released assignment to be modified, but unpredictable consequences may occur if students have started accepting assignments.

(f) *Student List.* For qualitative analysis assignments, a student list is provided for making individual assignments and to show the unknowns assigned to each student. The list shows three students. The middle student in the box is the currently selected student, and there is a student before and after. Student names in red indicate an assignment has not been given, whereas student names in blue indicate an assignment has been given. The up and down arrows are used to scroll through the list. When an assignment has been made (name in blue), the class and unknown are highlighted in the class and unknown scroll boxes, and the structure of the unknown is shown in the structure display box. Updating the assignment information as each student is accessed can take several seconds. Rapidly advancing through the students bypasses the assignment update for the intermediate students. Changes in the assignments can be made up until the release date.

(g) *Structure Display Box.* Mousing over a product or unknown listed in the product/unknown scroll box shows the structure of the compound in the structure display box. When a product has been selected, the structure is shown in the display box by default. For qualitative analysis unknowns, the structure of the unknown assigned to the selected student is shown by default in the display box.

(h) *Function Buttons.* The four function buttons are *Save, Cancel, Delete,* and *Help.* The *Save* button saves the current assignment. The *Cancel* button resets the current assignment to a blank assignment if it has not yet been saved; otherwise, it restores the assignment to its last saved state. The *Delete* button deletes an assignment that has not been released, and the *Help* button opens the help window for organic assignments.

Archiving and Retrieving Assignments

When defining a qualitative analysis assignment, the instructor is required to define a set of possible unknowns by selecting from the available set of compounds given in each class of unknown. This can be a time-consuming and laborious process, especially if these sets are large and need to be defined for several classes. To make this process more simple, these sets can be archived or saved and then retrieved using the *Archive Assignment* and *Retrieve Assignment* buttons. These buttons are only active for qualitative analysis assignments. Archiving is not possible for synthesis assignments.

To archive an assignment, define a qualitative analysis assignment following the steps and procedures that were described in the *Assignments* section. Pressing the *Archive Assignment* button will save the unknown set and the number of points allocated for the assignment. A dialog box will appear asking for a name for the archive and where to save it. The assignment archive can be stored anywhere, but the default location is the *Assignment /Organic* directory located where the database is stored. Any number of archives can be stored with any combination of unknowns.

To retrieve an assignment, a qualitative analysis assignment must first be created. Inside a qualitative analysis assignment, pressing the *Retrieve Assignment* button will bring up a dialog box where the instructor may select from any of the available archives. Selecting an archive will automatically define the set of unknowns based on the archive and allocate the number of points for the assignment if that was also saved as part of the archive. At this point, the release date and due date for the assignment must still be specified, and the actual unknowns must be assigned to the students by saving the assignment (pressing the *Save* button).

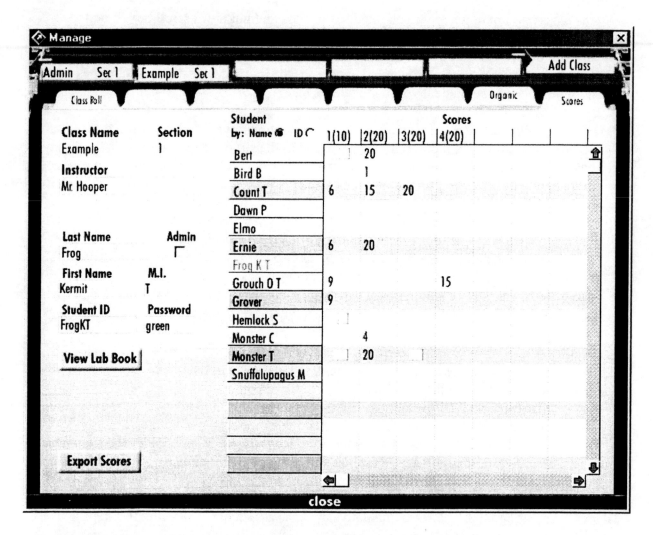

Figure 7. The Scores folder inside the Class Management drawer.

Scores

Overview

The scores folder (see Figure 7) shows the scores that have been earned by each student in the class for each assignment, allows these scores to be exported in a tab-delimited text file, shows the assignments that need to be graded, and allows the lab books to be inspected. The scores folder is divided into three areas: (1) class and student information, (2) function buttons, and (3) a spreadsheet view of student records. Each of these areas is described in the following sections.

Class and Student Information

Shown in Figure 7 is the class and student information area of the scores folder. Information on the currently selected class is given at the top, followed by detailed student information for the selected student in the spreadsheet. Class and student information cannot be modified in this folder.

Function Buttons

The two function buttons are *View Lab Book* and *Export Scores*. Selecting a student in the spreadsheet enables the *View Lab Book* button. Clicking *View Lab Book* brings up the lab book for the selected student starting in the *Practice* section. It is possible to record or modify scores for assignments that have been reported. See *Grading* for more details. The *Export Scores* button exports the current scores to a tab-delimited text file. A dialog box is used to specify the file name and path.

Student Records

The list of members is given in the spreadsheet with the assignments and points possible listed across the top. Members can be listed by Name or by ID (password). When an assignment has been reported by a student but has not been graded, a small lab book icon appears in the cell corresponding to the student and the assignment. The lab book icon indicates that an assignment is available for grading for that student. Clicking the lab book icon brings up the lab book for the student in the assignment section that needs to be graded. While in the lab book, it is possible to record a score for the assignment or simply view the lab book and then return to the scores folder. See *Grading* for more details. When a grade has been recorded for the assignment, the lab book icons are replaced with the actual score.

Grading

Overview

Each student is given an electronic lab book to record their notes and submit their results for grading. These lab books may be reviewed and graded (assigned a score) by (1) clicking the stack of lab books on the stockroom desk, (2) clicking a lab book icon in Scores, or (3) clicking the *View Lab Book* button in Scores. Each method launches the electronic lab book and allows the instructor to navigate through a student's notes, results, and conclusions and record grades for assignments. Each method differs, however, in how the students and assignments are selected.

The lab book is organized by sections and pages. The section name and current page number for the section is listed at the top of the page. The first section is labeled *Practice* and is always the section that is available to the student anytime an assignment is *not* out in the laboratory. When an assignment is accepted for the first time, a new section is created in the lab book (named with the assignment number) where only the notes associated with that assignment can be recorded. Each assignment will have its own section, and these sections can only be modified while the assignment is out in the laboratory. Once an assignment has been submitted for grading, no other modifications are allowed. After an assignment has been submitted, an extra page is added to the end of the section where grading information will be posted. This last page also contains the student's reported answers for unknowns.

Described in the following sections are the navigation tools for the lab book, recording scores, and the different methods the lab book can be accessed.

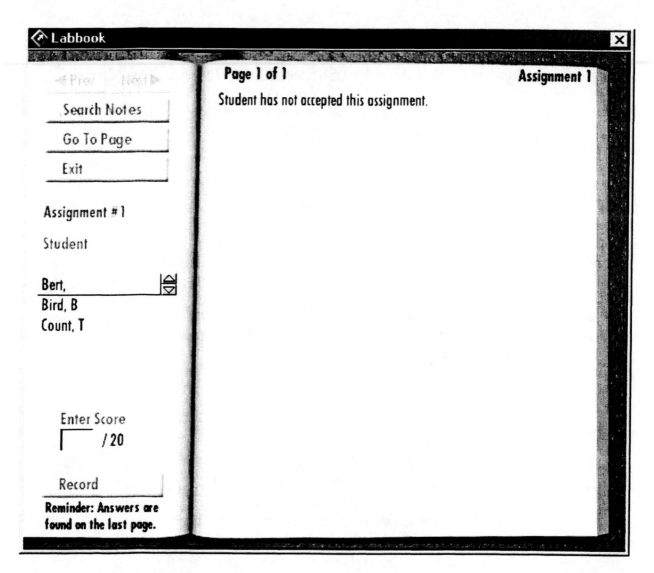

Figure 8.   The grading view of the lab book as accessed through the stack of lab books in the stockroom.

Navigation

Moving around inside the lab book from page to page and section to section is accomplished using the five buttons grouped at the top of the left page of the lab book. (See Figure 8.) The description of the functionality for each of these buttons follows.

The *Previous* and *Next* buttons are used to go to the previous or next page in the current section. If a page in either the downward or upward direction is not available in the section, the button is grayed out and not active.

The *Search Notes* button is used to specify a word or phrase that can be searched for in the current section or in the entire lab book. Shown on the right is the Search dialog area that is placed on the left page of the lab book when the *Search Notes* button has been pressed. The text box is used to enter the word or words that will be searched for in the current section or in all sections. The *Search* button initiates the search for the word or words typed in the text box. If a match is found, the page with the match will be shown on the right page of the lab book with the match highlighted. Pressing the *Search* button again will search for the next occurrence. After a match has been found, pressing the *OK* button will close the Search dialog and switch the lab book to the new page. Pressing the *Cancel* button closes the Search dialog and keeps the lab book on the old page. The *Current Section* and *All Sections* radio buttons specify whether the search is to be made on the current section or over all sections in the lab book, respectively.

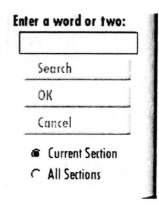

The *Go To Page* button is used to jump to any page in any of the sections in the lab book. Shown on the right is the Go To dialog box that is displayed when the *Go To Page* button is pressed. The first box lists the currently available sections in the lab book by name. Clicking one of these will then list the available pages for the highlighted section in the second box. Clicking one of the pages will switch the lab book to the indicated page and section. Pressing the *Cancel* button keeps the lab book on the old page.

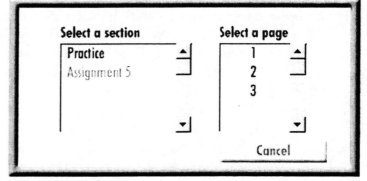

The *Exit* button exits the lab book.

Accessing the Lab Book

A student's lab book can be accessed in three ways.

1. *Stack of Lab Books*. Clicking the stack of lab books on the stockroom desk launches the electronic lab book with a dialog box (shown in the accompanying figure) that allows a specific class and assignment to be selected. The first box shows the current list of classes. Selecting one of these classes then lists in the second box the assignments that have been defined for the selected class. Selecting one of the assignments listed in the second box removes the dialog box and displays the lab book for the first student in the class with the lab book in the selected assignment section. (See Figure 8.) In the middle of the left page is a student list where the student shown in the box is the student to whom the current lab book belongs. Recording a score for this assignment

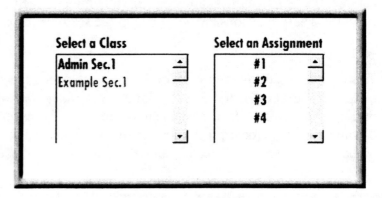

315

automatically advances the lab book to the next student. Other students in the class can also be accessed using the up and down arrow keys in the student list. Other assignments can be viewed or graded using the *Go To Page* button or the *Search Notes* button. Pressing *Exit* returns to the select class/select assignment dialog box.

2. *Lab Book Icon.* When an assignment has been reported by a student, but has not been graded, a small lab book icon is placed in the cell corresponding to the student and the assignment in the Scores spreadsheet. The lab book icon indicates that an assignment is available for grading for that student. Clicking the lab book icon brings up the lab book for the student in the assignment section that needs to be graded. Recording a score for the assignment replaces the lab book icon with the score in the spreadsheet.

3. *View Lab Book.* Selecting a student listed in the Scores spreadsheet and clicking the *View Lab Book* button brings up the lab book for the student starting in the *Practice* section. The assignment sections of the lab book can be accessed using the *Go To Page* button or the *Search Notes* button. Scores can be modified or recorded in the assignment sections.

Recording Scores

In assignment sections of the lab book, a score box and *Record* button are available at the bottom left page of the lab book. (See Figure 8.) If a score has already been recorded for the assignment, then the score is shown in the score box; otherwise, the score box is blank. A score is recorded or modified by (1) clicking the score box, typing the score, and pressing *Enter* or (2) clicking the *Record* button. A score can be recorded for an assignment even if the assignment has not been submitted; however, this will prevent the student from further work on the assignment even if the due date has not passed.

Utilities

Overview

Since the class lists, assignments, scores, and lab books are stored in a centralized database, basic backup and restore functions are available to protect against accidental or intentional corruption of the database. In addition to these database utilities, there is also a Message utility that allows an instructor to broadcast important information or reminders to the students of a selected class on the chalkboard in the organic laboratory or the chalkboard in the general chemistry laboratory. All of these functions are accessed by clicking the bottom drawer of the filing cabinet. Inside the utilities drawer are manila folders, each of which performs a specific utility function. These functions are described in the sections that follow.

Backup

The Backup folder contains a list of the 18 most recent backups listed by date and time with the most recent backups listed first. Clicking the *Perform Backup* button performs a complete backup of the current database. When the number of backups reaches 18, the oldest backup is discarded to make room for the newest backup. These backups are stored in the *Backup* directory in the *Virtual ChemLab* directory and, therefore, do not protect against hardware failures.

Restore All

The Restore All folder contains a list of the 18 most recent backups listed by date and time with the most recent backups listed first. Clicking one of the backups generates another list containing the classes that were stored in the selected backup. Clicking the *Restore All* button replaces the current database with the selected backup. A warning is given before the restore proceeds to delete the current database.

Restore Class

The Restore Class folder contains a list of the 18 most recent backups listed by date and time with the most recent backups listed first. Clicking one of the backups generates another list containing the classes that were stored in the selected backup. Unlike with Restore All, which restores an entire database, a single class can be selected and then restored by clicking the *Restore Class* button. A warning is given before the restore proceeds to delete the current class and replace it with a backup.

Reset

The reset folder simply contains a *Reset* button, which, when pressed, deletes the current database and resets it to a known state containing one class (Admin) and two members. One of the members has administrative privileges for access to the stockroom. It is important that after the reset operation, the new administrative password is either noted or changed so future access to the stockroom can be ensured.

Messages

When administering classes and assignments inside of *Virtual ChemLab*, it is sometimes necessary or useful to send out brief messages reminding the students of deadlines, giving them hints, or warning them of problems. The Messages folder (see Figure 9) allows an instructor to compose a message, select the classes where the message will be sent, and define at what time the message will be released to the student and when the message will expire. Messages that have been sent are displayed on the chalkboards in the general chemistry laboratory and in the organic laboratory. Multiple messages can be sent and made available to students at the same time. The process for creating and sending messages is divided into three steps: (a) Compose the message, (b) select the class or classes where the message will be sent, and (c) define when the message will be sent and when it will expire.

(a) *Composing a Message.* A new message is created by first clicking the *Create New Message* button (unless this is the first message, in which case the message area is already set up for a new message). The actual text to be sent to the students can be typed directly into the message box or can be pasted in from another program. The message can be as long as needed since scrolling will be available for the students at the chalkboards.

(b) *Selecting the Classes.* Once the message has been typed or entered, the classes for whom the message is intended must be selected. Located on the left of the Messages folder is a list of classes for the current database. Classes are selected by clicking the desired class. Multiple classes are selected by Ctrl-click (both for the Mac and PC) and a range of classes is selected by Shift-click.

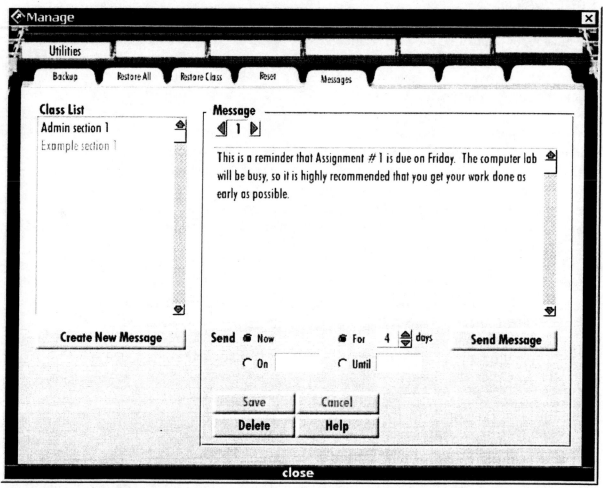

Figure 9.   The Messages folder as accessed from the Utilities drawer.

(c) *Sending the Message.* Once the message has been composed and the destination classes selected, the time of delivery for the message must be defined next. Below the message text box are the Send options. A message can be sent *Now* or *On* a specified date by selecting the appropriate radio button. If a date is specified, the date must follow the usual format of *MM/DD/YY,* where *MM* is a two-digit month, *DD* is a two-digit day, and *YY* is a two-digit year. The duration of the message or how long the message will be available to the selected classes is defined by specifying the number of days (from the send date) the message will be available or by specifying the *Until* date using the same format as described earlier. The message is not actually sent until the *Send Message* button is pressed.

(d) *Miscellaneous.* The number of the current message is shown in the message number box at the top of the folder. Messages that have already been created and saved can be accessed using the left and right arrows next to the box. It can take several seconds to update the message information as each message is accessed.

At the bottom of the Messages folder are the normal four buttons for *Save, Cancel, Delete,* and *Help*. The *Save* button will save the current message for later action. The *Cancel* button will cancel the current message or current changes and revert back to the previously saved state. The *Delete* button will delete the current message, and *Help* will access the Utilities Help screen.

Appendix A
INI Variables and Management Issues

Many of the functions and simulation parameters used in *Virtual ChemLab* are controlled by INI variables. INI variables are numerical or text settings that are contained in a small set of INI files found in the various *Virtual ChemLab* directories. These INI files are text-based files all with the extension ".ini" and can be viewed or edited in any simple text-based editor. It should be noted that in these INI files, variables are grouped together in sections by a header line with the format [*name*], where *name* is the name of the section. When adding INI variables to a file, the section names, if not already present in the file, must be added along with the new variables.

During the installation of *Virtual ChemLab*, these INI variables are set at what is considered to be the optimal settings for most applications. However, many of these INI variables can be changed to fit individual needs and applications. Given in this appendix is a description of most of these INI variables and how they fit within the greater scope of *Virtual ChemLab*. Along with a description of these INI variables, many issues associated with the management and implementation of *Virtual ChemLab* will also be discussed.

Database Path

When *Virtual ChemLab* is installed, a Chemlab.ini file is created in the main *Virtual ChemLab* directory that has the format

> [Database]
> DatabasePath = *path*\Data\   (PC)
> or
> DatabasePath = *path*:Data: (Mac)

where *path* is the path to the *Virtual ChemLab* directory chosen at the time of the installation. This INI variable points to the *Data* directory where the login, class management files, and electronic lab books are stored. For client installations, this variable points to the database on the server. For local installations, the variable points to the local database.

During a client installation, the installer creates this variable based on where the client installer was launched. If the installer was launched from the server in the *Virtual ChemLab* directory, then the variable should point to the correct database. If the client installer was copied to a removable media (say, a Zip drive), which is then used to install the client program, the INI variable will default to the removable media drive. During the installation, an option is given to enter the correct path for the server database. This path must include the \Data\ (:Data:) part of the path to the database.

Lab Book Issues

To increase the speed and reliability of the electronic lab book, a copy of the lab book is placed on the local drive of the computer when the lab book is opened in the laboratory or in *Instructor Utilities*. When this is done, a lock is placed on the file to prevent two users (the instructor and the student) from modifying the file at the same time. In the event of a hardware crash while the lab book is open, this lock remains in effect even when the program is restarted. This lock can be overridden by the instructor by opening the lab book inside *Instructor Utilities* using the *View Lab Book* button in the Score folder.

When a student has their lab book open in the laboratory, the lab book information is stored in memory. Saves of the lab book are made only at the time the lab book is exited, when an assignment is submitted, or when a grade is assigned. To protect against loosing data because of hardware crashes, the lab book is automatically saved every 5 minutes (300 seconds). The timer interval between automatic saves can be changed by adding the variable

> [Labbook]
> SaveTimer = *nnnn*

to the Chemlab.ini file, where *nnnn* is the time in seconds between saves. If this line is absent in the INI file, the time interval defaults to 300 seconds. If *nnnn* is set to zero, then automatic saving is turned off.

Inorganic INI Files

The inorganic simulation uses over 2500 pictures to represent the different test tube color combinations and 220 ten-second video clips to represent the flame tests. The combined size of these media is 150 MB. During the *Virtual ChemLab* installation these media are copied to the local drive for every local, client, and student installation. If disk space is at a premium, the *Media* directory inside the *ChemLabI* directory containing all these media files can be moved to a central location on a server that all client installations can share or to a CD (or Zip250) for a local installation. The INI variable that tells *Virtual ChemLab* where these media files are located is found in the ChemlabI.ini file inside the *ChemLabI* directory and has the format

> [Settings]
> MediaPath = *path*\Media\ (PC)
> or
> MediaPath = *path*:Media: (Mac)

where *path* is the path to *Media* directory. This path must include the \Media\ (:Media:) part of the path to the media directory. During installation, this path defaults to the user selected *Virtual ChemLab* location.

Quantum INI Files

The quantum simulation consists of a set of fundamental experiments that demonstrate the ideas and concepts leading up to the development of quantum mechanics. Much of the operation of the laboratory and the parameters defining the experiments is controlled using INI variables located in the files *Lab.ini*, *Video.ini*, *Spectro.ini*, *Phosphor.ini*, *KE.ini*, and *Diode.ini*. The variables in *Lab.ini* generally control aspects of the entire quantum simulation or experimental parameters that are in more than one experiment. The *Lab.ini* file is located in the *QuantumDB* directory in the *ChemLabQ* directory. The *Video.ini*, *Spectro.ini*, *Phosphor.ini*, *KE.ini*, and *Diode.ini* files contain INI variables that are specific to the operation of each of the indicated detectors. These variables generally control and define the operation of the various quantum experiments and are located in the *Detectors* directory in the *ChemLabQ* directory. There is one additional set of INI files and these define the preset experiments located on the stockroom clipboard and used in the quantum assignments. Described in each of the following sections are the INI variables contained in each of these INI files. The purpose for providing this information is to grant instructors the ability to change or adjust the quantum simulation to suit their own needs.

Lab.ini

INI Variables	Description
[Settings]	Required header line.
Move_Detector_Forward=1	For monitors with resolutions of 1024 x 768 or less, there may not be enough room for the main lab window and detector window to be open at the same time and comfortably see changes in the detector as changes are made in the lab. Setting this variable to 1 forces the detector window to be on top after any change is made in the lab. Setting this variable to 0 forces normal window operation.
IntenEGunDisp=1 e/s,10 e/s,100 e/s, 1000 e/s,1 nA,1 uA,1 mA,1 A	The electron gun allowed intensity values displayed on the LCD controller.
IntenEGunVal=1 e/s,10 e/s,100 e/s,1000 e/s, 0.05,0.3,0.7,1	The electron gun intensities assigned to the corresponding display values. It is not suggested that the e/s values be changed.
IntenLaserDisp=1 p/s,10 p/s,100 p/s,1000 p/s, 1 nW,1 uW,1 mW,1 W,1 kW,1 MW	The laser allowed intensity values displayed on the LCD controller.
IntenLaserVal=1 p/s,10 p/s,100 p/s,1000 p/s, 0.05,0.2,0.4,0.6,0.8,1	The laser intensities assigned to the corresponding display values. It is not suggested that the p/s values be changed.
IntenBulbDisp=1 nW,1 uW,1 mW,1 W,1 kW, 1 MW	The super light bulb allowed intensity values displayed on the LCD controller.
IntenBulbVal=0.05,0.2,0.4,0.6,0.8,1	The super light bulb intensities assigned to the corresponding display values.
WavelengthDisp=nm,um,mm	The allowed units displayed on the laser LCD controller.
WavelengthVal=1e-9,1e-6,1e-3	The multipliers assigned to the corresponding units on the laser LCD.
WavelengthMax=999	The maximum setting on the maximum scale on the laser LCD controller.
WavelengthMin=020	The minimum setting on the minimum scale on the laser LCD controller.
KEnergyDisp=me,eV,keV	The allowed units displayed on the electron gun LCD controller.
KEnergyVal=1e-3,1,1e3	The multipliers assigned to the corresponding units on the electron gun LCD.
KEnergyMax=050	The maximum setting on the maximum scale on the electron gun LCD controller.
KEnergyMin=001	The minimum setting on the minimum scale on the electron gun LCD controller.
AlphaKEnergy=5.4e6	The kinetic energy of the alpha particles from the alpha source in eV.
BDisp=uT,mT,T	The allowed units displayed on the magnetic field LCD controller.
BVal=1e-6,1e-3,1	The multipliers assigned to the corresponding units on the magnetic field LCD.
BMax=100	The maximum setting on the maximum scale on the magnetic field LCD controller.
BMin=0	The minimum setting on the minimum scale on the magnetic field LCD controller.

EDisp=V,kV	The allowed units displayed on the electric field LCD controller.
EVal=1,1e3	The multipliers assigned to the corresponding units on the electric field LCD.
EMax=005	The maximum setting on the maximum scale on the electric field LCD controller.
EMin=00	The minimum setting on the minimum scale on the electric field LCD controller.
HeatDisp=0 K	The allowed units displayed on the heater LCD controller.
HeatVal=10	The multipliers assigned to the corresponding units on the heater LCD.
HeatMax=400	The maximum setting on the maximum scale on the heater LCD controller.
HeatMin=30	The minimum setting on the minimum scale on the heater LCD controller.
SlitDisp=nm,um,mm	The allowed units displayed on the two-slit LCD controller.
SlitVal=1e-9,1e-6,1e-3	The multipliers assigned to the corresponding units on the two-slit LCD.
SlitMax=100	The maximum setting on the maximum scale on the two-slit LCD controller.
SlitMin=1	The minimum setting on the minimum scale on the two-slit LCD controller.
Laser_Open_Delay=75	The delay time in msec before the laser lid is removed during a mouse over.
T_Heat_Glow = 399	The temperature at which the heating element begins to glow in K.
T_Gas_XPLD = 700	The temperature at which the gas holder explodes.
T_Liquid_XPLD = 400	The temperature at which the liquid holder explodes.
T_Oil_XPLD = 450	The temperature at which the oil mist begins to smoke.
T_Red = 700	The temperature at which the foils turn dull red when heated.
T_Orange = 900	The temperature at which the foils turn orange when heated.
T_white = 1100	The temperature at which the foils turn white when heated.
Color_A=4096	The first of the visible light scaling parameters used in the spectrometer color window to simulate the sensitivity of the human eye.
Color_B=8.317766167	The second scaling parameter. The equation is $I_{obs} = I_{max}\left[\ln(I \cdot A)/B\right]$.
Setting_Delay=400	The delay time in msec before a change in any LCD controller is processed.
Gas_Glow=300	The AC voltage at which any gas will begin to emit.
PB_Gx=76.20	The distance, in cm, between position 7 and position 9 on the table. This is used to calculate the deflection of particles in any particle bending experiment.
PB_Ey=91.44	The distance, in cm, between position 9 and position 8 or 10 on the table. This is used to calculate whether a particle will hit a detector in position 8 or 10.
PB_n=40	The number of iterations to use when solving the differential equation while a charged particle moves through the electric or magnetic fields.
PB_EB_Length=0.050	The length of the electric and magnetic fields, in m, for the E and B modifiers in position 7 on the table. This is used in the particle bending experiments.
PB_E_Dist=0.050	The spacing between the electric plates for the E modifier in position 7. This is used for calculating the applied electric field using $E = V/d$.

Video.ini

INI Variables	*Description*

[Video]
OilYMin=29 — The *y* pixel position where the oil drops disappear from the screen.
OilYMax=379 — The *y* pixel position where the oil drops appear on the screen.
OilXMin=75 — The left-most pixel position (*xmin*) where the oil drops can fall.
OilXMax = 330 — The right-most pixel position (*xmax*) where the oil drops can fall.
PixelFactor=1 — The number of pixels used when calculating the speed of the oil drops per pixel.
Oil_Y_Pixel_D_nm=2857 — Defines the number of nm per pixel in the oil mist.
Oil_SlowMo_Factor = 5 — Defines the slow-motion factor when the slow-motion button is pressed.
Oil1=1.00e-06 — Defines the diameters of the 10 different oil drops in m.
Oil2=1.13e-06
Oil3=1.25e-06
Oil4=1.38e-06
Oil5=1.42e-06
Oil6=1.51e-06
Oil7=1.64e-06
Oil8=1.69e-06
Oil9=1.79e-06
Oil10=1.92e-06

Oil1_Size=01 — There are 10 graphics that depict 10 different size drops where 01 is the
Oil2_Size=01 — smallest drop and 10 is the largest. These variables assign the drop graphic for
Oil3_Size=01 — the 10 different size drops defined earlier.
Oil4_Size=01
Oil5_Size=02
Oil6_Size=02
Oil7_Size=02
Oil8_Size=02
Oil9_Size=03
Oil10_Size=03

MaxIntensity=1 — The intensity of the egun that blows away the oil drops.
EPlate_D=0.010 — The spacing of the electric plates in the oil mist chamber in m.
oilDensity=821 — Density of the oil in $kg \cdot m^{-3}$ for the oil mist.
airDensity=1.22 — Density of the air in $kg \cdot m^{-3}$ for the oil mist.
airVisc = 1.4607e-5 — Viscosity of the air in $kg \cdot m^{-1} \cdot s^{-1}$ for the oil mist.
atmoPres=1.00 — Air pressure in atmospheres for the oil mist.

SpotPixel=2 — The size of the spots for the two-slit single photon experiments.
PixelPerCM=50 — The number of pixels per cm in the *x* direction on the video screen for the two-slit experiment. Essentially defines the size of the screen.
Video_Slit_D=0.01 — The distance of the screen from the slits in m.
SlitTopY=126 — The top pixel position for the interference pattern.
SlitBottomY=239 — The bottom pixel position for the interference pattern.
SpotSqueeze=0.9 — Used to adjust a set of random numbers to give a gaussian distribution.
BaseIntensity=0.25 — The intensity of each spot as they hit the screen in the single photon experiment. Overlapping spots add intensity.
Spot_Dis_mSec=750 — The time, in msec, spots on the video screen persist before disappearing when

	not in Persist Mode.
BoxExtend=100	For some configurations, the outer fringes of an interference pattern can be very long. This variable sets an upper bound on this size for certain situations.
Large_Spot_Size=8	The size of a simple laser spot on the video camera in pixels.
Slit_Rect_W=400	The width of the white rectangle in a bulb/two-slit combination.
Slit_Rect_H=20	The height of the white rectangle in a bulb/two-slit combination.
Slit_Width_Pixel=187	The width, in pixels, the two-slit graphic can move.

Spectro.ini

INI Variables	Description
[Spectro]	
BB_Min = 10	The minimum wavelength, in nm, for the blackbody spectrum.
BB_Max = 5000	The maximum wavelength, in nm, for the blackbody spectrum.
Zoom_Min = 1	The maximum, full-scale zoom, in nm, for the blackbody experiment.
Graph_Resolution=300	The number of points to use to graph the blackbody curve.
Zoom_Min_PE=0.1	The maximum, full-scale zoom, in nm, for the photoemission experiment.
PE_Detail_Switch=5	The full-scale zoom, in nm, where a switch is made between the low-resolution and high-resolution photoemission files.
Adsorb_Detail_Switch=10	The full-scale zoom, in nm, where a switch is made between the low-resolution and high-resolution adsorption files.
Raman_Scale_Factor=1e4	The multiplication factor for the center Raman peak.
Raman_Broad_Factor=.10	The gaussian broadening parameter for the center Raman peak.
Raman_Sat_Scale_Factor=0.01	The multiplication factor for the satellite Raman peak.
Raman_Sat_Broad_Factor=.010	The gaussian broadening parameter for the satellite Raman peak.
Raman_Wave_Min_nm=110	The minimum laser wavelength where a Raman experiment will work.
Raman_Wave_Max_nm=999	The maximum laser wavelength where a Raman experiment will work.

Phosphor.ini

INI Variables	Description
[Phosphor]	
Spot_Diameter=10	The diameter, in pixels, for general spots that appear on the phosphor screen.
Spot_Remain_mSec=300	The time, in msec, spots persist on the phosphor screen when not in Persist Mode.
Spot_R=108	The R-value for a full-intensity spot.
Spot_G=165	The G-value for a full-intensity spot.
Spot_B=78	The B-value for a full-intensity spot.
Base_Intensity=0.2	The intensity of each spot as they hit the screen in the single particle experiments. Overlapping spots add intensity.
SpotPixel=2	The size of the spots for the two-slit single particle experiments.
PixelPerCM=50	The number of pixels per cm in the x direction on the phosphor screen for the two-slit experiment. Essentially defines the size of the screen.
Phosphor_Slit_D=0.01	The distance of the screen from the slits in m.
SlitTopY=108	The top pixel position for the interference pattern.
SlitBottomY=221	The bottom pixel position for the interference pattern.
SpotSqueeze=0.9	Used to adjust a set of random numbers to give a gaussian distribution.

BaseIntensity=0.25	The intensity of each spot as they hit the screen in the single particle, two-slit experiment. Overlapping spots add intensity.
Spot_Dis_mSec=750	The time, in msec, spots on the phosphor screen persist before disappearing when not in Persist Mode.
BoxExtend=100	For some configurations, the outer fringes of an interference pattern can be very long. This variable sets an upper bound on this size for certain situations.
Ruth_Diam=50	The base diameter, in pixels, for the forward scattering spot in the Rutherford experiment. Spot size changes size based on nuclear cross section.
Eo=5.4	The energy of the alpha particles in MeV.
Ruth_Intensity=1e5	The intensity of the alpha-particle flux in particles per second.
T=0.001	The thickness of the metal foil in cm.
Area_cm2=144	The area of the phosphor screen in cm^2.
DistB_cm=138.2	The distance from position 5 to position 1 in cm.
DistI_cm=81.3	The distance from position 5 to position 4 in cm.
DistE_cm=190.9	The distance from position 5 to position 8 in cm.
DistG_cm=172.7	The distance from position 5 to position 9 in cm.
Ruth_Spread=0.1	The fade parameter for the forward-scattering Rutherford spot.
Ruth_Dis=300	The time, in msec, the backscattering spots persist before disappearing when not in Persist Mode.
Ruth_Spot_Size=6	The size of the backscattering spots in pixels.
Ruth_Spot_Fade=12	The fade parameter for the backscattering spots.
Ruth_Spot_Power=3	A second fade parameter for the backscattering spots.
Sigma=100	A second fade parameter for the forward scattering spot.
PB_Base_Intensity=.25	The intensity of a single particle spot as it hits the screen in the particle-bending experiments. Overlapping spots add intensity.
PB_Spot_Dis_mSec=300	The time, in msec, spots on the phosphor screen persist before disappearing when not in Persist Mode.
PB_ScreenW=12	The screen width, in cm, for the particle-bending experiment.
PB_SpotSize=10	The size of a particle-bending spot in pixels.
PB_Fade=15	The fade parameter for a particle-bending spot.
Grid_Red=100	The gird color R-value.
Grid_Green=100	The gird color G-value.
Grid_Blue=100	The gird color B-value.
Grid_Space_CM=1	The spacing between major grid lines.

KE.ini

INI Variables	*Description*
PE_Min = 0	The minimum energy, in eV, for graphing on the bolometer.
PE_Max = 60	The maximum energy, in eV, for graphing on the bolometer.
PE_Zoom_Min = 2	The maximum, full-scale zoom, in eV, for the blackbody experiment.
PE_R=0	The graphing line color R-value.
PE_G=200	The graphing line color G-value.
PE_B=0	The graphing line color B-value.
Time_Interval_mSec=1000	The time interval between measurements in the integrated mode.
Time_Scale_Sec=60	The full-scale time in the integrated mode.

Diode.ini

INI Variables	Description
[Diode]	
Time_Interval_mSec=1000	The time interval between measurements.
Time_Scale_Sec=60	The full-scale time.
Line_R=25	The graphing line color R-value.
Line_G=25	The graphing line color G-value.
Line_B=25	The graphing line color B-value.
BB_Min=100	The wavelength to starting integrating the blackbody intensity.
BB_Max=5000	The wavelength to stop integrating the blackbody intensity.
BB_Resolution=3000	The number of points to use to perform the integration.

Preset Experiments

Located on the clipboard in the quantum stockroom is a set of 15 preset experiments listed by title. If allowed by the instructor, students can select one of these experiments and, upon returning to the laboratory, the selected experiment will be automatically set up and running. A preset experiment can also be used for assignments so a student can accept an assignment with the experiment already set up for them. Preset experiments are intended to provide flexibility for the instructor so the quantum simulation can be adapted to the level of the class or the individual teaching style of the instructor. Several experiments have already been defined and are installed with the software. This section describes how these files can be modified.

Each preset experiment is defined using an INI file. For the preset experiments on the clipboard, these files have the name *Experimentn.ini,* where *n* is a number between 1 and 15 and represents experiments 1 through 15 on the clipboard. These files are located in the *Presets* directory in the *ChemLabQ* directory. For the preset experiments used in assignments, these files must be located in the *Assignments/Quantum* directory and can have any name, but must have the extension ".*ini*". Information on how to use preset experiments in assignments is given in the "Quantum Assignments" section. Note that in client installations, any modified preset experiments for the clipboard must be modified for each client installation.

Given subsequently is a description of a preset experiment INI file and the variables that are used to define an experiment. Before reviewing the INI file information, here are some important points to keep in mind: (a) All of the variables described have default values, so variables may be left blank or not used at all. An experiment can be set up or defined to any degree desired by the instructor. (b) Some variables are mutually exclusive; that is, the use of one variable may mean another variable cannot be used. Some error checking exists for such situations, but the error checking is not comprehensive. (c) The LCD control boxes for various pieces of equipment use three different INI variables to define their initial settings: one for the numeric value on the LCD box, one to define the location of the decimal place, and the other to define the units. Not all of these need to be used to define the initial settings. (d) Positions on the table are defined using numbers from 1 to 10 as indicated in the following figure:

1	4	8
2	5	7 9
3	6	10

Positions 1, 2, and 3 are for sources, position 5 is for samples, position 5 is also for electric or magnetic field modifiers or heat, position 7 is for electric or magnetic field modifiers, and positions 1, 3, 4, 6, 8, 9, and 10 are for detectors.

The following two tables show the INI variables used in preset experiments. The first lists all the variables that can be used and their allowed values. Default values are given in red. The second is an example of a preset experiment for the Millikan Oil Drop Experiment to show how the variables can be used.

Complete Preset Experiment INI Variable List

INI Variables	Description
[Title]	
Title=Experiment Title	Defines the title of the experiment as shown on the clipboard. Not used for preset assignments.
[Source]	
Source=none, alpha, bulb, egun, laser	Defines the source for the experiment. The allowed values are shown.
Position=1, 2, 3 *(Default = stockroom counter)*	Defines the position for the source.
On_Off=on, off	Sets the source initially on or initially off.
Intensity= *(Default = lowest intensity)*	Sets the source intensity. See *Lab.ini* file for allowed values.
Setting=*nnn (Default = lowest value)*	Sets the three digits on the LCD source control box.
Setting_Units= *(Default = smallest units)*	Sets the units on the LCD source control box. See *Lab.ini* file for allowed values.
Setting_Decimal_Position=1, 2, 3	Sets the decimal place on the LCD source control box. 1 is after the first digit, 2 the second digit, and 3 is after the right-most digit.
[Sample]	
Holder=none, oil mist, liquid, metal, gas, two slit	Defines the sample holder that will be used in the experiment. The allowed values are shown.
Sample= *(Default = empty)*	Defines the liquid, metal, or gas sample to be used. Allowed values are given in the *Liquid, Metal, or Gas Tables* found in the *QuantumDB* directory.
Position=5 *(Default = stockroom counter)*	Defines the position for the sample. 5 is the only allowed position.
Spacing=*nnn (Default = lowest value)*	Sets the three digits on the LCD spacing control box for the two-slit sample.

Spacing_Units=nm, um, mm	Sets the units on the LCD spacing control box. The allowed values are shown.
Spacing_Decimal_Position=1, 2, 3	Sets the decimal place on the LCD spacing control box. 1 is after the first digit, 2 is after the second digit, and 3 is after the right-most digit.

[Detector]

Detector=none, phosphor, spectro, video, diode, bolometer	Defines the detector that will be used in the experiment. The allowed values are shown.
Position=1, 3, 4, 6, 8, 9, 10 (Default = stockroom counter)	Puts the detector in the specified position. The allowed values are shown.
On_Off=on, off	Turns the detector initially on or initially off.

[Modifiers]

Modifier=none, heat, E_field, B_field, E_B_field	Defines the modifiers that will be used in the experiment. The allowed values are shown. To use an electric and magnetic field combination, utilize the E_B_field value. Heat cannot be used in combination with another modifier.
Position=5, 7 (Default = stockroom counter)	Puts the modifiers in position 5 or 7. Heat can only be in position 5. The electric and magnetic fields must be in the same position.
E_Setting=nnn (Default = lowest value)	Sets the three digits on the LCD electric field control box.
E_Setting_Units=V, kV	Sets the units on the LCD electric field control box. The allowed values are shown.
E_Setting_Decimal_Position=1, 2, 3	Sets the decimal place on the LCD electric field control box. 1 is after the first digit, 2 is after the second digit, and 3 is after the right-most digit.
B_Setting=nnn (Default = lowest value)	Sets the three digits on the LCD magnetic field control box.
B_Setting_Units=uT, mT, T	Sets the units on the LCD magnetic field control box. The allowed values are shown.
B_Setting_Decimal_Position=1, 2, 3	Sets the decimal place on the LCD magnetic field control box. 1 is after the first digit, 2 is after the second digit, and 3 is after the right-most digit.
H_Setting=nnn (Default = lowest value)	Sets the temperature on the heat modifier. The units of the specified temperature must be in Kelvin and the ones digit must be 0 (zero).

An Example of a Millikan Oil Drop Preset Experiment

INI Variables | Description

[Title]

Title=Millikan Oil Drop Experiment	Defines the title of the experiment shown on the clipboard. Not used for preset assignments.

[Source]

Source=eGun	Defines the source as the electron gun.
Position=2	Puts the source at position 2.
On_Off=on	Turns the source on initially.
Intensity=1 nA	Sets the source intensity to 1 nA.
Setting=100	Sets the electron gun energy to 100 on the LCD box.
Setting_Units=me	Sets the electron gun energy units to meV.
Setting_Decimal_Position=3	Puts the electron gun energy decimal place to the right-most position.

[Sample]

Holder=oil mist	Defines the holder as the oil mist.
Position=5	Puts the oil mist in position 5.

[Detector]

Detector=video	Defines the detector as the video camera.
Position=9	Puts the video camera in position 9.
On_Off=on	Turns the video camera on.

[Modifiers]

Modifier=E_field	Defines the modifier as the electric field.
Position=5	Puts the modifier in position 5.
E_Setting=0	Sets the electric field initially to zero.
E_Setting_Units=V	Sets the units on the electric field LCD box to volts (V).
E_Setting_Decimal_Position=3	Puts the decimal place to the right-most position.

Appendix B
List of Organic Synthesis Assignments

A list of products that can be assigned for organic synthesis experiments for each named reaction.

Esterification

1. Methyl acetate

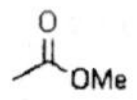

2. Ethyl acetate

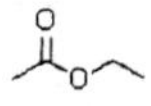

3. 3-Methylbutyl acetate

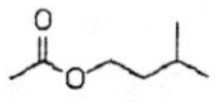

4. Methyl butanoate

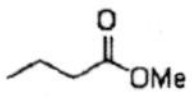

5. Ethyl butanoate

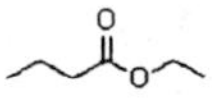

6. 3-Methylbutyl butanoate

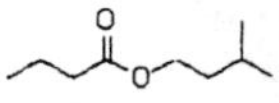

7. Methyl phenylacetate

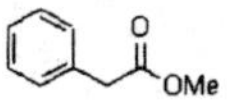

8. Ethyl-2-phenyl acetate

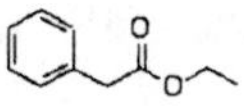

9. 3-Methylbutyl phenylacetate

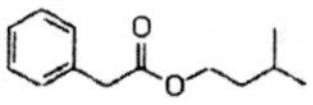

10. Butanol

11. 2-Phenyl ethanol

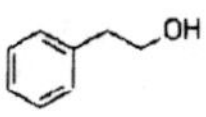

12. 4-Nitrobenzeneacetic acid

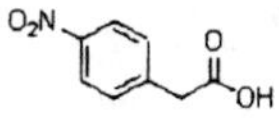

13. 2-Nitrobenzeneacetic acid

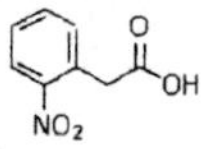

14. 2,4-Dinitrophenylacetic acid

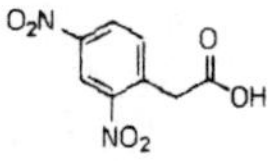

15. Formic acid

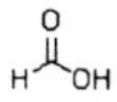

16. 3-Methyl butanoic acid

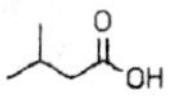

17. Ethanal

18. 3-Methyl butanal

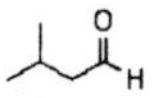

19. 1-Chloro-3-methylbutane

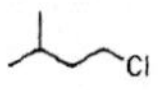

20. 2-Chloro-3-methylbutane

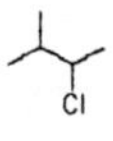

21. Diisopentyl ether

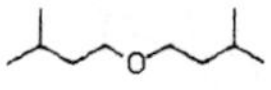

22. Benzoic acid

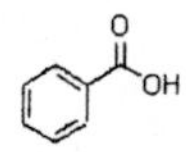

23. Bromo-phenyl-acetic acid

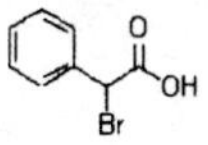

Alcohol Halogenation

1. Chlorocyclohexane

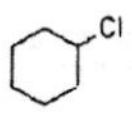

2.   Chlorophenylmethane

3.   2-Chloro-2-methyl propane

4.   1-Chloro-3-methylbutane

5.   2-Chloro-3-methylbutane

6.   3-Methyl butanoic acid

7.   3-Methyl butanal

8.   Benzoic acid

9.   Benzaldehyde

10.   Cyclohexanone

11.   Cyclohexene

12.   Diisopentyl ether

13.   Dibenzyl Ether

14.   1,1-Oxybis-cyclohexane

15.   Di-tert-butyl ether

16.   Benzyl ethyl ether

Alkyl Halide Solvolysis

1.   Benzyl alcohol

2.   2-Methyl-2-propanol

3.   exo-Bicyclo[2.2.1] heptane-2-ol

4.   Tetrahydrofuran

5.   1,4-Butanediol

6.   1-Chloromethyl-4-nitro-benzene

7.   1-Chloromethyl-2-nitro-benzene

8.   1-Chloromethyl-2,4-dinitro-benzene

9.   4-Nitro-benzyl alcohol

10.   2-Nitro-benzyl alcohol

11.   Benzyl ethyl ether

12.   Benzyl methyl ether

13.   2-methyl-2-ethoxy-propane

14.  1-Methoxy butane

2. 1-Phenylethanol

15. 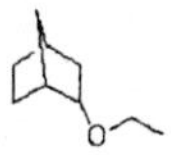 5-Ethoxybicyclo[2.2.1]heptane

3. 1-Methyl-cyclohexanol

16.  Bicyclo[2.2.1]hept-2-ene

4. 2,3-Dimethyl-2-butanol

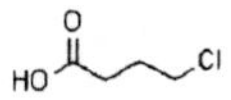

17. 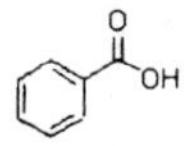 Benzoic acid

5. 1-Hexanol

18. 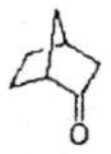 Bicyclo[2.2.1]heptan-2-one

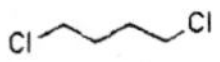

6. 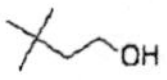 3,3-Dimethyl-1-butanol

19. 4-Chloro-butanoic acid

7. 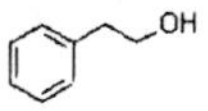 2-Phenyl ethanol

20. 4-Chloro-butyraldehyde

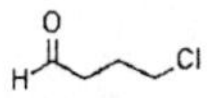

8. 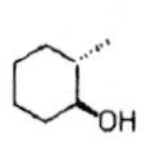 trans-2-methyl-cyclohexanol

21. 1,4-Dichlorobutane

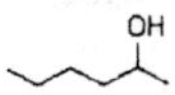

9. 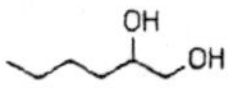 Hexane-1,2-diol

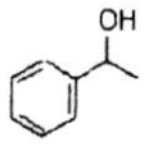

22. Butanol

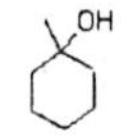

10. 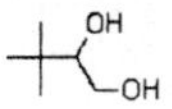 3,3-Dimethyl-1,2-butane diol

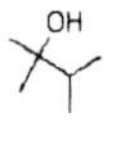

23. 2-Benzyl-benzyl chloride

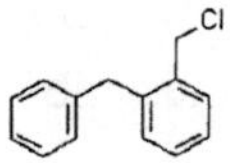

11. 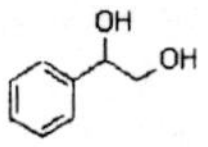 1-Phenyl-ethane-1,2-diol

24. 4-Benzyl-benzyl chloride

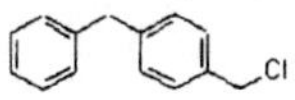

12. 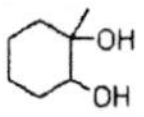 cis-1-Methyl-cyclohexane-1,2-diol

25. Benzyldiisopropylamine

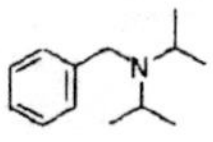

13. 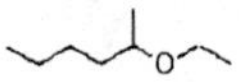 Ethyl 2-hexyl ether

26. Butyldiisopropylamine

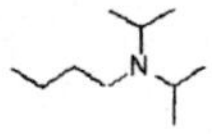

14. 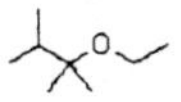 2-Ethoxy-2,3-dimethyl-butane

Alkene Hydration

15. 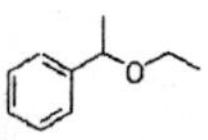 Ethyl-(1-phenyl-ethyl)-ether

1. 2-Hexanol

16. 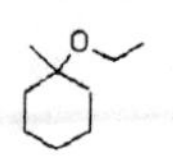 1-Ethoxy-1-methyl-cyclohexane

17. 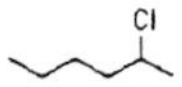 2-Chloro-hexane

18. 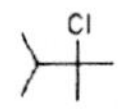 2-chloro-2,3-dimethyl butane

19. 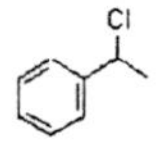 1-Chloro-1-phenylethane

20. 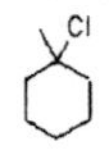 1-Chloro-1-methyl-cyclohexane

21. 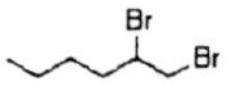 1,2-Dibromo-hexane

22. 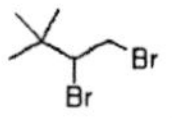 1,2-Dibromo-3,3-dimethyl-butane

23. 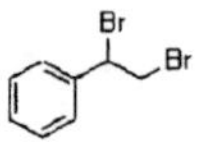 (1,2-Dibromoethyl)-benzene

24. 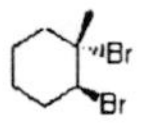 1,2-Dibromo-1-methyl-cyclohexane

25. 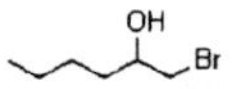 1-Bromo-2-hexanol

26. 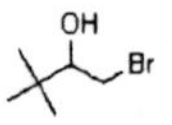 1-Bromo-3,3-dimethyl-2-butanol

27. 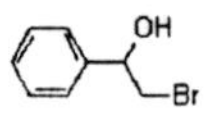 2-Bromo-1-phenyl-ethanol

28. 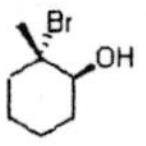 2-Bromo-2-methyl-cyclohexanol

29. 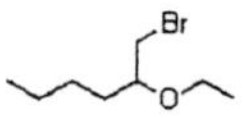 1-Bromo-2-ethoxy-hexane

30. 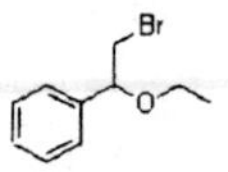 Ethyl-(2-bromo-1-phenyl-ethyl)-ether

31. 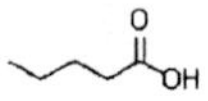 Pentanoic acid

32. 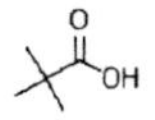 2,2-Dimethylpropanoic acid

33. 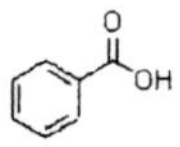 Benzoic acid

34. 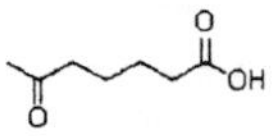 6-Oxo-heptanoic acid

35. 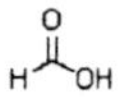 Formic acid

36. 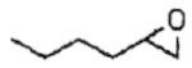 1,2-Epoxyhexane

37.  3,3-Dimethyl-1,2-epoxy butane

38. 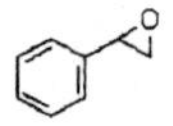 1,2-Epoxyethylbenzene

39. 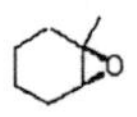 1-Methyl-1,2-epoxycyclohexane

40. 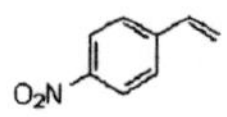 4-Nitro-styrene

41. 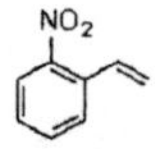 2-Nitro-styrene

42. 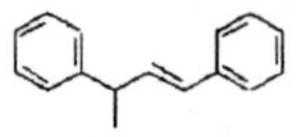 1,3-Diphenyl-1-butene

Hydroboration

1. 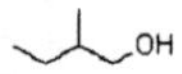 2-Methyl-1-butanol

2. 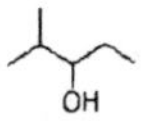 2-Methyl-3-pentanol

3. 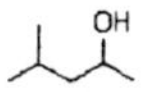 4-Methyl-2-pentanol

4.  1-Hexanol

5. 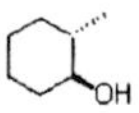 trans-2-methyl-cyclohexanol

6. 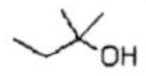 2-Methyl-2-butanol

7.  2-Methyl-2-pentanol

8. 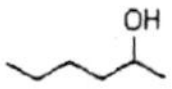 2-Hexanol

9. 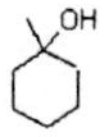 1-Methyl-cyclohexanol

10. 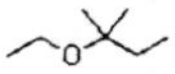 2-Ethoxy-2-methylbutane

11. 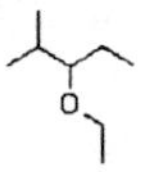 3-Ethoxy-2-methyl-pentane

12. 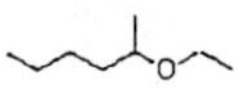 Ethyl 2-hexyl ether

13. 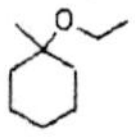 1-Ethoxy-1-methyl-cyclohexane

14. 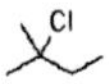 2-Methyl-2-chlorobutane

15.  2-Chloro-2-methylpentane

16. 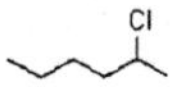 2-Chloro-hexane

17.  1-Chloro-1-methyl-cyclohexane

18. 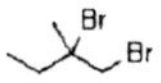 1,2-Dibromo-2-methyl-butane

19. 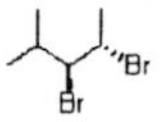 2,3-Dibromo-4-methyl-pentane

20. 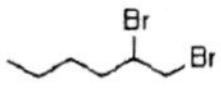 1,2-Dibromo-hexane

21. 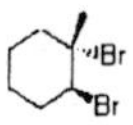 trans-1,2-Dibromo-1-methyl-cyclohexane

22. 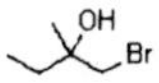 1-Bromo-2-methyl-butan-2-ol

23. 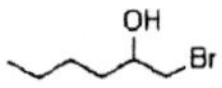 1-Bromo-2-hexanol

24. 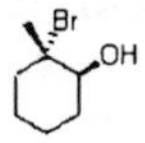 trans-2-Bromo-2-methyl-cyclohexanol

25. 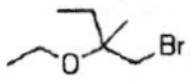 1-Bromo-2-ethoxy-2-methyl-butane

26. 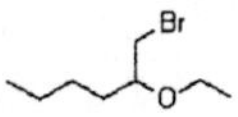 1-Bromo-2-ethoxy-hexane

27. 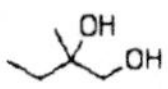 2-Methyl-butane-1,2-diol

28. 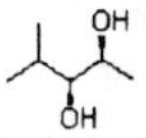 syn-4-Methyl-pentane-2,3-diol

29. 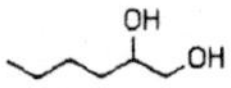 Hexane-1,2-diol

30. cis-1-Methyl-cyclohexane-1,2-diol

31. 1,2-Epoxy-2-methyl-butane

32. 2,3-Epoxy-4-methyl-pentane

33. 1,2-Epoxyhexane

34. 1-Methyl-1,2-epoxycyclohexane

35. 2-Butanone

36. 2-Methyl-propionic acid

37. Acetic acid

38. Pentanoic acid

39. 6-Oxo-heptanoic acid

40. Formic acid

41. 2-Methyl-2-pentene

Alkene Bromination

1. 1,2-Dibromo-hexane

2. 3,4-Dibromo-1-butene

3. 1,4-Dibromo-2-butene

4. trans-2,3-Dibromo-butane

5. (1R)-trans-1,2-Dibromo-cyclohexane

6. 2-Hexanol

7. 3-Buten-1-ol

8. 2-Butanol

9. 1-Cyclohexanol

10. 1-Hexanol

11. Ethyl 2-hexyl ether

12. 3-Ethoxy-1-butene

13. 1-Ethoxy-2-butene

14. 2-Ethoxy-butane

15. Ethoxy-cyclohexane

16. 2-Chloro-hexane

17. 3-Chloro-1-butene

18. 1-Chloro-2-butene

19. 2-Chloro-butane

20. Chlorocyclohexane

21. 1-Bromo-2-hexanol

22. anti-3-Bromo-butan-2-ol

23. trans-2-Bromo-cyclohexanol

24. 1-Bromo-2-ethoxy-hexane

25. 4-Bromo-3-ethoxy-but-1-ene

26. anti-2-Bromo-3-ethoxy-butane

27. trans-1-Bromo-2-ethoxy-cyclohexane

28. Hexane-1,2-diol

29. But-3-ene-1,2-diol

30. syn-Butane-2,3-diol

31. cis-Cyclohexane-1,2-diol

32. 1,2-Epoxyhexane

33. 3,4-Epoxy-but-1-ene

34. 2,3-Epoxy-butane

35. 1,2-Epoxy-cyclohexane

36. Pentanoic acid

37. 2-Propenoic acid

38. Acetic acid

39. Hexanedioic acid

40. Formic acid

Alkene Dihydroxylation

1. 2-Methyl-butane-1,2-diol

2. Hexane-1,2-diol

3. cis-Octahydro-naphthalene-4a,8a-diol

4. cis-Cyclohexane-1,2-diol

5. 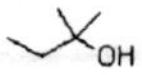   2-Methyl-2-butanol

19.   1,2-Dibromo-2-methyl-butane

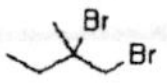

6. 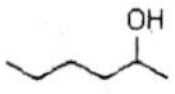   2-Hexanol

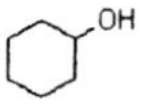

20.   1,2-Dibromo-hexane

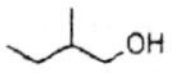

7. 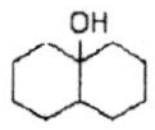   Bicyclo[4.4.0]decane-1-ol

21. 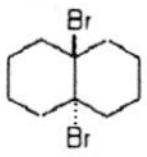   4a,8a-Dibromo-decahydro-naphthalene

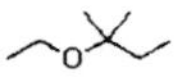

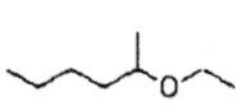

8.   1-Cyclohexanol

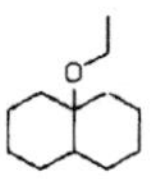

22. 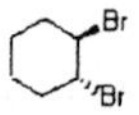   (1R)-trans-1,2-Dibromo-cyclohexane

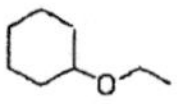

9.   2-Methyl-1-butanol

23. 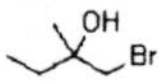   1-Bromo-2-methyl-butan-2-ol

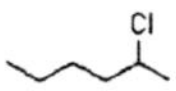

10.   1-Hexanol

24. 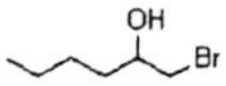   1-Bromo-2-hexanol

11.   2-Ethoxy-2-methylbutane

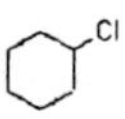

25. 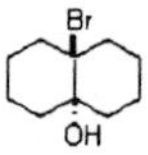   9-Bromo-10-hydroxy-trans-decalin

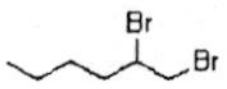

12.   Ethyl 2-hexyl ether

26. 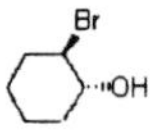   trans-2-Bromo-cyclohexanol

13.   trans-9-Ethoxydecalin

27. 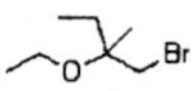   1-Bromo-2-ethoxy-2-methyl-butane

14.   Ethoxy-cyclohexane

28. 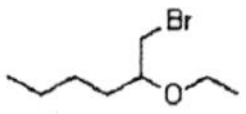   1-Bromo-2-ethoxy-hexane

15.   2-Methyl-2-chlorobutane

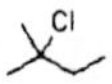

29. 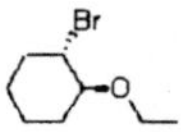   trans-1-Bromo-2-ethoxy-cyclohexane

16.   2-Chloro-hexane

30.    1,2-Epoxy-2-methyl-butane

17.   4a-Chloro-decahydro-naphthalene

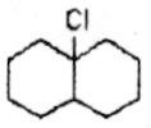

31. 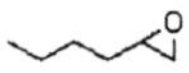   1,2-Epoxyhexane

18.   Chlorocyclohexane

32. 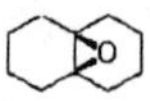   4a,8a-Epoxy-decahydro-napthalene

33. 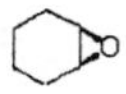   1,2-Epoxy-cyclohexane

34. 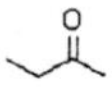   2-Butanone

35. 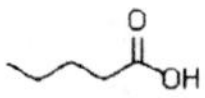   Pentanoic acid

36. 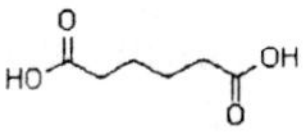   Hexanedioic acid

37. 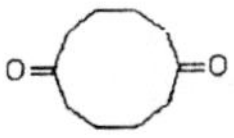   Cyclodecane-1,6-dione

38. 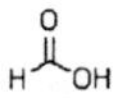   Formic acid

Epoxidation

1.    2,3-Epoxy-butane

2. 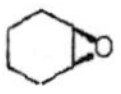   1,2-Epoxy-cyclohexane

3. 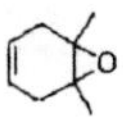   1,2-Dimethyl-1,2-epoxy-cyclohex-4-ene

4. 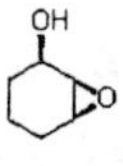   2,3-Epoxy-cyclohexanol

5. 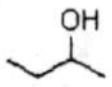   2-Butanol

6. 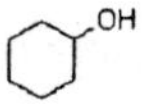   1-Cyclohexanol

7. 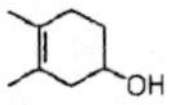   3,4-Dimethyl-cyclohex-3-enol

8. 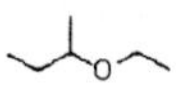   2-Ethoxy-butane

9. 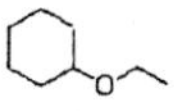   Ethoxy-cyclohexane

10. 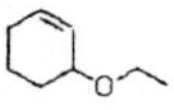   3-Ethoxy-cyclohexene

11. 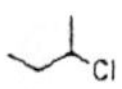   2-Chloro-butane

12. 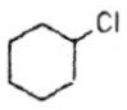   Chlorocyclohexane

13. 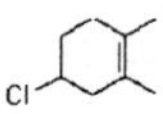   4-Chloro-1,2-dimethyl-cyclohexene

14. 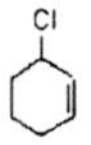   3-Chloro-cyclohexene

15. 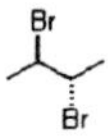   trans-2,3-Dibromo-butane

16. 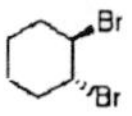   (1R)-trans-1,2-Dibromo-cyclohexane

17. 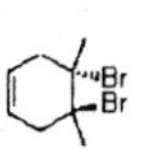   4,5-Dibromo-4,5-dimethyl-cyclohexene

18. 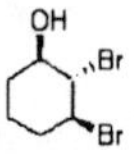   2,3-Dibromo-cyclohexanol

19. 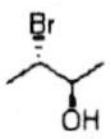   anti-3-Bromo-butan-2-ol

20. 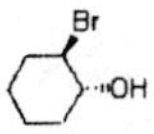   trans-2-Bromo-cyclohexanol

21. 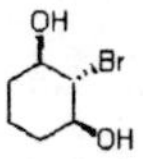   2-Bromo-cyclohexane-1,3-diol

22. 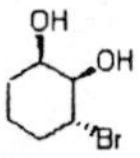   3-Bromo-cyclohexane-1,2-diol

23. 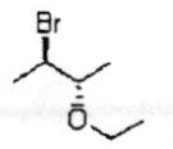 anti-2-Bromo-3-ethoxy-butane

24. 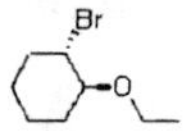 trans-1-Bromo-2-ethoxy-cyclohexane

25. 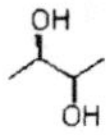 syn-Butane-2,3-diol

26. 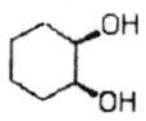 cis-Cyclohexane-1,2-diol

27. 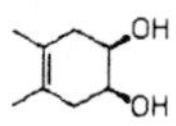 cis-4,5-Dimethyl-cyclohex-4-ene-1,2-diol

28. 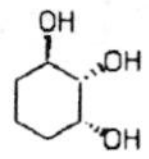 Cyclohexane-1,2,3-triol

29. 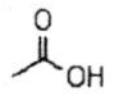 Acetic acid

30. 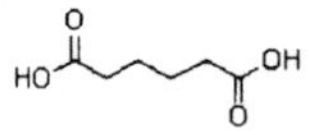 Hexanedioic acid

31. 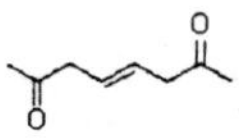 Oct-4-ene-2,7-dione

32.  2-Cyclohexen-1-one

33. Cyclohexa-1,3-diene

Diels Alder

1. 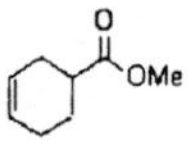 Cyclohex-3-enecarboxylic acid methyl ester

2. 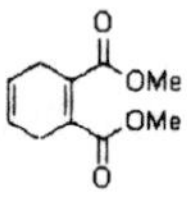 Cyclohexa-1,4-diene-1,2-dicarboxylic acid dimethyl ester

3. 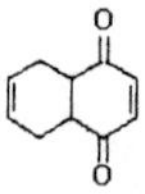 4a,5,8,8a-Tetrahydro-[1,4]naphthoquinone

4. 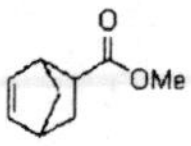 Bicyclo[2.2.1]hept-5-ene-2-carboxylic acid methyl ester

5. 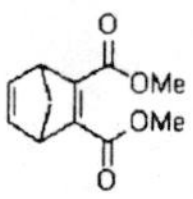 Bicyclo[2.2.1]hepta-2,5-diene-2,3-dicarboxylic acid dimethyl ester

6. 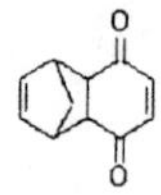 1,4,4a,8a-Tetrahydro-1,4-methano-naphthalene-5,8-dione

7. 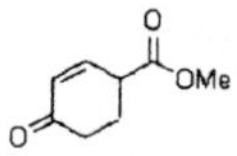 4-Oxo-cyclohex-2-ene carboxylic acid methyl ester

8. 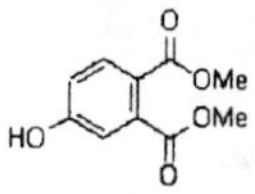 4-Hydroxy-phthalic acid dimethyl ester

9. 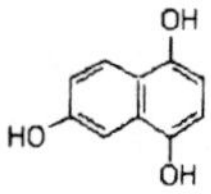 Naphthalene-1,4,6-triol

10. 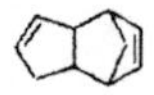 3a,4,7,7a-Tetrahydro-4,7-methano-indene

11. 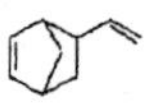 5-Vinylbicyclo[2.2.1]hept-2-ene

12. 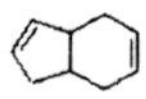 Bicyclo[4.3.0]nona-3,7-diene

13. 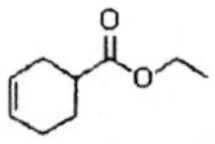 Cyclohex-3-enecarboxylic acid ethyl ester

14. 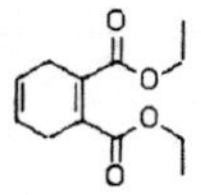 Cyclohexa-1,4-diene-1,2-dicarboxylic acid diethyl ester

15. 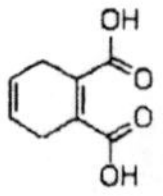 Cyclohex-1,4-diene-1,2-dicarboxylic acid

16. 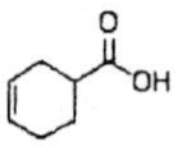 Cyclohex-3-enecarboxylic acid

17. 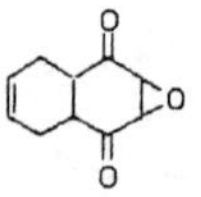 2,3-Epoxy-2,3,4a,5,8,8a-hexahydro-[1,4]naphthoquinone

18. 5,6-Epoxy-3a,4,5,6,7,7a-hexahydro-4,7-methano-indene

19. 1,2-Epoxy-1,2,3a,4,7,7a-hexahydro-4,7-methano-indene

20. 2-Bicyclo[2.2.1]hept-5-en-2-yl-oxirane

21. 6-vinyl-3-oxa-tricyclo [3.2.1.02,4]octane

22. 2,2a,3,5a,6,6a-hexahydro-1aH-1-oxa-cyclopropa [f]indene

23. 7-Oxa-bicyclo[4.1.0]hept-3-ene-3,4-dicarboxylic acid dimethyl ester

24. 3,4-Epoxy-cyclohexane carboxylic acid methyl ester

25. 1,2,3,4,4a,8a-hexahydro-1,4-methano-2,3-epoxy-naphthalene-5,8-dione

26. 3-Oxa-tricyclo[3.2.1.02,4] oct-6-ene-6,7-dicarboxylic acid dimethyl ester

27. 3-Oxa-tricyclo[3.2.1.02,4] octane-6-carboxylic acid methyl ester

28. 3-Buten-1-ol

29. 2-Cyclopenten-1-ol

30. 3-Ethoxy-1-butene

31. 1-Ethoxy-2-butene

32. Cyclopent-2-enyl ethyl ether

33. 3-Chloro-1-butene

34. 1-Chloro-2-butene

35. 3-Chloro-cyclopentene

36. 3,4-Dibromo-1-butene

37. 1,4-Dibromo-2-butene

38. trans-3,4-Dibrom-cyclopentene

39. 3,5-Dibromo-cyclopentene

40. 2,3-Dibromo-propanoic acid methyl ester

41. trans-5-Bromo-cyclopent-2-enol

42. 3-Bromo-2-hydroxy-propionic acid methyl ester

43. 4-Bromo-3-ethoxy-but-1-ene

44. Buta-3-ene-1,2-diol

45. cis-Cyclopent-3-ene-1,2-diol

46. 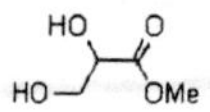 2,3-Dihydroxy-propionic acid methyl ester

47. 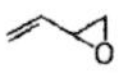 3,4-Epoxy-but-1-ene

48.  3,4-Epoxy-cyclopentene

49. 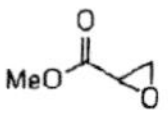 Oxirane-2-carboxylic acid methyl ester

50. 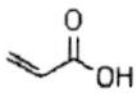 2-Propenoic acid

51. 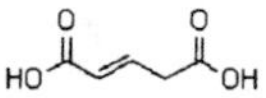 Pent-2-ene-1,5-dioic acid

52. 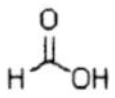 Formic acid

53. 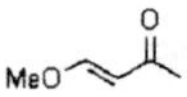 4-Methoxy-but-3-en-2-one

54. 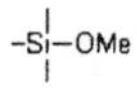 Methoxy-trimethyl-silane

55. 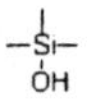 Trimethylsilanol

56. 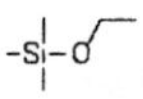 Ethoxy-trimethyl-silane

57. 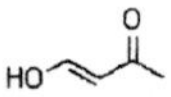 4-Hydroxy-but-3-en-2-one

58. 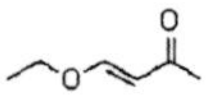 4-Ethoxy-but-3-en-2-one

59. 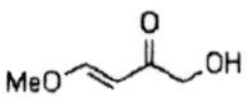 1-Hydroxy-4-methoxy-but-3-en-2-one

60.  Hydroquinone

61.  But-2-ynedioic acid

62. 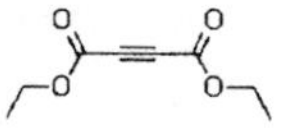 But-2-ynedioic acid diethyl ester

63. 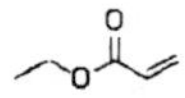 2-Propenoic acid, ethyl ester

Aldol

1. 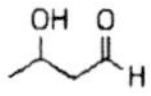 3-Hydroxybutanal

2. 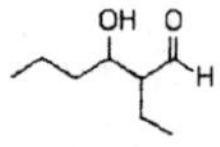 2-Ethyl-3-hydroxy-hexanal

3. 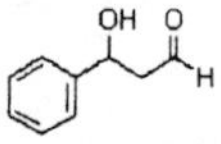 3-Hydroxy-3-phenyl-propanal

4. 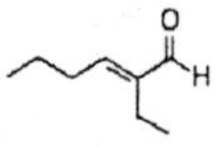 2-Ethyl-hex-2-enal

5. 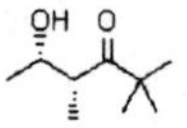 5-Hydroxy-2,2,4-trimethyl-hexan-3-one

6. 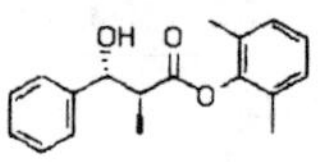 3-Hydroxy-2-methyl-3-phenyl-propionic acid 2,6-dimethyl-phenyl ester

7. 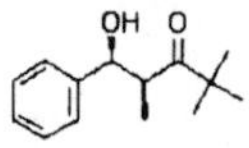 1-hydroxy-2,4,4-trimethyl-1-phenyl-pentan-3-one

8. 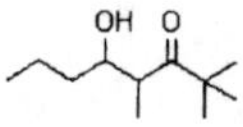 5-Hydroxy-2,2,4-trimethyl-octan-3-one

9. 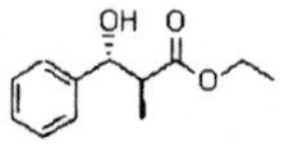 anti-3-Hydroxy-2-methyl-3-phenyl-propionic acid ethyl ester

10. 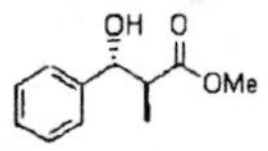 3-Hydroxy-2-methyl-3-phenyl-propionic acid methyl ester

11. 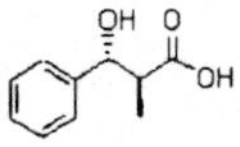 anti-3-Hydroxy-2-methyl-3-phenyl-propionic acid

12. 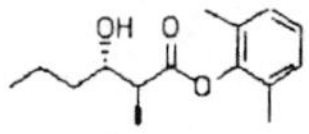 anti-3-hydroxy-2-methyl-hexanoic acid-2,6-dimethyl-phenyl ester

13. 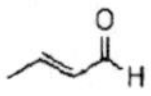 But-2-enal

14. 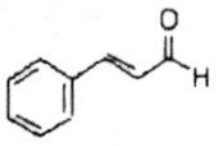 3-Phenyl-propenal

15. 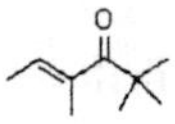 2,2,4-Trimethyl-hex-4-en-3-one

16. 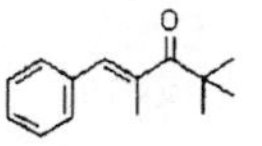 2,4,4-Trimethyl-1-phenyl-pent-1-en-3-one

17. 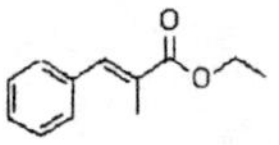 2-Methyl-3-phenyl-acrylic acid ethyl ester

18. 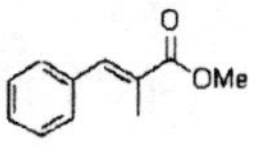 2-Methyl-3-phenyl-acrylic acid methyl ester

19. 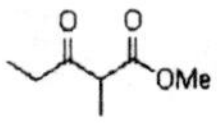 2-Methyl-3-oxo-pentanoic acid methyl ester

20. 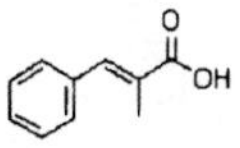 2-Methyl-3-phenyl-acrylic acid

21. 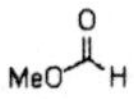 Formic acid methyl ester

22. 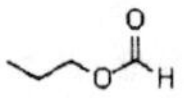 Formic acid propyl ester

23. 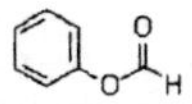 Formic acid phenyl ester

24. 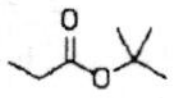 Propanoic acid, 1,1-dimethylethyl ester

25. 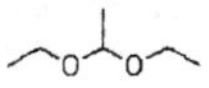 1,1-Diethoxy-ethane

26. 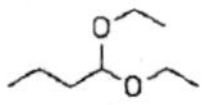 1,1-Diethoxy-butane

27. 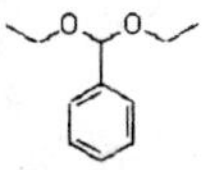 Benzaldehyde diethylacetal

28. 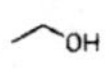 Ethanol

29.  Butanol

30. 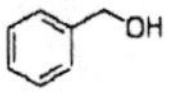 Benzyl alcohol

31. 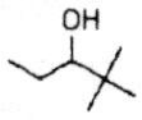 2,2-Dimethyl-pentan-3-ol

32. 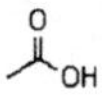 Acetic acid

33. 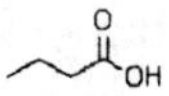 Butanoic acid

34. 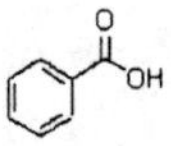 Benzoic acid

35. 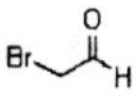 Bromo-acetaldehyde

36. 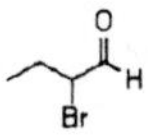 2-Bromo-butanal

37. 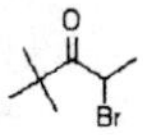 4-Bromo-2,2-dimethyl-pentan-3-one

38. 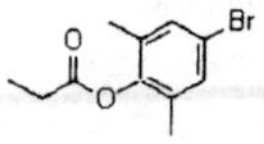 Propionic acid-2,6-dimethyl-4-bromo-phenyl ester

39. 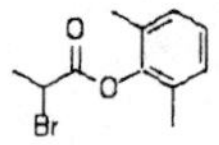 2-Bromo-propionic acid 2,6-dimethyl-phenyl ester

40. 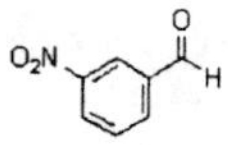 3-Nitro-benzaldehyde

41. 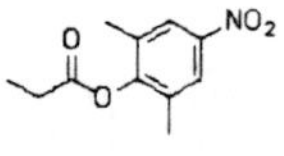 Propionic acid-2,6-dimethyl-4-nitro-phenyl ester

42. 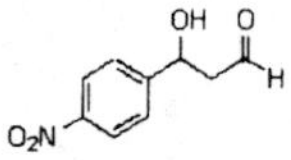 3-Hydroxy-3-(4-nitro-phenyl)-propanal

43. 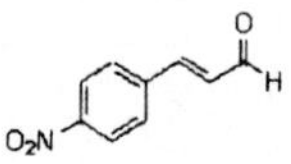 3-(4-Nitro-phenyl)-propenal

44. 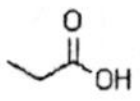 Propionic acid

45. 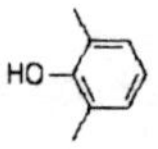 2,6-Dimethyl-phenol

46. 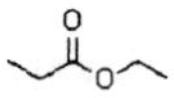 Propionic acid ethyl ester

Grignard Addition

1. 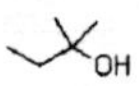 2-Methyl-2-butanol

2. 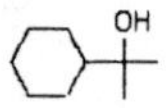 2-cyclohexyl-propan-2-ol

3. 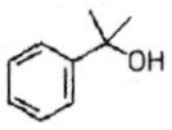 2-Phenyl-2-propanol

4. 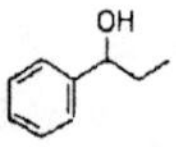 1-Phenyl-1-propanol

5. 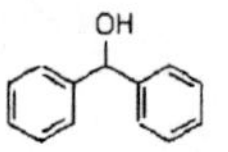 Diphenyl-methanol

6. 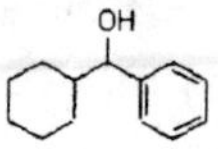 Cyclohexyl-phenyl-methanol

7. 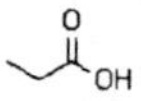 Propionic acid

8. 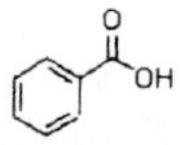 Benzoic acid

9. 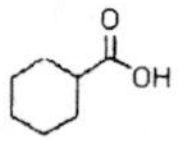 Cyclohexane carboxylic acid

10. 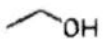 Ethanol

11. Propan-2-ol

12. 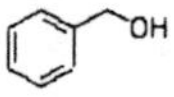 Benzyl alcohol

13. 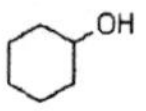 1-Cyclohexanol

14. 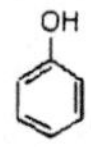 Phenol

15. 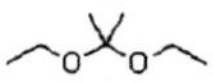 2,2-Diethoxy-propane

16. 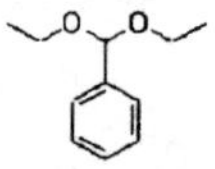 Benzaldehyde diethylacetal

17. Ethyl bromide

18. 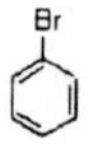 Bromobenzene

19. 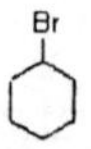 Bromocyclohexane

20. 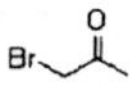   1-Bromo-propan-2-one

21. 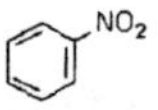   nitro-Benzene

22. 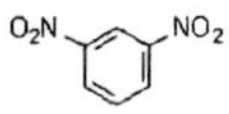   1,3-Dinitrobenzene

23. 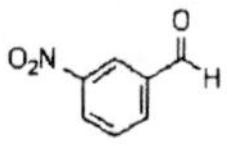   3-Nitro-benzaldehyde

24. 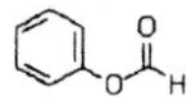   Formic acid phenyl ester

25. 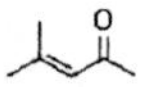   4-Methyl-pent-3-en-2-one

26. 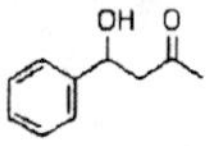   4-Hydroxy-4-phenyl-butan-2-one

27. 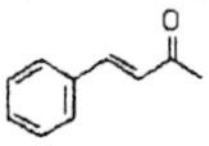   4-Phenyl-but-3-en-2-one

28. 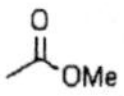   Methyl acetate

Benzene Nitration

1. 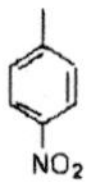   1-Methyl-4-nitro-benzene

2. 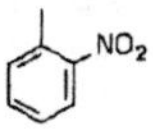   1-Methyl-2-nitro-benzene

3. 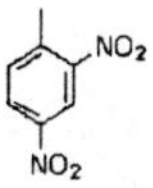   1-Methyl-2,4-dinitro-benzene

4. 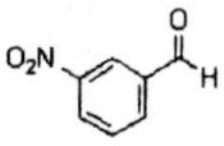   3-Nitro-benzaldehyde

5. 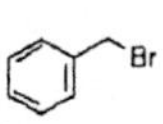   Bromomethyl-benzene

6. 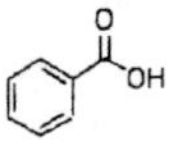   Benzoic acid

7. 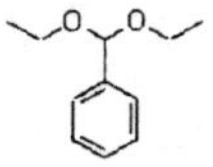   Benzaldehyde diethylacetal

8. 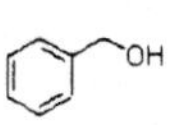   Benzyl alcohol

9. 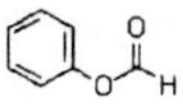   Formic acid phenyl ester

Friedel-Crafts

1. 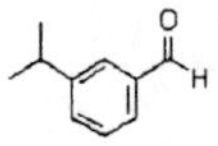   3-Isopropyl-benzaldehyde

2. 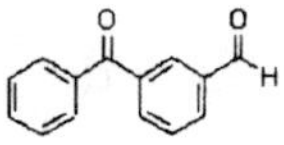   3-Benzoyl-benzaldehyde

3. 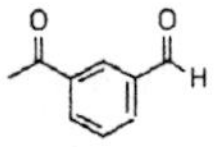   3-Acetyl-benzaldehyde

4. 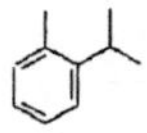   1-isopropyl-2-methyl-benzene

5. 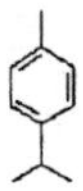   1-Isopropyl-4-methyl-benzene

6. 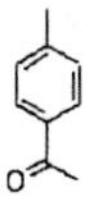   4-Acetyltoluene

7. 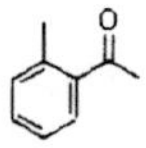   2-Acetyltoluene

8. 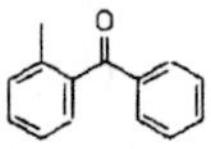   2-Methyl-benzophenone

9. 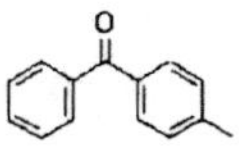   4-Methyl-benzophenone

10. 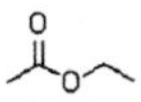   Ethyl acetate

11. Methyl acetate

12. Benzoic acid ethyl ester

13. Benzoic acid methyl ester

14. Bromoacetic acid ethyl ester

15. Acetic acid

16. Benzoic acid

17. Bromoacetic acid

18. 2,2-Diethoxy-propane

19. Benzaldehyde diethylacetal

20. Propan-2-ol

21. Benzyl alcohol

22. N,N-Diisopropyl-acetamide

23. N,N-Diisopropyl-benzamide

24. 1-Methyl-4-nitro-benzene

25. 1-Methyl-2-nitro-benzene

26. 1-Methyl-2,4-dinitro-benzene

27. 3-Nitro-benzaldehyde

28. 3-Nitro-benzoic acid

29. Bromomethyl-benzene

30. Formic acid phenyl ester

31. 2-Ethoxy-propane

32. 2-Propanone

Acid Chloride

1. Acetyl chloride

2. Benzoyl chloride

3. Heptanoyl chloride

4. Ethyl acetate

5. Benzoic acid ethyl ester

6. Ethyl heptanoate

7. Ethanol

8. Benzyl alcohol

9. 1-Heptanol

10. 3-Nitro-benzoic acid

Carbonyl Reduction

1. Benzyl alcohol

2. 1-Cyclohexanol

3. 3-Hydroxy-butyric acid methyl ester

4. Benzaldehyde diethylacetal

5. 1,1-Diethoxy-cyclohexane

6. 2-Bromo-cyclohexanone

7. 2-Bromo-3-oxo-butyric acid methyl ester

8. Benzoic acid

9. Formic acid phenyl ester

10. Oxepan-2-one

11. 3-Oxo-butyric acid

12. 3-Oxo-butyric acid ethyl ester

13. 3-Nitro-benzaldehyde

14. Bicyclohexyliden-2-one

15. 2-(Hydroxy-phenyl-methyl)-cyclohexanone

16. 2-Benzylidene-cyclohexanone

17. 2-Acetyl-3-phenyl-acrylic acid

18. 4-Phenyl-but-3-en-2-one

19. 2-Acetyl-3-phenyl-acrylic acid methyl ester

20. 2-Acetyl-3-phenyl-acrylic acid ethyl ester

21. 2-Cyclohexylidene-acetoacetic acid

22. 1-Cyclohexylidene-propan-2-one

23. 2-Cyclohexylidene-3-oxo-butyric acid methyl ester

24. 2-Cyclohexylidene-3-oxo-butyric acid ethyl ester

Claisen Condensation

1. 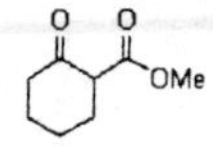 2-Oxo-cyclohexane carboxylic acid methyl ester

2. 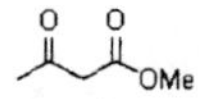 3-Oxo-butyric acid methyl ester

3. 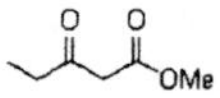 3-Oxo-pentanoic acid methyl ester

4. 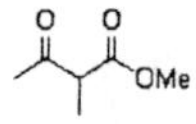 2-Methyl-3-oxo-butyric acid methyl ester

5. 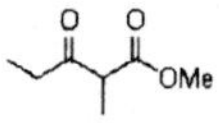 2-Methyl-3-oxo-pentanoic acid methyl ester

6. 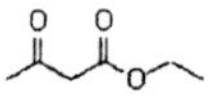 3-Oxo-butyric acid ethyl ester

7. 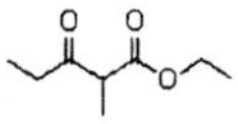 2-Methyl-3-oxo-pentanoic acid ethyl ester

8. 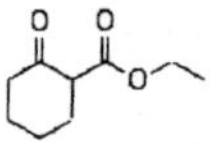 2-Oxo-cyclohexane carboxylic acid ethyl ester

9. 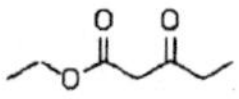 3-Oxo-pentanoic acid ethyl ester

10. 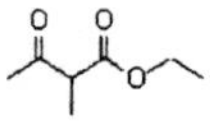 2-Methyl-3-oxo-butyric acid ethyl ester

11. 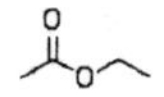 Ethyl acetate

12. 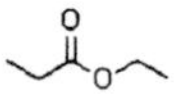 Ethyl propionate

13. 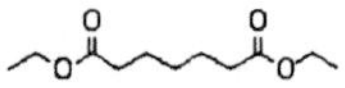 Heptanedioic acid diethyl ester

14. 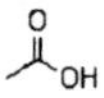 Acetic acid

15. 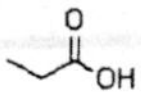 Propionic acid

16. 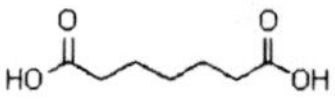 Heptanedioic acid

17. 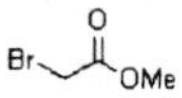 Bromo-acetic acid methyl ester

18. 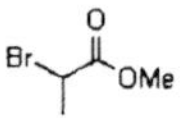 2-Bromo-propanoic acid methyl ester

19. 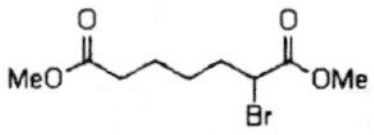 2-Bromo-heptanedioic acid dimethyl ester

Alcohol Oxidation

1. 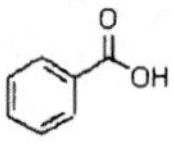 Benzoic acid

2. 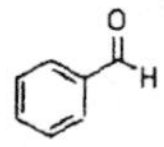 Benzaldehyde

3. 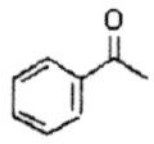 Acetophenone

4. 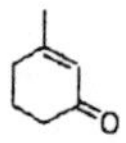 3-Methyl-cyclohex-2-enone

5. 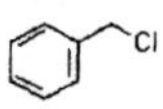 Chlorophenylmethane

6. 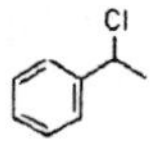 1-Chloro-1-phenylethane

7. 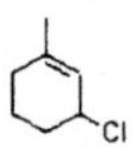 3-Chloro-1-methyl-cyclohexene

8. 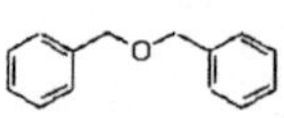 Dibenzyl Ether

9. 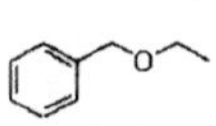 Benzyl ethyl ether

10. bis-(1-Phenyl-ethyl)-ether

11. Ethyl-(1-phenyl-ethyl)-ether

12. Benzyl-(1-phenyl-ethyl)-ether

13. 1-Methyl-cyclohexane-1,2,3-triol

14. 2-Hydroxy-2-methyl-hexanedioic acid

15. 1-Methyl-2,3-epoxycyclohexanol

Appendix C
List of Organic Qualitative Analysis Unknowns

A list of organic qualitative analysis unknowns that can be assigned arranged by unknown class.

Alkenes

1.  1-Hexene

2. 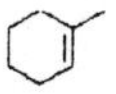 1-Methyl-cyclohexene

3. 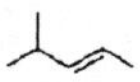 4-Methyl-2-pentene

4. 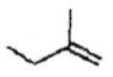 2-Methyl-1-butene

5. 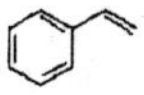 Styrene

6. 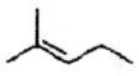 2-Methyl-2-pentene

7. 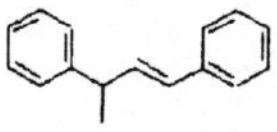 1,3-Diphenyl-1-butene

8. Benzene

9. 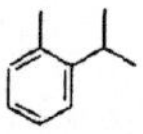 1-isopropyl-2-methyl-benzene

10. 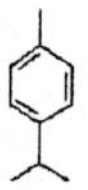 1-Isopropyl-4-methyl-benzene

11. 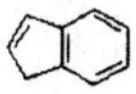 Indene

12. Cyclohexene

13. 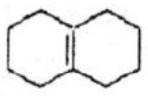 1,2,3,4,5,6,7,8-Octahydro-naphthalene

14. 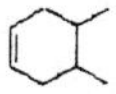 4,5-Dimethyl-cyclohexene

15. Cyclohexa-1,3-diene

16. Cyclopenta-1,3-diene

17. 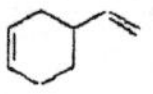 4-Vinyl-cyclohexene

18. 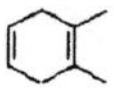 1,2-Dimethyl-cyclohexa-1,4-diene

19.  Bicylo[2.2.1]hept-2-ene

20. 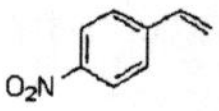 4-Nitro-styrene

21. 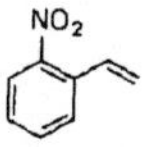 2-Nitro-styrene

22. 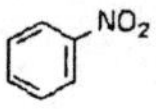 nitro-Benzene

23.  Cyclohex-2-enol

24.  2-Buten-1-ol

25. 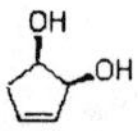 cis-Cyclopent-3-ene-1,2-diol

26. cis-4,5-Dimethyl-cyclohex-4-ene-1,2-diol

27. But-2-enal

28. 3-Phenyl-propenal

29. 2-Ethyl-hex-2-enal

30. 4-Methyl-pent-3-en-2-one

31. 2,5-Cyclohexadiene-1,4-dione

32. 3-Methyl-cyclohex-2-enone

33. 2-Propenoic acid, methyl ester

34. 2-Propenoic acid, ethyl ester

35. Cyclohex-3-enecarboxylic acid methyl ester

36. 2-Propenoic acid

37. 3-Chloro-cyclohexene

38. 3-Chloro-1-butene

39. 1,4-Dibromo-2-butene

40. 1,2-Dimethyl-1,2-epoxy-cyclohex-4-ene

41. 1-Ethoxy-2-butene

42. N-Allylaniline

43. Acrylamide

44. Cinnamamide

45. 1-Bromo-but-3-en-2-ol

46. 4-Bromo-3-ethoxy-but-1-ene

Alcohols

1. Benzyl alcohol

2. 3-Methyl-1-butanol

3. 2-Methyl-2-propanol

4. 2-Methyl-butane-1,2-diol

5. Methanol

6. Ethanol

7. Butanol

8. 1-Hexanol

9. 1-Heptanol

10. 2-Methyl-1-butanol

11. 2-Phenyl ethanol

12. 4-tert-Butylbenzyl alcohol

13. 2-Butanol

14. 2-Hexanol

15. 1-Phenylethanol

16. Diphenyl-methanol

17. 1-Phenyl-1-propanol

18. Propan-2-ol

19. 2,2-Dimethyl-pentan-3-ol

20. 2-Methyl-3-pentanol

21. 4-Methyl-2-pentanol

22. 1-Cyclohexanol

23. trans-2-methyl-cyclohexanol

24. 2,3-Dimethyl-2-butanol

25. 2-Phenyl-2-propanol

26. 2-Methyl-2-pentanol

27. 2-Methyl-2-butanol

28. 1,4-Butanediol

29. Hexane-1,2-diol

30. syn-Butane-2,3-diol

31. syn-4-Methyl-pentane-2,3-diol

32. cis-Cyclohexane-1,2-diol

33. cis-1-Methyl-cyclohexane-1,2-diol

34. Phenol

35. Benzene-1,3-diol

36. 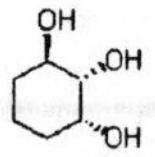 Cyclohexane-1,2,3-triol

37. 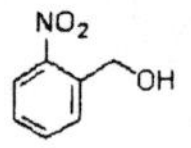 2-Nitro-benzyl alcohol

38. 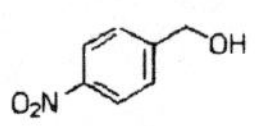 4-Nitro-benzyl alcohol

39. 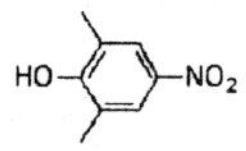 2,6-Dimethyl-4-nitro-phenol

40. 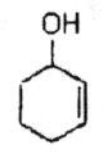 Cyclohex-2-enol

41.  2-Buten-1-ol

42. 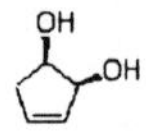 cis-Cyclopent-3-ene-1,2-diol

43. 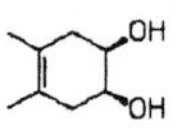 cis-4,5-Dimethyl-cyclohex-4-ene-1,2-diol

44. 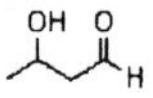 3-Hydroxybutanal

45. 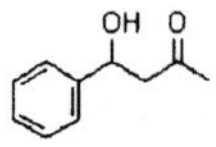 4-Hydroxy-4-phenyl-butan-2-one

46. 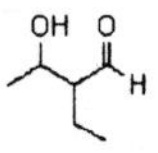 2-Ethyl-3-hydroxy-butyraldehyde

47. 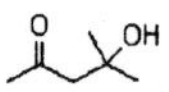 4-Hydroxy-4-methyl-pentan-2-one

48. 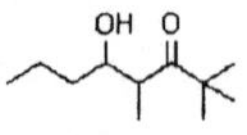 5-Hydroxy-2,2,4-trimethyl-octan-3-one

49. 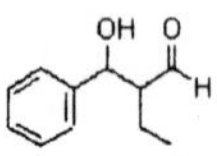 2-(Hydroxy-phenyl-methyl)-butyraldehyde

50. 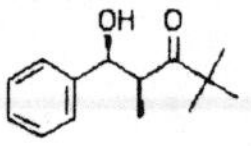 1-hydroxy-2,4,4-trimethyl-1-phenyl-pentan-3-one

51.  4-Chloro-1-butanol

52. 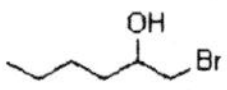 1-Bromo-2-hexanol

53. 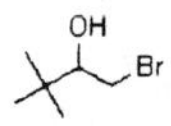 1-Bromo-3,3-dimethyl-2-butanol

54. 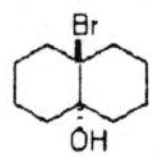 9-Bromo-10-hydroxy-trans-decalin

55. 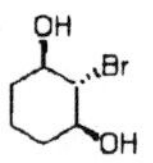 2-Bromo-cyclohexane-1,3-diol

56. 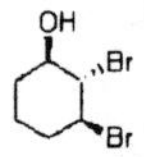 2,3-Dibromo-cyclohexanol

57. 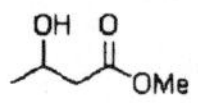 3-Hydroxy-butyric acid methyl ester

58. 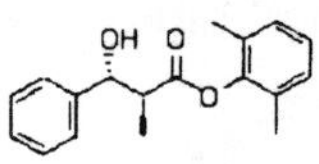 3-Hydroxy-2-methyl-3-phenyl-propionic acid 2,6-dimethyl-phenyl ester

59. 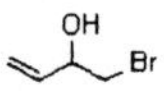 1-Bromo-but-3-en-2-ol

60. 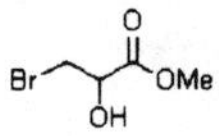 3-Bromo-2-hydroxy-propionic acid methyl ester

Aldehydes

1. 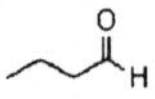 Butyraldehyde

2. 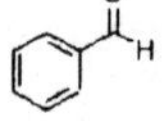 Benzaldehyde

3. 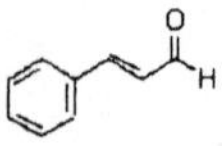 3-Phenyl-propenal

4. 3-Methyl butanal

5. 3-Isopropyl-benzaldehyde

6. 4-Nitrobenzaldehyde

7. 3-Nitro-benzaldehyde

8. But-2-enal

9. 2-Ethyl-hex-2-enal

10. 3-Acetyl-benzaldehyde

11. 3-Hydroxybutanal

12. 3-Hydroxy-3-phenyl-propanal

13. 2-Ethyl-3-hydroxy-butyraldehyde

14. 2-(Hydroxy-phenyl-methyl)-butyraldehyde

15. Bromo-acetaldehyde

16. 4-Chloro-butyraldehyde

17. 4-Chloro-benzaldehyde

18. 4-Acetamidobenzaldehyde

Ketones

1. 1-Phenyl-ethanone

2. Cyclohexanone

3. 2-Propanone

4. 2-Butanone

5. 2,2-Dimethyl-pentan-3-one

6. 4-Acetyltoluene

7. 2-Acetyltoluene

8. 4-Methyl-benzophenone

9. Cyclodecane-1,6-dione

10. Bicyclo[2.2.1]heptan-2-one

11. 4-Methyl-pent-3-en-2-one

12. 2-Cyclohexen-1-one

13.		3-Methyl-cyclohex-2-enone	3.		Formic acid
14.		2,5-Cyclohexadiene-1,4-dione	4.		Acetic acid
15.		3-Acetyl-benzaldehyde	5.		Propionic acid
16.		4-Hydroxy-4-phenyl-butan-2-one	6.		Butanoic acid
17.		4-Hydroxy-4-methyl-pentan-2-one	7.		Pentanoic acid
18.		1-hydroxy-2,4,4-trimethyl-1-phenyl-pentan-3-one	8.		2-Methyl-propionic acid
19.		5-Hydroxy-2,2,4-trimethyl-octan-3-one	9.		3-Methyl butanoic acid
20.		2-Bromo-cyclohexanone	10.		2,2-Dimethylpropanoic acid
21.		3-Oxo-butyric acid	11.		2-Phenylacetic acid
22.		2-Oxo-propionic acid	12.		Cyclohexanecarboxylic acid
23.		3-Oxo-butyric acid methyl ester	13.		Ethane-1,2-dioic acid
24.		2-Oxo-cyclohexane carboxylic acid methyl ester	14.		Propanedioic acid
			15.		Hexanedioic acid

Acids

1.		Benzoic acid	16.		Heptanedioic acid
2.		Heptanoic acid			

17. 3-Nitro-benzoic acid

18. 4-Nitro-benzoic acid

19. 2-Nitrobenzeneacetic acid

20. 2,4-Dinitrophenylacetic acid

21. 2-Propenoic acid

22. Bicyclo[2.2.1]hept-5-ene-2-carboxylic acid

23. 3-Oxo-butyric acid

24. 2-Oxo-propionic acid

25. 2-Bromo-butanoic acid

26. m-Chlorobenzoic acid

27. N-Acetylanthranilic acid

Esters

1. Ethyl-2-phenyl acetate

2. 3-Methylbutyl acetate

3. Methyl propionate

4. Methyl acetate

5. Ethyl acetate

6. Propionic acid ethyl ester

7. Propanoic acid, 1,1-dimethylethyl ester

8. Methyl butanoate

9. Ethyl butanoate

10. 3-Methylbutyl butanoate

11. Benzoic acid methyl ester

12. Benzoic acid ethyl ester

13. Methyl phenylacetate

14. 3-Methylbutyl phenylacetate

15. Ethyl heptanoate

16. Acetic acid 1-phenyl-ethyl ester

17. Formic acid methyl ester

18. Formic acid propyl ester

19. Formic acid phenyl ester

20. Propionic acid 2,6-dimethyl-phenyl ester

21. Dihydro-furan-2-one

22. Oxepan-2-one

23. 1,7-Dimethyl-heptanedioate

24. Heptanedioic acid diethyl ester

25. 3-Nitro-benzoic acid ethyl ester

26. Propionic acid-2,6-dimethyl-4-nitro-phenyl ester

27. 2-Bromo-heptanedioic acid dimethyl ester

28. 2-Propenoic acid, methyl ester

29. 2-Propenoic acid, ethyl ester

30. Cyclohex-3-enecarboxylic acid methyl ester

31. But-2-ynedioic acid ethyl ester methyl ester

32. 3-Oxo-butyric acid methyl ester

33. 3-Oxo-butyric acid ethyl ester

34. 2-Oxo-cyclohexane carboxylic acid methyl ester

35. Methyl 2-chloropropionate

36. 3-Hydroxy-butyric acid methyl ester

37. 3-Bromo-2-hydroxy-propionic acid methyl ester

38. 3-Hydroxy-2-methyl-3-phenyl-propionic acid 2,6-dimethyl-phenyl ester

Amines

1. Benzylamine

2. Diisopropyl amine

3. Triethyl amine

4. Methyl amine

5. Propyl amine

6. n-Heptylamine

7. n-Octylamine

8.	Isopropylamine	22.	Quinoline
9.	sec-Butylamine	23.	N-Allylaniline
10.	Aniline		

Amides

11.	Diethylamine	1.	N,N-Diisopropyl-acetamide
12.	N-Methylpropylamine	2.	Acetanilide
13.	N-Ethylisopropylamine	3.	Formamide
14.	N-Methylaniline	4.	Butyramide
15.	N-Methyldibutylamine	5.	Cyclohexanecarboxamide
16.	Butyldiisopropylamine	6.	N-Ethylacetamide
17.	Benzyldiisopropylamine	7.	2,2-Dimethyl-propionamide
18.	Triisopropylamine	8.	N,N-Dimethylacetamide
19.	N,N-Dimethylaniline	9.	Formanilide
20.	Cyclobutylamine	10.	N,N-Diphenylformamide
21.	1-Phenylpiperidine	11.	1-Acetylpiperidine

12. Cinnamamide

13. 2-Bromopropionamide

14. 4-Acetamidobenzaldehyde

15. 2-Bromo-N-phenylpropionamide

16. N-Acetylanthranilic acid

Halides

1. Chlorophenylmethane

2. 2-Chloro-2-methyl propane

3. Chlorocyclohexane

4. 1-Chloro-3-methyl butane

5. 1,4-Dibromo-2-butene

6. Chlorobutane

7. 1-tert-Butyl-4-chloromethyl-benzene

8. Ethyl bromide

9. Bromomethyl-benzene

10. 2-Chloro-hexane

11. 2-Chloro-butane

12. 2-Chloro-3-methylbutane

13. 2-Chloro-4-methyl pentane

14. 3-Chloro-2-methyl pentane

15. exo-2-Chloro-bicyclo[2.2.1]heptane

16. Bromocyclohexane

17. 2-Chloro-2-methylpentane

18. 4a-Chloro-decahydro-naphthalene

19. 1,2-Dibromo-hexane

20. 1,2-Dibromo-2-methyl-butane

21. 1,2-Dibromo-1-methyl-cyclohexane

22. 4a,8a-Dibromo-decahydro-naphthalene

23. 1-Chloromethyl-2-nitro-benzene

24. 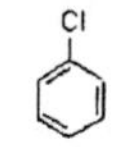 Benzene Chloride

25. 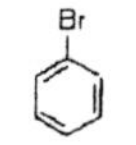 Bromobenzene

26. 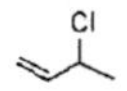 3-Chloro-1-butene

27. 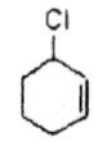 3-Chloro-cyclohexene

28.  4-Chloro-1-butanol

29. 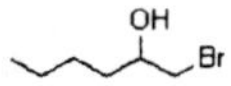 1-Bromo-2-hexanol

30. 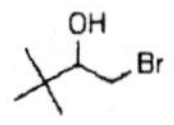 1-Bromo-3,3-dimethyl-2-butanol

31. 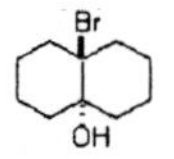 9-Bromo-10-hydroxy-trans-decalin

32. 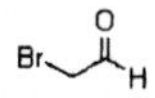 Bromo-acetaldehyde

33. 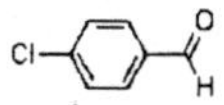 4-Chloro-benzaldehyde

34. 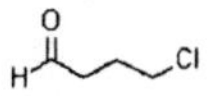 4-Chloro-butyraldehyde

35. 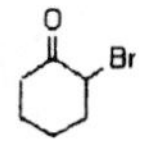 2-Bromo-cyclohexanone

36. 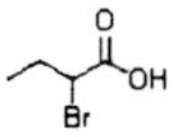 2-Bromo-butanoic acid

37. 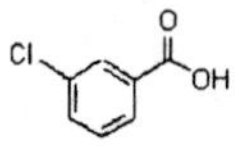 m-Chlorobenzoic acid

38. 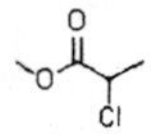 Methyl 2-chloropropionate

39. 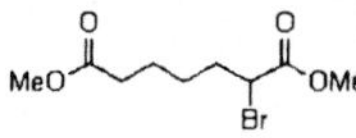 2-Bromo-heptanedioic acid dimethyl ester

40. 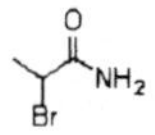 2-Bromopropionamide

41. 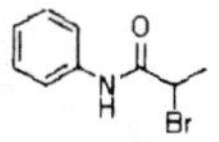 2-Bromo-N-phenyl propionamide

42. 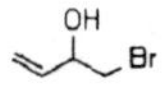 1-Bromo-but-3-en-2-ol

43. 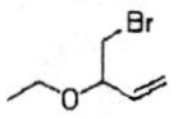 4-Bromo-3-ethoxy-but-1-ene

44. 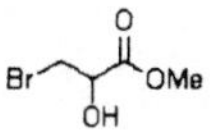 3-Bromo-2-hydroxy-propionic acid methyl ester

45. 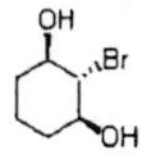 2-Bromo-cyclohexane-1,3-diol

46. 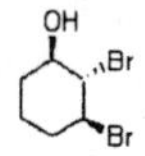 2,3-Dibromo-cyclohexanol

Ethers

1. 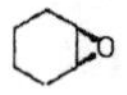 1,2-Epoxy-cyclohexane

2. 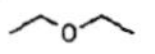 Diethyl ether

3. 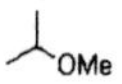 2-Methoxypropane

4. 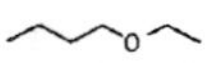 1-Ethoxy-butane

5. 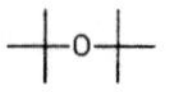 Di-tert-butyl ether

6. 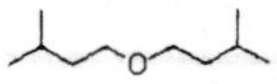 Diisopentyl ether

7. 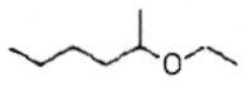 Ethyl 2-hexyl ether

8.  2-Methoxy-2-methyl-propane

9. 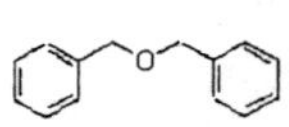 Dibenzyl Ether

10. 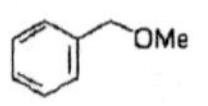 Benzyl methyl ether

11. 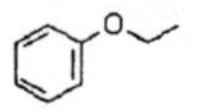 Ethyl phenyl ether

12. 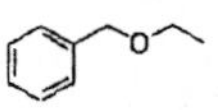 Benzyl ethyl ether

13. Tetrahydrofuran

14.  2,3-Epoxy-butane

15. 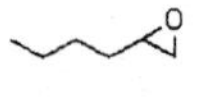 1,2-Epoxyhexane

16. 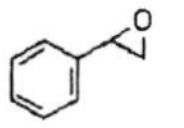 1,2-Epoxyethylbenzene

17. 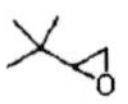 3,3-Dimethyl-1,2-epoxybutane

18.  1,2-Epoxy-2-methyl-butane

19. 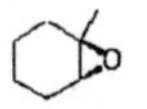 1-Methyl-1,2-epoxycyclohexane

20. 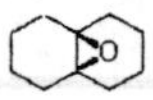 4a,8a-Epoxy-decahydro-napthalene

21. 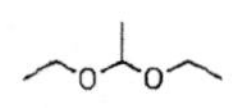 1,1-Diethoxy-ethane

22. 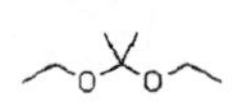 2,2-Diethoxy-propane

23. 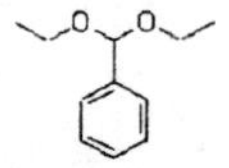 Benzaldehyde diethylacetal

24. 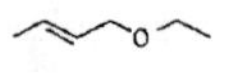 1-Ethoxy-2-butene

25. 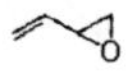 3,4-Epoxy-but-1-ene

26. 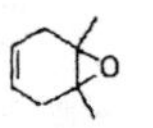 1,2-Dimethyl-1,2-epoxy-cyclohex-4-ene

27. 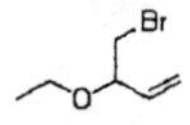 4-Bromo-3-ethoxy-but-1-ene

Natural Products

1. 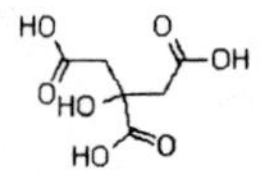 Citric Acid

2. 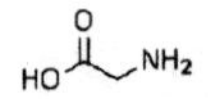 Glycine

3. 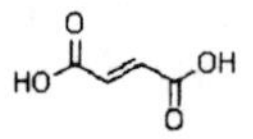 Fumaric Acid

4. 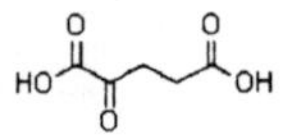 Alpha-ketogluteric Acid

5. 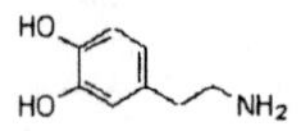 Dopamine

6. 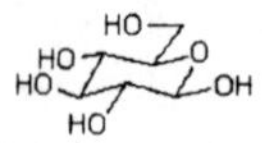 D-Glucose

7. 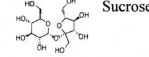 Sucrose

8. Vanillin

9. Capsaicin

10. Cocaine

11. Cholesterol

Appendix D
Quantum Equations

The experiments in the quantum simulation are based on actual experimental measurements, as is the case for the emission and adsorption experiments or on equations that are derived from fundamental principles. Given in this section is a description of some of these equations that an instructor may wish to pass on to the students in the class. It is beyond the scope of this User Guide to detail how these equations were derived. Most of the supporting information for these equations can be found in a good undergraduate physics text. In the case of the Millikan Oil Drop Experiment, the equations used in the simulation were developed from Millikan's original paper.

Photoelectric Effect. In the photoelectric experiment, the kinetic energy of the electron ejected from a metal due to an incident photon is calculated using the equation, $E_{kinetic} = h\nu - \Phi$, where h is Planck's constant, ν is the frequency of the photon, and Φ is the work function for the metal. Values of the work function used for all the available metals are given in the *Metal Table* found in the *QuantumDB* directory. In this experiment, no multiple photon events are allowed to occur.

Blackbody Radiation. In the quantum simulation, each available metal can be heated up to its melting point, where it is then allowed to melt. Before the metal melts, each metal is treated as a perfect blackbody emitter and follows Planck's blackbody radiation formula. The equation that is used in the simulation is given in terms of the intensity (not the energy density, which is normally the case) and is $I(\lambda) = N \times \dfrac{8\pi hc}{T \cdot \lambda^5} \left(\dfrac{1}{e^{hc/\lambda k_B T} - 1} \right)$ where $I(\lambda)$ is the intensity of the radiation as a function of wavelength, λ; N is a normalizing factor set to 0.2 to keep the intensity within the bounds of 0 to 1; and the other variables take on their normal values.

Thompson Experiment. In the Thompson Experiment, the charge-to-mass ratio, q/m_e, for an electron can be calculated by measuring the deflection of a beam of electrons on a phosphor screen caused by an applied electric field and then measuring the magnitude of a perpendicular magnetic field required to bring the deflected beam back to the center of the phosphor screen. The setup and geometry of the experiment has an incident beam of electrons with a given kinetic energy (velocity), which passes through an electric field of strength E and a perpendicular magnetic field of strength B. Initially, B is set to 0 (zero), and the incident beam is deflected on the phosphor screen by applying a voltage across the electric plates. The deflection and voltage must be measured. The deflected beam is then brought back to the zero (or middle) of the phosphor screen by applying the magnetic field. From these measurements and using values specified in the INI variables, the charge-to-mass ratio for an electron, q/m_e, can be calculated.

The derivation of the following equations is straightforward, but involves more detail than is necessary here. The charge-to-mass ratio, q/m_e, is calculated using the equation

$$\frac{q}{m_e} = \frac{2Ez}{B^2l^2}, \text{ where}$$

q = the charge on the electron in coulombs,

m_e = the mass of the electron in kg,

E = is the magnitude of the electric field calculated using $E = V/d$,

V = voltage applied to the electric plates in volts,

d = the spacing between the electric plates in m and is specified as an INI variable in *Lab.ini* (default setting = 0.050 m),

z = the deflection of the electron beam as the beam exits the electric and magnetic fields,

B = the applied magnetic field in T, and

l = the length of the electric and magnetic fields. (This is also specified as an INI variable in *Lab.ini*. The default setting is 0.050 m.)

The deflection of the electron beam as the beam exits the electric and magnetic field, z, cannot be measured directly, but must be calculated using the measured deflection on the phosphor screen, x. The equation that calculates z from x is straightforward to derive and reduces to

$$z = \frac{x}{1 + 2b/l}, \text{ where}$$

z = the deflection of the electron beam as the beam exits the electric and magnetic fields,

x = the deflection of the electron beam as measured at the phosphor screen,

b = the distance from the electric and magnetic field to the phosphor screen and is specified as an INI variable in *Lab.ini* (default setting = 0.762 m),

l = the length of the electric and magnetic fields. (This is also specified as an INI variable in *Lab.ini*. The default setting is 0.050 m.)

Millikan Oil Drop Experiment. In the Millikan Oil Drop Experiment, the charge of an electron is measured using the following process: (1) A random number of electrons (between 0 and 5) are deposited on very fine oil mist droplets using an electron gun. (2) The mass of an individual droplet is calculated by measuring the terminal velocity of the drop. (3) The drop is then suspended (or stopped from falling) by adjusting the voltage across the electric plates. (4) From the mass of the drop and the voltage required to suspend the drop, the charge on the drop can be calculated. The following equations are required for this calculation.

To calculate the radius of the oil droplet from the terminal velocity, the first approximation of the radius, is

$$r = \sqrt{\frac{9 \cdot \eta_{air} \cdot v_t}{2 \cdot g \cdot (\rho_{oil} - \rho_{air})}},$$

which can then be used to calculate a more accurate value using the equation

$$r = \sqrt{\frac{9 \cdot \eta_{air} \cdot v_t}{2 \cdot g \cdot (\rho_{oil} - \rho_{air})} \cdot \left(\frac{1}{1 + b/pr}\right)^{1/2}},$$

where r on the right side of the equation is the radius acquired from the first approximation and the new r is used for the second iteration and so on until the answer converges. The variables are defined as follows:

v_t = terminal velocity;

g = 9.81 m·s^{-2}, acceleration due to gravity;

ρ_{oil} = density of oil = 821 kg·m^{-3} (set as an INI variable in *Video.ini*);

ρ_{air} = density of air = 1.22 kg·m^{-3} (set as an INI variable in *Video.ini*);

η_{air} = viscosity of air = 1.4607 × 10^{-5} kg·m^{-1}·s^{-1} (set as an INI variable in *Video.ini*);

b = correction for small drop size = 8.1184 × 10^{-8} m·atm;

p = atmospheric pressure in atm = 1 (set as an INI variable in *Video.ini*).

From this, the mass of the droplet can be calculated from the equation

$$m = \frac{4\pi}{3} \cdot r^3 \cdot \rho_{oil}.$$

If a voltage is applied such that the drop is stationary, then the force due to gravity is balanced by the force due to the electric field, or

$$qE = mg.$$

Rearranging and using $E = V/d_{plates}$ yields

$$q = \frac{d_{plates} \cdot m \cdot g}{V} \quad \text{or} \quad Q(n) \cdot C = \frac{d_{plates} \cdot m \cdot g}{V}, \text{ where}$$

q = total charge on the drop,

$Q(n)$ = number of electrons on the drop (an integer),

C = the fundamental charge of an electron,

E = electric field = V/d_{plates},

V = voltage across the plates, and

d_{plates} = the distance between the voltage plates = 0.010 m (set as an INI variable in *Video.ini*).

To do a more refined calculation of q, or to calculate it for a nonzero velocity for an applied field, the equation

$$q = \frac{4 \cdot \pi \cdot d_{plates}}{3 \cdot V} \cdot \left(\frac{1}{g(\rho_{oil} - \rho_{air})} \cdot \left(\frac{9 \cdot \eta_{air}}{2} \right)^3 \right)^{1/2} \cdot \left(\frac{1}{1 + b/pr} \right)^{3/2} \cdot \left(v_t - v_{field} \right) \cdot \sqrt{v_t}$$

can be used, where the only new variable not described previously, v_{field}, is the velocity of the drop in the applied electric field.

Appendix E
Frequently Asked Questions by Students

This appendix contains a list of questions frequently asked by students as they use the *Virtual ChemLab* simulations. The questions are divided into four parts: *Lab Book Questions, Organic Questions, Inorganic Questions*, and *Quantum Questions*. The *Help* mode is available for additional questions. Simply click the pull-down TV handle, click the *Help* mode, and then select *Overview*. This section should get you started and give you a good overview of the program and how to use it. You can also visit *chemlab.byu.edu* for up-to-date information.

Lab Book Questions

Q: What is the purpose of the lab book? Why is it useful?
A: The lab book allows you to write and save experimental procedures and observations. Through the lab book, results and notes are submitted to the instructor for grading.

Q: How can I save my notes in the lab book easily?
A: The program saves the contents of the lab book when you close or exit the lab book and during various other lab book operations. The program is also set up to save the contents of the lab book automatically every five minutes.

Q: How can I maneuver around the lab book?
A: Use the top four buttons on the left page to move around inside the lab book. The functions of these buttons are described in the *Navigation* section of the lab book *Help*.

Q: What can I do so that the lab book is more user friendly?
A: Here are a few commands that will help:
- Ctrl-c copies selection.
- Ctrl-v pastes selection.
- Home goes to the first page of the assignment.
- End goes to the last page of the assignment.
  You can write in any part of your lab book, but you can only use Ctrl-c and Ctrl-v in the current active section of your lab book. The current active section of your lab book is either the assignment section for the current unknown in the lab room or the practice section if there is no unknown in the lab room. If you want to copy part of the practice section into an assignment section, copy the practice section while the unknown is in the stockroom. Then retrieve the unknown, and paste your selection into the assignment section.

Q: When I use my lab book, how can I make sure the grader sees what I see? (This question deals with how to add pages to the lab book and allowing word wrap around each line.)
A: Always open a new page when you get close to the bottom of the original page. The grader cannot see anything typed past the last line (even though you can continue to type

below the last line). Detailed information on how to use the lab book is located in the lab book itself.

Q: How can I use the lab book simultaneously with the rest of the program (rather than having the window move behind the others)?

A: The lab book window and the lab window can be moved on the desktop to any location that is most convenient for your particular needs. If the screen resolution is insufficient, most monitors may be adjusted to give a higher resolution resulting in smaller windows.

Q: Why can't I write in different portions of my lab book at the same time?

A: After submitting an assignment, nothing can be written or changed for that assignment. However, while working on an assignment, all sections are available for reference, and the practice section is still available to write in. Keep in mind that only the assignment section will be submitted to your instructor.

Q: Whenever I re-opened my lab book or whenever I left the stockroom, my lab book would automatically return to "Page 1." Is there any way I can keep this from happening?

A: The program does not store what page you were on when you were last in the lab book; there is nothing you can do to avoid this.

Organic Questions

Functionality/Usage

Q: What do I do if I have trouble logging on?

A: Make sure you are not typing in your password too fast. Also, note that all ID's (or passwords) are case sensitive. If you still are having trouble logging in, check with your lab assistant or instructor to make sure you are using the correct ID.

Q: Where can I go to get some help using the program?

A: A good source to visit is the TV screen in the lab. Then click *Help*. Here you will find most of the answers to your questions. If you still have questions go to your TA or instructor for help, or you can visit *chemlab.byu.edu* for up-to-date information.

Q: How do I begin starting on something new in the lab?

A: In *Organic Chemlab,* you are only allowed to work on one experiment at a time. To start a new experiment (either a synthesis or qualitative analysis experiment), you need to clear the lab first by clicking the red disposal bucket and then proceed to the stockroom. If you need help setting up an experiment in the stockroom, click the bell on the stockroom counter.

Q: How can I easily add reagents to my flask?

A: All reagents for a synthesis experiment must be added before the reaction is started. Reagents are added to the flask by clicking the selected reagent and dragging the indicated icon to the reaction flask, or you can double-click the selected reagent.

Q: How can I easily use the lab equipment?

A: If you want to use the IR or NMR equipment, simply click the selected analytical tool and drag the icon to the reaction flask. (This equipment is available after workup.) You can use TLC at anytime during the reaction by clicking the TLC jar and dragging the TLC plate icon to the desired flask. Other lab equipment for building a synthesis experiment, workup, or purification is accessed by clicking and dragging or by double-clicking.

Q: How can I start over quickly?

A: To start over, the lab must be cleared first by clicking the red disposal bucket. Then proceed to the stockroom to set up a new experiment.

Q: What is the difference in throwing away test tubes and clearing the lab?

A: If you throw away a test tube, it only disposes of the aliquot in the test tube. The qualitative assignment is still open, and you can continue to bring over new aliquots for further testing. If you clear the lab (using the red disposal bucket), it will dispose of the flask containing the qualitative analysis unknown and force you to go to the stockroom to start a new experiment.

Q: How do I stop a reaction?

A: The reaction stops when you use the separatory funnel and then quench the reaction by adding a workup reagent. In an actual lab, this step is analogous with removing the flask from the heat source and doing extractions on the reaction mixture.

Q: How do I switch between different procedures (like going from refluxing to doing a workup)?

A: Switching between procedures is simply done by choosing the next step. For example, if you want to stop the reaction, choose the separatory funnel and then follow with the appropriate workup reagent. To purify a liquid, you must have the flask on the stir plate and then select the distillation equipment and N_2 gas. To purify a solid, you select the crystallization dish and add the flask to the dish. For more details on the procedures, use the *Help* button located on the TV screen.

Q: How can I expand the possibilities of *ChemLab Organic* with the limited number of reagents?

A: The short answer is you can't. However, keep in mind that *ChemLab Organic* has over 50 starting materials, which can be combined in combinations of one or two, and any of the 15 reagents can be used with these starting materials combinations. That is a lot of chemistry to explore and learn.

Q: What do I do if the computer locks up?

A: We have found that *Organic Chemlab* does not cause system freeze-ups. If your computer locks up, simply reboot the computer. Please note it is good practice to always save your lab book during the experiment. (Simply close or exit your lab book to save.) In addition, the program automatically saves the lab book every five minutes.

Analyzing Data

Q: What do I do if some peaks on the IR or the NMR are wrong or missing?

A: Students need to know that the IR and NMR spectra are actual data of the specific compounds and not theoretical or idealized. The developers of the program obtained spectra from precise instruments and took great care in the accuracy of each particular compound. Always check the integration of each of the peaks, and make sure to account for each hydrogen atom.

Q: What do I do if the pieces of my analysis do not fit together as I think they should?

A: Usually when this occurs, some part of your analysis is not accurate. You need to always check the data a few times before concluding there is error within the program. Again, great care and accuracy went into the creation of the *Organic Chemlab*.

Q: How do I know if I have a heteroatom?

A: The easiest way to know is by the C–H analysis posted on the chalkboard. The C–H analysis tests only for carbon and hydrogen. Therefore, if the C–H percentages do not add up to 100%, the unknown has at least one heteroatom present.

Q: What do I do if the C and H percentages are wrong on my qualitative unknowns?

A: The C–H percentages were calculated based on the actual chemical formula of the unknown and have been thoroughly checked for accuracy. You should always presume the data to be correct. Most students make the mistake of thinking they "know" what the unknown is before analyzing all the data given. Do not try to "fit" the data to your presumption of the unknown. First, analyze the data and then come up with a number of possibilities the unknown might be.

Q: What can I do if my unknown is too difficult for me to identify?

A: If you have spent a significant amount time analyzing all the data given and still have not come to any conclusions, contact your lab assistant or instructor. They will help you identify your unknown and any mistakes you might have made in your analysis.

Q: How do I know if a test for my qualitative analysis occurs "fast" or "moderate"?

A: Use the TV screen, and click *Help* to answer questions regarding qualitative analysis. The details for each functional group test are listed in *Help*.

Q: How can I make sure a test is positive, even though it is difficult to interpret?

A: First you need to familiarize yourself with qualitative analysis and the practice unknowns. The purpose of the practice unknowns is to allow you to explore the possible positive and negative results for the 15 functional group tests for the different classes of unknowns. In *Help*, you can read about qualitative analysis and the 15 different functional group tests.

Reporting Data

Q: Where can I go if I have difficulty naming compounds?

A: You can always refer to your organic chemistry textbook, an Aldrich catalog, or your lab assistant or instructor.

Q: When I use my lab book, what can I do to make sure my journal entries do not disappear?

A: The program is set up to save the contents of the lab book every five minutes. It is always good practice to save your lab book after adding more information. (This is done by closing or exiting the lab book.) The lab book has the function to print, so you can save a hard copy of your journal entries.

Q: What do I do if I loose my information when I try to report my results?

A: This problem is old and has been fixed on more recent versions of *Organic Chemlab*.

Inorganic Questions

Stockroom Issues

Q: How can I move between the stockroom and the lab?

A: Simply click the stockroom at the top right of the interface to access the stockroom. To return to the lab, click the *Return to Lab* arrow at the top right of the stockroom.

Q: What is the stockroom? How do I use the stockroom?

A: The stockroom contains test tubes, all the cations, the practice unknowns, and the assignments (assigned unknowns). Click the bell in the stockroom to learn more about how to use the stockroom and stockroom features.

Computer Issues

Q: What do I do if I have trouble logging on?

A: Make sure you are not typing in your password too fast. Also, note that all ID's (or passwords) are case sensitive. Another common problem is using the numeric key pad to type in numbers when the <u>Num Lock</u> key has not been pressed. If you still are having trouble logging in, check with your lab assistant or instructor to make sure you are using the correct ID.

Q: What do I do if the computer crashes or locks up?

A: If your computer locks up, simply reboot the computer. Please note it is good practice to always save your lab book during the experiment. (Simply close or exit your lab book to save.) In addition, the program automatically saves the lab book every five minutes.

Q: What do I do if the font in the pull-down TV menu is too small to read?

A: This can be a problem sometimes when the screen or monitor resolution is high or the monitor is low quality. To fix this problem, the screen resolution can be reduced, which will increase the window size.

Reporting Data

Q: How can I report my unknown?

A: After each step in identifying your unknown, write what you did. Staying on top of the lab book will help you identify your unknown; a good lab book will track procedures and results, helping you see connections between known solutions and your unknown. When you have identified your unknown, click the *Report* button and then select the cations present in your unknown. After clicking *Submit*, all notes and your reported cations are submitted to your instructor, and no changes can be made to that lab book section.

Maneuverability Issues

Q: How can I easily access the right lab assignment?

A: Click the stockroom (the right top of the lab room), and your assignment will be in the left slot of the unknown rack (located at the right). Click and drag your unknown assignment to the test tube holder, and then click *Done* or the *Return to Lab* arrow.

Q: Why can't I work on a practice unknown at the same time as my assigned unknown?

A: The program only allows one unknown to be out in the lab at any one time. A practice unknown should be done before, not simultaneously with, an assigned unknown. However, if you have started an assigned unknown, but you feel like you need more practice, you can dispose of the assigned unknown and bring a practice unknown into the lab room. After disposing of all of the test tubes associated with the practice unknown, you can go to the stockroom to retrieve the same assigned unknown as before.

Q: How can I easily label the test tubes?

A: Click the label area on the test tube, type an appropriate description, and then press *Enter*.

Q: What is the difference in "clear all" and just throwing away one test tube?

A: Throwing away a test tube (by dragging it to the red disposal bucket) disposes only that test tube. If you "clear all" by clicking the red disposal bucket, all the test tubes in the lab room will be thrown away.

Q: ChemLab is hard for me to navigate. How can I look at the interface of ChemLab so that it is more intuitive to me?

A: Click the pull-down TV handle at the top left corner of the interface. Click the *Help* mode, and then select *Overview*. This section should get you started and give you a good overview of the program and how to use it. You can also visit *chemlab.byu.edu* for up-to-date information.

Instructor/Help Menu Support or Other Implementation Problems

Q: What is the Tutorial mode used for? Will it help me complete my assignments faster? If so, how?

A: The tutorial mode displays the list of cations (in whatever form they may be) in the active test tube. This list reflects the changes to the cations as various reagents are added to the test tube or other laboratory manipulations are performed. This list is the main tutorial or learning tool when exploring the chemistry of the cations. By using the tutorial, you will be able to learn methods for separating and identifying cations. The tutorial mode is not active for assignments or practice unknowns, but your preparation and lab notes will help you complete your assignment.

Q: What can I do if I feel like I'm spending too much time completing an assignment?

A: If you have spent a significant amount of time experimenting with your unknown and analyzing your data, and you still have not come to any conclusions, contact your lab assistant or instructor. They will give you ideas and clues on how to develop a method for identifying your unknown. Remember, the purpose of *ChemLab* is to help you develop problem solving strategies by allowing you to experiment and try different approaches. The key to an inorganic qualitative analysis experiment is being systematic to discover the chemistry that will allow you to separate and identify each cation in your unknown.

Q: What is the difference between practice mode and assignment mode?

A: The practice unknown gives you the opportunity to create an unknown similar to the assignment unknown (the unknown created by your instructor) and practice your scheme or approach to discovering the cations in your unknown without the penalty of loosing points. The practice unknown also prevents you from "cheating" by looking at the TV in tutorial mode.

Q: How can I create a practice unknown?

A: Select the *Help* mode on the pull-down TV, and then select *Practice Unknowns*. This help section explains how to create a practice unknown.

Q: Where can I go for help on how to use the program?

A: The *Help* mode on the pull-down TV in the lab is a good source for help. Here you will find most of the answers to your questions. If you still have questions, go to your TA or instructor for help, or you can visit *chemlab.byu.edu* for up-to-date information.

Q: How can I know what options I have for a particular procedure I'd like to follow? For example, can I combine the solutions from two test tubes?

A: Any reagent can be added and any laboratory manipulation can be performed at any time to test tubes in the lab room, but test tubes cannot be mixed together or taken back into the stockroom to add more cations. However, keep in mind that in the stockroom any cation can be added in any combination to a test tube, and any test tube can have any of the 11 reagents added to the test tube in any combination. This results in over 10^{16} possible combinations. That is a lot of chemistry to explore.

Q: Some of the chemicals I wanted to use were not available. Where can I go to receive more instruction on how to make substitutions?

A: There is a way to separate and/or identify each cation with the available reagents. Remember, the purpose of *ChemLab* is to allow you to learn and discover the necessary chemistry to identify your unknown quickly and safely, not to provide the outcomes for any possible chemical route. In *ChemLab*, we do not want a "cookbooking" mentality; rather, your job is to explore and experiment with the available reagents, finding ways to identify and separate cations. In the program, there are 26 cations, 11 reagents, and 10 different laboratory manipulations. The reagents and laboratory manipulations can be added or performed to any combination of the cations, which provides a lot of chemistry to explore and learn.

Q: Can I leave the heat on while I centrifuge or decant?

A: Yes. In fact, this may be an important option to use while separating cations. Whenever the hotplate is on the lab table, it is on, but it does not restrict any of the other nine buttons for laboratory manipulations.

Q: I didn't know I needed to divide my practice unknown—each time I threw the test tubes away, the computer would generate a new unknown. What can I do to keep the same practice unknown?

A: In order to let you practice more, the program generates a different unknown each time you retrieve a practice unknown from the stockroom. Just remember to divide your unknown so that you have enough to sufficiently analyze your unknown in case of mistakes.

Procedures

Q: Decanting was confusing because there is still liquid in my test tube; what is *that* liquid and where did my supernatant go?

A: The decant option puts the supernatant, or liquid, from the active test tube into a new test tube placed in the first available slot in the test tube rack. Any precipitate that is left behind is rinsed with an appropriate solution at the right pH so that the precipitate does not dissolve—that is the liquid you see after decanting.

Q: When I was adding reagents, I didn't know how much was added – one drop, two drops, etc. How do I know if I added "enough" of the solution? Does this matter for completing assignments?

A: The reagents, or anions, that you add are always added in excess for precipitates to form. The only time that adding a reagent twice will actually change the solution is when you add Na_2CO_3 to HNO_3 or you add HNO_3 to Na_2CO_3; combining these reagents first results in H_2O, CO_2, and a more neutral solution, but the second addition of HNO_3 or Na_2CO_3 will result in an acidic or basic solution. The purpose of the pH buffers is to replace the need for drop wise addition of acid or base to adjust the pH.

Q: When I work on my assignments, how can I get enough copies of my unknown so that I don't have to keep returning to the stockroom to get more?

A: Before you start working with your unknown, make a copy by simply clicking the *Divide* button (fifth button from the left). Before you use this copy, make another copy by clicking the *Divide* button again.

Q: When a reagent was added to my test tube, sometimes it didn't look like it was added: My solution didn't change colors, my solution didn't precipitate, or the reagent didn't show up in the Tutorial mode. Does this mean that there was a bug in the program?

A: The Tutorial mode displays the list of the cations (in whatever form they may be), but it does not display reagents. Simply clicking the reagent will add the reagent to the active test tube, but remember that many reagents will not react with the cations in the test tube.

Troubleshooting Techniques

Q: What can I do if I can't see or distinguish between the flame tests?

A: The videos of the flame tests are actual footage taken in the laboratory. If you are not sure whether the flame is indicative of the cations you suspect in the solution, compare the flame with several known solutions. (Go to the stockroom, and make solutions of the cations you suspect in your unknown.) Remember to use your original solution for flame tests since adding most reagents will add Na^+, which gives a strong yellow flame.

Q: Where can I go to learn more chemistry, so that I can make the simulation do what I want?

A: You can learn more chemistry by experimenting with the simulation and discovering the chemistry yourself. The simulation is designed to teach the thinking processes that are the foundation of an inorganic qualitative analysis laboratory. The simulation is unrestrictive, allowing you to explore and learn for yourself. You could always refer to a book containing solution chemistry in order to predict the chemistry, or you could just use the simulation to discover the chemistry yourself.

General Problems

Q: How can I undo my mistakes?

A: Just like in the actual laboratory, you cannot simply remove a reagent. However, you can divide your test tube at different points during your analysis. By doing this, you can revert back to the divided solution instead of the original solution if you make a mistake.

Q: How can I determine the degrees of solubility when every precipitate looks the same?

A: The best way to determine the solubility of a precipitate is to change the pH to find the conditions in which the precipitate will dissolve.

Q: How can I easily keep track of my test tubes on my rack?

A: Label your test tubes and keep track of your work in the lab book.

Q: How can I write subscripts and superscripts into my notes?

A: There is no easy way to use superscripts and subscripts in the lab book. However, if you really want to go the extra mile there is an Accessory program on most PC and Mac computers, which allows you to bring up the character set for each installed font on the computer. *ChemLab* does not actually install a font permanently on the computer, but only installs it temporarily while the program is running. If you bring up the character set, you will see a font called *ChemLab*. Choose this font, and you will see the superscripted and subscripted characters we use in the program.

Q: What can I do if the QuickTime videos are not working?

A: There are usually three causes for this: (1) There is an INI variable in the *ChemLabI* directory that points to where the videos are located. If this path is wrong, then neither the videos nor the pictures will work. (2) QuickTime 5.0 or later has not been installed on your computer. (3) For unknown reasons on some PC machines, the default settings for the QuickTime player do not work correctly. Try going into the QuickTime settings from the Control Panel and setting the video properties to Safe Mode.

Quantum Questions

Stockroom Issues

Q: How can I move between the stockroom and the lab?

A: Simply click the stockroom at the top center of the interface to access the stockroom. To return to the lab, click the *Return to Lab* arrow at the top right of the stockroom.

Q: What is the stockroom? How do I use the stockroom?

A: The stockroom is used to select the equipment for a particular experiment that will be carried out on the optics table in the laboratory. Click the bell in the stockroom to learn more about how to use the stockroom and stockroom features.

Laboratory Set-up

Q: I don't understand what all the equipment does. Where can I go to become more familiar with what each piece of equipment does?

A: Click the pull-down TV handle, click on *Help* mode, and then select *The Simulation*. Pages 3-11 of this section contain descriptions (including the degree of idealization) for all the equipment in the stockroom.

Q: How do I set up an experiment?

A: Experiments can be set up by selecting equipment in the stockroom. This equipment is placed on the stockroom counter while in the stockroom. From the laboratory, this equipment can be clicked and dragged from the counter and placed in selected locations on the optics table to perform an experiment. It is up to the user to design the experiment, arrange the equipment appropriately, and set the correct values on the instruments. When allowed by the instructor, the clipboard gives access to a list of 15 fundamental experiments that are predefined and ready to run. To select one of these experiments, click the clipboard, and then click the desired experiment; the necessary equipment will be automatically selected and placed on the stockroom counter. Clicking the *Return to Lab* arrow will then automatically place the equipment on the optics table in the laboratory and start the experiment.

Q: What is the purpose of the optics table?

A: The optics table is where all the equipment is placed to perform an experiment. In an actual laboratory, an optics table is used to isolate the experiment from the vibrations of the building.

Q: How realistic is this laboratory? Is this really how these experiments are done?

A: The actual experiments are not so simplistic. Most of the equipment is highly idealized in order to simplify the simulation to within the general scope of the *Virtual ChemLab* series. The *Help* mode describes all the idealizations and assumptions. Click the pull-down TV handle, click the *Help* mode, and then select *The Simulation*. Pages 3-11 of this section contain descriptions of the degree of idealization for all the equipment in the stockroom. Other important idealizations and assumptions of the laboratory are listed on page 12.

Q: Does an electron gun really look like it does in the simulation?

A: An electron gun is a virtual instrument. An electron source does not exist that can produce a collimated beam of electrons over the range of energies and with a range of intensities that the virtual electron gun has. In addition, as actual laboratory experiment would require that these electrons be contained in a vacuum; otherwise, the electrons would ionize the air at high intensities and energies or collide with the air molecules at low intensities and be absorbed.

Q: Does a laser really look and function like it does in the simulation?

A: The image used for this laser was modeled after an actual laser. The insides of this laser can be seen by mousing over the laser while it is on the optics table and turned off. Lasers do exist that can produce light over a range of wavelengths, but not even close to the range that this "virtual" laser can produce. The range of intensities covered by this laser is also significantly wider than what can be produced by a real laser.

Q: The detectors can be placed at several different angles. Why does the detector monitor always look the same?

A: The detector monitor always faces forward towards you no matter what direction the detector is facing on the optics table.

Q: What is the purpose of the spectrum chart? Can I use it in for any experiments?

A: The spectrum chart is provided as a reference in the virtual laboratory. It depicts the different regions of the electromagnetic spectrum. Clicking the chart will bring up an expanded view in a separate window. When the laser is out in the laboratory and turned on, arrows will be displayed on the chart showing the wavelength set on the laser in relation to the rest of the electromagnetic spectrum.

Saving Data

Q: When I save the spectrometer screen to the lab book, why does it come up in wavelength units if I save it in frequency units?

A: Hitting the record button saves the current detector output according to the intensity and setting controllers of the equipment. The record button does not save the settings for the detector monitor. However, after clicking the saved link, you can change the settings on the detector monitor.

Q: When I open a saved graph from the lab book, why does the current monitor sometimes disappear?

A: Only one monitor for each detector can be displayed at the same time. Thus, if you are currently using the phosphor screen and you open saved data on a phosphor screen, your current phosphor screen monitor will be turned off.